AF323548

GENDER AND COSMOPOLITANISM IN EUROPE

In memory of Hanna Behrend
Born in Vienna in 1922 and passed away in Berlin in 2010

Gender and Cosmopolitanism in Europe

A Feminist Perspective

ULRIKE M. VIETEN
Vrije Universiteit Amsterdam, The Netherlands

ASHGATE

Published by
Ashgate Publishing Limited
Wey Court East
Union Road
Farnham
Surrey, GU9 7PT
England

Ashgate Publishing Company
Suite 420
101 Cherry Street
Burlington
VT 05401-4405
USA

www.ashgate.com

British Library Cataloguing in Publication Data
Vieten, Ulrike.
   Gender and cosmopolitanism in Europe : a feminist
   perspective. -- (The feminist imagination -- Europe and
   beyond)
   1. Cosmopolitanism--Europe. 2. Social justice--Europe.
   3. Discrimination--Law and legislation--Europe. 4. Group
   identity--Europe. 5. Women's rights--Europe. 6. Feminist
   theory.
   I. Title II. Series
   305'.01–dc23

Library of Congress Cataloging-in-Publication Data
Vieten, Ulrike.
   Gender and cosmopolitanism in Europe : a feminist perspective / by Ulrike
M. Vieten.
     p. cm.
   Includes bibliographical references and index.
   ISBN 978-1-4094-3383-5 (hbk) -- ISBN 978-1-4094-3384-2 (ebook)
   1. Feminism--Europe. 2. Cosmopolitanism--Europe. I. Title.
   HQ1587.V54 2011
   305.42094–dc23

                                      2011052539

ISBN 9781409433835 (hbk)
ISBN 9781409433842 (ebk)

Printed and bound in Great Britain by the
MPG Books Group, UK.

Contents

Acknowledgements

The idea to engage with *cosmopolitanism* came up in 2003 when I attended a lecture at the London School of Economics and Political Science (LSE) in London; and guess, who gave the talk? The focus was on *European cosmopolitanism* and I was wondering why cosmopolitanism should be bounded by any territorial notion? As part of an ensuing intellectual journey, I submitted my PhD thesis in 2007 at the University of East London. I am still very grateful to Nira Yuval- Davis, my supervisor during these years, for the inspiration I received from her and for providing an academic environment that encouraged critical thinking. This book is partly based on the findings of my research, adding subsequent insights and giving it a more provocative twist. Foremost, I would like to thank my Irish and Italian colleagues Patrick O'Donovan and Laura Rascaroli for providing first, an interdisciplinary space at the conference they organised at University of Cork in 2005 (*The Cause of Cosmopolitanism in Europe and Beyond*) and second, for inviting me to contribute to their edited collection later on; I cherish very much having presented, discussed and explored some of the theoretical considerations that evolved and took shape. Also, I would like to mention my closest German friends; Gabi Kapitzki and Ulrike Waltemathe (Oldenburg), Ane El Assal (Hamburg; now Belfast), Anja Burghardt (Hamburg, now Salzburg), Ilona Paula Themann and Christa Anders (Bremen). Sharing an *autonome* (anarchist) political spirit and being engaged in feminist activities for ages they all helped me through these transnational years with their warm friendship and hospitality while I took the notion of mobility, migration and cosmopolitanism to heart when moving to England (London) in 2002. Living in Leeds (since 2008) and working at the *Vrije Universiteit* in Amsterdam (since 2009) simultaneously meant more travelling in-between and across European nation states and cultures. As the years are unfolding many lovely people contributed to the crafting of the book, among them I would like to thank and name, also: Elizabeth Mason, who read my drafts and was enthusiastic about them, Halleh Ghorashi (VU Amsterdam), who was sympathetic to and supportive of my writing project as part of the 'Inclusive Thinking' Research Group, Neil Jordan, my editor, who liked the idea of 'Gender and Cosmopolitanism in Europe' instantly, and encouraged me through the entire process. Thanks go particularly to my London-based friend Cigdem Esin, whose piece of art on the cover of the book gives some visual sense of feminist vernacular cosmopolitanism. The picture was created at the workshop 'You're here: East London Self-Portraits' held by the artist Chila Kumari Burman and academic Corinne Squire (UEL). Like Cigdem, Anat Pick further shared her home, food for thought and time with me when I was writing at the British Library in London in summer 2011, and on several occasions beforehand. Last but not least, Dagmar, for making a home with me abroad and elsewhere, cheering me up and listening to my thoughts, keeping our life filled up with love, humour, work and passion for politics and social justice.

Introduction
Gendered Cosmopolitanism:
The Scope of this Book

'New' cosmopolitanism has been on the cultural, social and political agenda for more than 20 years. What cosmopolitanism might be about remains largely vague and more often contested. Understood in lay terms cosmopolitan habits are often identified with western city lifestyles regarding taste, culture and the mixture of diverse populations. Further, the notion of *cosmopolitan* could be a cocktail, the image of any metropolitan city either in Europe or in other parts of the world, or the brand of a fashion magazine. If we might think of the latter it promotes a certain personal style of dress and make-up as a cosmopolitan attitude projected on the female gender. By contrast, the academic debate concerning new cosmopolitanism, as political community outlook unfolds predominantly as male business.[1] Hence, it appears that gendered dividing lines characteristic of 'the' nation state and its societies are carried on to the perspectives on cosmopolitanism. However, the idea of global humanity is much too exciting to leave it to a 'boys' playground' for conceptualising policy perspectives of a new European belonging. Thus, this book presents a feminist perspective that engages with cosmopolitanism as a source that can strengthen female resistance to oppression and supports an alternative social-cultural framework for bonding people, globally.

Looking at contemporary discourses on cosmopolitanism we recognise a renaissance of interest in cosmopolitan visions since 1990.[2] 1989 makes a significant ideological turning point as the Cold War ended and the Communist system collapsed. The terrorist attacks on US soil on 9/11 2001[3] mark a second symbolic date and ideological turning point that is influential in terms of the

---

1 The *Cosmopolitanism Reader*, published in December 2010 includes 25 essays four of which are authored by women. Martha Nussbaum contributes two essays; one based on her famous writing on patriotism and cosmopolitanism, and a second one examining Kant's oeuvre in the context of cosmopolitanism; likewise Onora O'Neill's essay discusses Kant's impact on human rights and global redistributive justice. I will come back to this in the final chapter of this book. The third female is LSE scholar Mary Kaldor discussing the theme of war/humanitarian intervention and cosmopolitanism.

2 See for example, Hannerz 1990; Held 1995; Nussbaum 1996; Brennan 1997, 2001; Derrida 2001; Appiah 1998; Nava 2002, 2007; Heater 2000; Beck 2000c; Calhoun 2002a, 2002b, 2007; Pollock, Bhabha, Breckenridge and Chakrabarty 2002; Archibugi 2003; Fine 2007, Werbner 2008; Mandel 2008; Delanty 2009.

3 I will refer in the following chapter to this with '9/11'.

reception and production of cosmopolitan thinking. In the aftermath of various terrorist attacks since 2001 an internationally racialising discourse became apparent, targeting, in particular, Islamist Muslims and orthodox Muslim communities as the 'threatening Other'. Any rhetoric of a cosmopolitan openness towards *the Other* has to be tested against the racialising discourse that has arisen significantly in the wake of the 9/11 aftermath.

Against the background of these considerations the overall aim of this book is to offer a critical and timely reading of European discourses of new cosmopolitanism and to unmask the gendered dynamics maintained in these discourses. In doing this it proposes a feminist counter perspective arguing for *transversal conversations on cosmopolitanism* in the plural, in and beyond Europe. So we could ask, what do feminists do when they look at the world or, for our purpose here, at cosmopolitanism? It appears that we share as Marsha Meskimmon (2011: 1) puts it nicely, 'developing sensitivity to places where sexual difference is of critical significance to the production of meaning and yet not signified.' Hence, it is something that is out there but not quite visible or extracted. Further, feminism as an optimistic political trajectory is committed to the analysis of transnational spaces (Levitt and Glick-Schiller 2004). Different streams of feminism aim to transcend fixed borders and boundaries and while proposing a 'politics of becoming' (Kannabiran 2006: 55) interrogate finite identities and homogenised nation containers. 'The impact of feminist praxis on the concept of cosmopolitanism is especially strong where connections are made between the macro-level of a politics of a world citizenship and micro-level of explorations of making ourselves at home in the world' (Meskimmon 2011: 7).

This introduction will sketch the theoretical feminist framework that is needed to analyse contemporary discourses on cosmopolitanism. Further, focusing on Britain and Germany, it is argued that new cosmopolitanism is embedded in different historical horizons of cosmopolitanism in Europe. It will make the claim that it matters in what ways academic interventions in debates on cosmopolitanism re-territorialise and accordingly, develop a discourse of *Europeanisation* that keeps gendered symbolic boundaries of political community belonging in place. Finally, there will be an outline of the subsequent chapters of the book.

The term 'cosmopolitanism' can be broken down to 'cosmos' and 'polis' and in doing so we can see the two dimensions of the concept: on the one hand cosmopolitanism suggests a privileged belonging to a particular political community (polis), and on the other hand the imagination of its extension to world scale (cosmos). The tension between these two angles poses theoretical questions that are worth asking. Firstly, does cosmopolitanism take for granted a privilege of citizenship and does this have to remain gendered? Secondly, if this kind of citizen's cosmopolitanism were extended to a world scale, what then does cosmopolitanism actually mean to those who are *citizens* of nowhere and/ or de-classed non-citizens? And further, in what ways are gendered symbolic boundaries of national and ethnic communities still relevant to the meaning of cosmopolitanism? While approaching these questions we have to take on board that the recent renaissance of interest in cosmopolitanism indicates the fundamental crisis of established notions of national borders and boundaries and a longing for a new utopia that binds humanity. Above all, it gives hope to broader efforts to imagine a more just and economically less uneven world.

Zygmunt Bauman (2005: 2) traces back the meaning of utopia to the two Greek words *eutopia* ('good society') and *outopia* ('nowhere'). European visions of a better future, however, have generally been either confined to modern humanist ontology or to religious discourse. Religion is dominated in Europe by Christian traditions on the one hand, and the narrative of enlightenment and humanism deeply intertwined with the particular European discourse of secularism and democratic progress, on the other. According to Jeff Spinner-Halev (1994: 36), 'Marx argued that those who celebrated the political emancipation of Jews did not care about the Jews' human emancipation'. Thus, the division of the State from religion constitutes a hegemonic structure which separates the public from the private while perpetuating secularism from a very Western and Christian perspective. Encompassing this division is the ideological bias of public and private affairs, which feminists (i.e. Pateman 1986, 1989, Lister 1997a, 1997b) regard as a gendered power realm. Ruth Gavinson (1992) emphasises that the disapproval of this bias by feminists primarily addresses the social and economic arrangements surrounding it. Building on this critical discourse of classed, ethnic and above all gendered divisions within national states we have to ask whether social divisions, symbolic boundaries and accordingly, structural exclusions are also characteristic to visions of cosmopolitanism. Hence, the central epistemic interrogation has to be directed at cosmopolitan claims to be emancipatory. Can these claims be upheld?

It is argued here that the potential of cosmopolitanism lies far beyond ideas that aim to integrate perplexity, multidimensionality and diversity into modified, but otherwise continuing, unjust social and economic political orders. Relevant to the emancipatory content of cosmopolitanism is the formation of a situated imagination that starts from a contingent historical angle. According to Amanda Anderson (2001: 64), cosmopolitan detachment has historically been assumed to be working 'against' certain political orders. In antiquity cosmopolitanism was set 'against the restricted perspective and interests of the polis'; in the Enlightenment vision 'against ... religion, class ... the absolutist state' and by the 19th century 'against ... nationalism' (ibid.). Hence, the contemporary debate on new cosmopolitanism needs to reflect the meaning of this detachment 'against' the timely transformation of the territorially bounded democratic nation state and the global stage of transnational capitalistic flows.

Feminist concepts as proposed by theorists Iris Marion Young and Nancy Fraser, for instance, are helpful in tackling this new stage of spatial transitions while looking at the gender paradox more systematically and further, leaving options to engage with contemporary debates on cosmopolitanism in Europe and beyond. I will adopt Young's critique of *normalisation* processes that determine her reading of an 'inclusive democracy' (2000, 2006) and Fraser's 'post-socialist' analytical framework of a transformative space as capable of resolving some of the problems concerning the fundamental 'redistribution-recognition dilemma' (1997: 11). These feminist analytical angles are maintained throughout the book when considering the 'cosmopolitan' promise to open up towards collective difference and 'the Other'. When referring to normalisation Young (2006: 96) writes, 'I refer to processes that construct experiences and capacities of some social segments into standards against which all are measured and some found wanting or deviant.' Mica Nava (2007) positively claims the normalisation of difference as far as 'visceral cosmopolitanism' in London is concerned. However, a more critical perspective on normalisation processes, needs to discuss global processes as an impact beyond 'a politics of difference in national culture or religion, on the one hand, and difference that arises primarily from structural relations in sexuality, divisions of labour, or the deviance of kinds of bodies, on the other' (Young 2006: 101). Further, agreeing with Young's focus on a strong *structural societal* level I link her perspective regarding the inclusion of *the Other* to Fraser's concern with 'distributive justice'. Fraser distinguishes analytically *gender* and *race* as those socially constructed groups[4] which are held more profoundly in a 'redistribution and recognition dilemma'. This might be a provocation to feminists, who prioritise individual intersecting identities as liberal perceptions of trans-gender choices. What is interesting beyond feminist disputes is the question of how cosmopolitanism as a utopian project could respond to the challenge of how to change existing structural exploitation regarding gendered race relations in concrete localities, states, regions and various parts of the world. From a feminist perspective a non-excluding identification with *any* Other determines a broader social perspective towards alternative visions of solidarity, justice and world community while incorporating cultural difference. Pnina Werbner (2006: 2) argues that cosmopolitan practices should be regarded as 'cosmopolitan consciousness, the reflexive awareness of this experience of toleration which often arises when taken-for-granted every-day cosmopolitan practices are threatened.' This definition captures the potential power of cosmopolitanism as an every-day habit based on resistance to norms that reflect social closure. In this regard cosmopolitan consciousness upholds the political potential to change social reality. Nava proposes acknowledging the gendered though racialised gaze on the Other in discourses of cosmopolitanism (2002, 2005, 2006, 2007). This evaluation is helpful in order to understand the impact of interrelated layers of social power and the role non-belonging, longing, desire and identification with marginalised difference play in discourses on cosmopolitanism. It accentuates the meaning of curiosity and rebellion against strict or authoritarian community boundaries.

As the notion of the Other is crucial to any utopian all-inclusive visions of cosmopolitanism, a deeper knowledge about the ideological construction of

---

4   Fraser differentiates these two groups from Gay men and Lesbians as primarily struggling with recognition, and working class citizens as primarily struggling with redistribution (Fraser 1997: 16–23).

national frames that organise patterns of differences is needed, too. The two national discourses in Britain and Germany are taken as examples of specific and significant European traditions with particular reference to notions of democracy, representation, and social integration. John Urry (2000), Andreas Wimmer and Nina Glick-Schiller (2002) as well as Ulrich Beck (2000c, 2006b), for example, expose the problematic aspects of methodological nationalism and demand that the current social reality should be analysed and understood according to a cosmopolitan methodological research frame. However, criticising a nation state anchored methodological lens does not automatically indicate the closing stages of nationalised knowledge horizons. The ideological dimension of *othering difference*, as a constitutive and racialising moment of differently nationalised contexts, is rather underestimated even when it affects the debate on cosmopolitanism. As it stands, the Holocaust separates continental Europe, in particular Germany, from Britain. The Holocaust as the institutionalised extinction of ethnic otherness is the turning point in the perception of collective difference in 20th- and 21st-century Europe (Levy and Sznaider 2002; see also Beck and Sznaider 2006). Thus, it is crucial for a critical discourse on contemporary cosmopolitanism to obtain a deeper understanding of difference, its tension to racialised otherness and the ideological implications of notions of territoriality. In a German publication, Natan Sznaider (2008) engages with cosmopolitanism and Europe, insisting on the need to anchor *cosmopolitanism* in Europe historically. Otherwise a cosmopolitan Europe would turn into an illusion like the Kafkaesque *Schloss* (2008: 83-84). My book submits that it is here where differences in our memory lead to differing consequences for our present time, that have to be reflected on in order to further cosmopolitan ideals beyond a parochially binding and ideologically bonding 'European' community.

To clarify the direction of my interest: I bring to mind and I am going to work on different terminologies that emerged in Britain and Germany. It makes a difference whether a '*Weltbürger*' (citizen of the world) or a '*Kosmopolit*' is mentioned in a German cultural context. Whereas, for example, the cosmopolite (*Kosmopolit*) as a term became an anti-Semitic idiom in 19th-century Germany, the '*Weltbürger*' connoted the ideological link between the 'citizens of the world' and a culturally laden, but hegemonic ethno-national identity of bourgeois Germans at the turn of the 19th to the 20th century. In addition, both terms were ascribed differently in discussions of social mobility (*Weltbürger*) or migration (*Kosmopolit*). Hence, due to their different meanings and ideological anchoring, the terms *Kosmopolit* and *Weltbürger* convey biased social positions attached to possibilities of cosmopolitan attitudes. As a consequence it is meaningful firstly to explore the extent to which these distinguished notions have emerged and shifted in Germany, and also to explore what it means that they did not evolve in Britain. Secondly, the comparison of current British and German discourses on new cosmopolitanism could help to identify the continuity of racialising categories, or alternatively, the disappearance of this distinction in the contemporary context. This is highly important as the cultural, political and social fusion of different countries with regard to the economic-political project of the European Union transforms the analytical understanding and construction of social divisions across its Member States but also beyond (Vieten 2009). In terms of the German and the English language, for example, the German phrase *Kultur* and the English world 'culture' relate to notions of European civilisation and its 'missions' in distinctive and peculiar ways. That indicates problematic tension as these notions are equipped with distinctive hegemonic knowledge.

According to Iris Marion Young (2000: 86), hegemony 'refers to how the conceptual and normative framework of the members of a society is deeply influenced by premises and terms that make it difficult to think critically about aspects of their social relations or alternative possibilities of institutionalisation and action'. We could respond to this by saying that the idea of challenging hegemony appears to be an absurd task given that any outlook is inevitably merged into the structure of hegemony. However, the circulation of knowledge in general, and the disappearance of certain streams of knowledge in particular, might prove the assumption that there is an imbalance in the social order and that there are different ways of getting access to power and to participation in the public sphere. Consequently, a notion of 'common sense'[5] underlies a definition of hegemony as the most powerful, constructed *Weltanschauung.*[6] This 'common sense' has to be regarded as in flux. Nonetheless, it conveys aspects of *normalisation.* Denounced by Young (2006), it hints at a broader acceptance of values and attitudes arising in a particular contingent situation as systems of knowledge which are taken for granted. To challenge these processes of normalisation as part of hegemonic knowledge production is one of the tasks when tracing back notions of new cosmopolitanism as historical journeys across Europe. In an effort to follow up these intellectual passages the contributions of particular academics engaging with cosmopolitanism is discussed against the archaeology of historical discourses on cosmopolitanism in the aforementioned two countries.

The choice of the specific academics whose pre- and post-9/11 texts are explored is based on the *international recognition* of some who have contributed to the emergence of a transnational and European discourse field of cosmopolitan studies on the one hand (here: David Held; Homi K. Bhabha; Jürgen Habermas; Ulrich Beck), and two feminist voices, who challenge the dominant perception of liberal cosmopolitan ideas and ideals, e.g. Chantal Mouffe and Hanna Behrend, on the other. All the British intellectuals that I am looking at are familiar with German ideology or merged their reading of German philosophy and social thinking into own distinctive conceptual frameworks. All the German intellectuals I refer to have

---

5   'According to Alfred Schütz (1967), social science should analyse the practice how the world and taken-for-granted phenomena are *subjectively* experienced and produced by members (common sense) and dissidents (the stranger)' (Vieten 2003: 8; MA Dissertation, University of Greenwich).

6   I use the German term as it is most central to my own situated background. It could be translated in English as 'philosophy of life' or view on the world though it does not capture the content adequately.

published in English though their transnational experience evolved under very different generational, historical and ideological circumstances. As I will explore more specifically, their different voices do not *represent* national cultures, but are *situated* in specific national histories. Calling Held, Mouffe and Bhabha 'British' authors suggests that contemporary academic voices in Britain reflect a history of migration, hybridity and diversity that emerged as a process of immigration and acculturation that was not fundamentally disrupted by German National Socialism and European Totalitarianism. Both Mouffe and Bhabha moved to Britain from abroad and thus bring with them a continental European (Mouffe) and a Commonwealth (Bhabha) layer of experiences. Held, who is Jewish and English, also studied for a while in continental Europe (France and Germany). Whereas Behrend might be rather unknown to a broader and international audience, Habermas and Beck are recognised internationally. Habermas is famous as the leading contemporary German *Frankfurt School* social theorists and Beck, likewise, is well known for his book on 'The Risk Society' and publications on cosmopolitanism in recent years. While the two male writers grew up and lived predominantly in West Germany, Behrend, racialised as a Jew in the 1930s, re-migrated from her exile in England after the liberation of Nazi Germany to East Berlin and so began living and working in the communist German Democratic Republic (GDR). Whereas Habermas was born in the Rhineland, Beck is a descendent of Germans who lived in Poland, and grew up in West Germany after his family fled the Communist Red Army at the end of World War II.

Finally, this book aims to highlight some of generational and social divisions and also illustrates the transformation, connections and constructions of new transnational epistemic communities. It will shed more light on marginalised knowledge, especially feminist interventions that propose alternative outlooks on cosmopolitanism.

Chapter 1 maps out the need to analyse contemporary discourses on cosmopolitanism as evolving from particular national horizons and specific memories in Europe. Importantly, the shifting meaning of territorial space, e.g. the transformation of borders and boundaries, will be discussed in terms of its impact on the notion of cultural-civic belonging and social solidarity. In a first step, a semiotic reading of the two collapsed structures (the Berlin Wall and the Twin Towers) in the context of 1989 and 9/11 will visualise the ideological meaning of 'liberty' symbols in the context of borders and boundaries. To clarify the consequences of these shifts also in terms of the notion of symbolic boundaries for community building, the chapter proposes the analytical differentiation between difference and otherness with reference to Levinas's notion of the 'indefinite Other'. This differentiation is essential in order to grasp the political implications of the current transformations of symbolic boundaries of nation states in Europe that transgress modern notions of difference.

In contrast to an understanding that assumes that cosmopolitanism challenges state nationalism it is argued in Chapter 2 that a novel form of *regional cosmopolitanism* is underway in Europe, evolving through peculiar legal measures by the European Union. In order to illustrate the contradictory EU policies towards difference as far as gender/sex, sexuality, religion and ethnicity are concerned, this chapter discusses positive strategies of including 'otherness', for example through granting civil rights to homosexual couples. In order to explicate a rift and an emerging contrast, the chapter discusses negative strategies of excluding 'otherness', too. Here, it problematises the tendency in some European nation states to target Muslims institutionally as representing minority faith orthodoxy and underclass ethnicity. As examples, policies of banning and penalising women who wear the *nijab* and the limits of anti-discrimination policy as far as the transnational community of European Roma is concerned are subjected to critical analysis. In both regards, a radical shift in the comprehension of difference and inclusion is of concern. This contradictory development regarding *accepted difference* and *targeted otherness* is crucial to discourses of new cosmopolitanism in Europe. Hence it is argued, finally, that we have to go back to different historical emanations of cosmopolitanism and nationalism in Europe, in Britain and Germany respectively, in order to grasp the critical stand of contemporary cosmopolitanism in challenging these modified racialised boundaries.

Chapter 3 starts by discussing some poignant historical emanations of discourses on cosmopolitanism in Germany. Against the background of *völkisch* nationalism we are confronted with a split of positively and negatively ascribed labels of cosmopolitan subjectivity at the end of the 19th century. The pair of *Weltbürger* (citizens of the world) on the one hand and the *Kosmopolit* (cosmopolitan), which was racially coined as an anti-Semitic idiom, on the other, is decisive in that regard. Further, the specific correlation between a federal state structure and different stages of homogenising populations as a cohesive political community are explored in this context. It is argued that the Holocaust of the 20th century and previous institutional anti-Semitism is enshrined in an ethnic meaning of secular democracy and at the roots of national identity. These are central legacies to the contemporary debate on cosmopolitanism in Germany. With reference to moral claims regarding the Other as well as political trajectories concerning the European Union, the first part of this chapter ends by making clear in what ways the tension between a territorially framed understanding of political unity and social cohesion still dominates the construction of gendered and symbolic 'national' boundaries in 21st-century Germany. In the second part of this chapter the work of Habermas and Beck is discussed against the background of this historical framing and the distinctive notions of plurality and alterity as exposed in Chapter 1. After an introduction of the individual research biographies, the texts by the two authors in the 1990s are analysed in greater depth. At that stage and with respect to the national knowledge horizon, this is done while bringing in the feminist-socialist as well as marginalised East German and Jewish voice of Hanna Behrend. In a third section, the post 9/11 engagements with cosmopolitanism are discussed in comparison with each other. In particular, the obstacles of an all-inclusive cosmopolitanism are subject to this inquiry which focuses on the gendered dimensions in their arguments.

As part of the historically anchored analysis of contemporary interventions into new discourses on cosmopolitanism, Chapter 4 reviews the emergence, content and features of discourses of cosmopolitanism in Britain since the middle of the 19th century. Thus, the first part of this chapter sketches some of the relevant cornerstones in the perception of British discourses on cosmopolitanism that prepare the subsequent analysis of the intellectual interventions by Held and Bhabha. A set of core questions leads the investigation: did global trade with its commercial and colonial encounters shape the notion of cosmopolitanism in Britain in significant ways? What are the social and spatial consequences of the economic and political centralism on the city of London? Finally, it reflects on cultural and political spaces of resistance and ideological transformations with reference to multiculturalism. All in all, the first part of this chapter illustrates the nuanced and complex potential of discourses on cosmopolitanism in Britain. It explores in its second part the explicit writings on cosmopolitanism by Held and Bhabha as specific examples of a British legacy of commercial and colonial cosmopolitanism. Given that discourses on cosmopolitanism span different disciplines, social backgrounds and ideological corners, what different academics have to say on cosmopolitanism is highly influenced by their original research subject and discipline; thus a brief researcher biography is introduced at the beginning as in Chapter 3. Then we turn to a discussion of the writings in the 1990s that are relevant to discourses on cosmopolitanism after the fall of the 'Iron Curtain'. As a second crucial step, the writings on cosmopolitanism after 9/11 are considered while exploring in what ways an 'opening'/'closure' nexus can be detected and whether there is a modification of exclusionary boundaries. The two analytical layers of difference, 'plurality' and 'alterity', are decisive in this regard. Furthermore, Held's and Bhabha's writings are analysed with reference to the feminist post-Marxist interventions by Chantal Mouffe.

Chapter 5 undertakes an intra- and international comparison between the differing British and German archaeologies of cosmopolitanism. Here, the chapter looks for symbolic legacies inherited by the different pairs of male mainstream authors and their female feminist contenders. Significantly, the historically different position of individual authors to the notion of the 'nation' is decisive. Whereas Bhabha, for example, gives voice to a postcolonial perspective that also contributes to the public discourse of a cosmopolitan 'multicultural Britain' in the 1990s, an alternative vision of a *non-ethnic German nation* remains largely a taboo in Germany. The theme of a 'German nation' is banned from a left wing and mainstream public debate. This contrasts with the emergence of a popular 'fun nationalism', which was pushed in the successful hosting of the 2006 World Cup and an anti-Muslim European secular democracy regime still on the populist horizon. Alternatively, the discourse of cosmopolitanism, i.e. cosmopolitan Europe, proposes a 'plain' identity box for German belonging supposedly cleared of nationalistic aspirations. European cultural identity, however, is equated with the polity project of the European Union, which reflects to a certain degree the hegemonic German history of 'federalisation' as segmentation. This chapter maps out the way in which a transnational 'European' debate is mainstreamed: Held, Habermas and Beck likewise advocate a 'cosmopolitan' Europe as a 'federal' European Union. Though Mouffe criticises the liberal notion of cosmopolitanism she equally regards an overlap of territorial belonging and political community bonds as essential for democratic participation and social cohesion. Accordingly, the contemporary hegemonic discourse of European cosmopolitanism unfolds as crossing 'classic' ideological lines. In total, the outlook on a common European community future enmeshes supra-territorial borders with a heuristic and nostalgic form of international politics and manageable instruments of social solidarity. It is argued that 'European cosmopolitanism' links to a hyper-*nationalising* discourse, which conveys 'othering' and 'racializing' dynamics and does not overcome Eurocentric state nationalism.

In the concluding chapter (Chapter 6), I review the notion of *subaltern cosmopolitanism* looking at the difference made by different feminist and postcolonial voices. Against the way *mainstreaming 'European' cosmopolitanism* works on state-centred frames of democracy and inclusion I explore the degree to which transversal feminist and post-colonial outlooks can be recognised as advocating counter perspectives. Here the interventions by Nina Glick-Schiller, Nira Yuval-Davis as well as Boaventura de Sousa Santos are considered, for example, bringing in greater social complexity to the understanding of new cosmopolitanism. These critical perspectives matter, particularly, as they enhance *transversal conversations* about roots and routes of cosmopolitanism and national liberations in Europe, and beyond.

Chapter 1
Who Belongs? Who is the Other?

Some of us might remember the images of East Germans climbing up the Berlin Wall, jumping over and landing on the other side. People all over the world celebrated *their* liberation enthusiastically in 1989. Let's pause this memory for a minute and try to feel this deep sympathy with strangers, who were literally contained behind the so called *Iron Curtain*, whether it was in the GDR, in Poland or in Hungary.

Looking back the stubborn dissidence of East Europeans, their largely peaceful protest and the decision of their leaders to give in to the people's demand for change led to the final collapse of the state communist system. We have to keep this in mind, over 20 years later. In February 2011 the peaceful protest of Egyptians and their victory, equally transmitted via visual images to our homes in different parts of the world, and then the subsequent protests in various Middle Eastern countries, remind us of the power of *the people*. Whereas the revolutionary spirit in North Africa seems to be unstoppable, the violent and cruel responses of various oligarchs against citizens' uprisings are not. Nor is there an end to her-story curious to understand the ways in which any change of local-national regimes might foster gender equality and do justice to issues of discrimination at large. Nonetheless, the year 2011 appears to mark another turning point in the perception of what counts as *national society* and *international solidarity* as well as the meaning of *local democracy* related to the meaning of borders and boundaries. Do we have another cosmopolitan moment more than twenty years after 1989 and more than ten years after 9/11? As Etienne Balibar (2010: 318) argues, the 'phenomenology of borders is essential to understand the cosmopolitan issue.'

This chapter starts with a semiotic reading of two falling structures: the *Berlin Wall* and the *Twin Towers* in New York. Men made and built the former for policing purposes against liberal Western capitalism, and the latter to symbolise liberal capitalism and its 'superiority'. At first glance, these locations belong to far away continents, but on closer inspection we see that both are connected through antagonistic hegemonic claims. There will be a brief exploration of the ways in which these two monuments acquired political significance as stepping-stones of contemporary global history and as defining our decades. In what ways does the second monument reverse the meaning of the first, conveying collective anxieties and thus being used notoriously as a reference point for a gated world community? How does global bonding work? What about particular memories and gendered positions at the threshold of these collapsing symbols that demarcate different areas?

In the second part of this chapter, the rise of new cosmopolitan spirit post 1989 and its structural altering into a civic boundary function via post 2001 anxieties is scrutinised against a theoretical framework that distinguishes between 'difference'/plurality and 'otherness'/alterity. This analytical differentiation should help to understand the running argument of the book: in the last decade a paradigm shift took place when talking about a cosmopolitan openness towards the Other. This paradigm shift is related to '*racialised boundaries*' (Anthias and Yuval-Davis 1992) adjusting to modifications of a worldwide westernised 'civic imagined' community. Changed versions of racialised boundaries accompany transformed gendered communalising projects and transgress to a global discourse of late modern civic boundary. Key entries to this contemporary discourse are 'cosmopolitan civic citizenship' and 'modern femininity'.

Bonding by Ideological B(l)inding: The Gendered Dimension of Falling Monuments

First, we have to take on board the transformed space of territorial borders and community boundaries: the 'border' that was gone (the Iron Curtain) and the 'boundary' that was destroyed (The Twin Towers) both illuminate the power of collective global symbols. Whereas the people's protest altered an outdated societal, economic and political container, ultimately longing for freedom, the latter poses the violent question of the degree to which national democracies, their claim of peace, and the privileges they give to their citizens still exist or rather fail them. Zygmunt Bauman (2002: 87) argues that 'the 11 September 2001 terrorist attacks on US soil could be regarded as a symbolic end to the era of space'. If we take this remark seriously, we are thrown into the narrative production of the one and only *united* global collective memory as facilitated by mass media. Maurice Halbwachs (1950: 6) argues that 'every collective memory unfolds within a spatial framework'. This spatial framework refers to physical environments; concrete place, time and the specificities of both (ibid.). 1989 and 2001 have become turning points in the perception of space and political community. As value laden collective symbols they are embedded in a broader project of claiming global presence while dismissing divided pasts and contested futures. What matters to the construction of boundaries is that there is a choice of events (Halas 2008) triggering global identification for political purpose. According to Elzbieta Halas (2008: 112), 'A good example of that problem in interpreting the transformation in Europe after communism is the symbolic function of the Fall of the Berlin Wall in 1989, which in the global politics of collective memory became a dominant symbol at the expense of the symbolism of 'Solidarity' that in 1980 challenged the communist regime.' We could argue that the amnesia towards the Polish trade unionist Lech Wałeşa's and the *Solidarność* driven resistance corresponds to the Western ideology of liberal capitalist societies having liberated the communist east bloc. Halas argues that the choice of one symbol and the rejection of the other 'is related to ideological principles of constructing the dominant commemorative narratives that dramatise the transition from one period to the other' (ibid.). In a similar way, Hilary Cunningham (2004: 332) stresses that 'the post-September 11th proliferation of border imagery appears to reflect a profound reorganization of the global imaginary.' As ideologically laden symbols the fall of the Berlin Wall and the falling Twin Towers convey synonymously a cause of global identification with particular local fate. In what ways are we facing a new dialectics of global bonding?

According to Maree Stenglin (2008: 426), 'Binding is a scale that organizes spaces along a restricted to unrestricted continuum from openness to extreme closure … Bonding complements Binding and is concerned with the communing potential of spaces. The basic function of Bonding is to align people into groups with shared dispositions.' In that respect the masterminded mass murder of air travellers on the US planes and their misuse as a flying weapon against the World Trade Center members of staff accelerates anxieties to keep local order and global power in place. Also, it provokes us to think about the arbitrary rule of becoming a victim - at home and elsewhere. At the same time, the 'singularity' of this catastrophe transmits the fiction of its extra-ordinary and particular meaning to a worldwide audience. In contrast to uncountable wars, innumerable female victims and millions of starving people across the world, the collapsing towers and the US American local victims demand civic loyalty, which in effect claims US hegemonic global binding. In his essay 'The spirit of Terrorism' (2001), Jean Baudrillard resonates:

> Though it is (this superpower) that has, through its unbearable power, engendered all that violence brewing around the world, and therefore this terrorist imagination which – unknowingly – inhabits us all. That we have dreamed of this event, that everybody without exception has dreamt of it, because everybody must dream of the destruction of any power hegemonic to that degree – this is unacceptable for Western moral conscience, but it is still a fact, and one which is justly measured by the pathetic violence of all those discourses which attempt to erase it. It is almost they who did it, but we who wanted it. If one does not take that into account, the event lost all symbolic dimension to become a pure accident, an act purely arbitrary, the murderous fantasy of a few fanatics, who would need only to be suppressed. But we know very well that this is not so. Thus all those delirious, counter-phobic exorcisms: because evil is there, everywhere as an obscure object of desire. Without this deep complicity, the event would not have had such repercussions, and without doubt, terrorists know that in their symbolic strategy they can count on this unavowable complicity.[1]

Globally screened, and repeated as images up for consumer grabs, the falling Twin Towers remind us of fictional fantasy and horror films, too; it seems as if the script was already out there; only the actors had to be chosen (or choose themselves). Somehow, surreal reality transgresses the boundaries between the

---

1   http://www.egs.edu/faculty/jean-baudrillard/articles/the-spirit-of-terrorism/.

'here' and the 'before'. In one of her brilliant essays, 'The Imagination of Disaster', Susan Sontag (2009, 1961) discusses the cultural longing for controlled spectacles that have underlain the viewer's voyeuristic interest in the genre of science fiction and horror films since the 1950s. She writes: 'There is a vast amount of wishful thinking in science fiction films, some of it touching, some of it depressing. Again and again one detects *the hunger for a "good war,"*[2] which poses no moral problems, admits no moral qualifications' (2009: 219). Further, in this controlled imaginary there is always the one (male) hero (and I would add here, his, perhaps, mixed race and gendered team) able to rescue *our* Western civilisation; a happy ending here means overcoming the final threat – in the end.

Susannah Radstone (2002) argues that 9/11 evokes both trauma and fantasy, but in contrast to those who might call it 'unimaginable', the shocking reality that was pictured as a real documentary had already been depicted by film scripts (New York is frequently targeted as a whole cityscape in the fictional text). As we know, the 9/11 attack on the Towers/New York was used rhetorically by the then US American president George W. Bush to launch further classic international wars (e.g. Afghanistan; Iraq), new imperial wars that claim old gender territory: the 'public' western goal to defend the freedom of women (and children) means killing civilians on the ground; anonymously, women and children are executed. Largely, these killing fields are invisible to Western eyes. 'Fantasies of invulnerability and of battle between different orders of paternal power appear to leave women on the margins of a "war" that is at once political, psychic, and cultural' (Radstone 2002: 469). There is a gendered division to these different spatial sites of ideological proliferations and real time scenarios; the gendered male still signifies the noisy war code of aggression and action (only marginally disrupted by the fact that women sometimes act as suicide bombers and soldiers) and the gendered female as epitomising calm empathy and patience. Male destination and decision ranks high whereas female fluidity and confusion ranks low. Also, we find the shape of the tower as echoing phallic erection as the artificial resonance to male power; destroying this symbol of hegemony means hitting at a deep *Angst* regarding its vulnerability and its temporality. Digging deeper into the sphere of symbolic representations concerning the collective unconsciousness we come across a very explicit feminist interpretation of the notion of the Tarot card 'Tower' ('The Tower of Destruction', Semetsky 2010: 112). According to Inna Semetsky (2010: 112), 'the image of "The Tower" signifies radical intervention, revolution and the overthrowing of false consciousness, violent social conflict and change, destruction of the old order on a grand scale, and release from imprisonment in the patriarchal structure during the very process of its demolition.'

Semiotics as the systematic study of signs refers to the way a culture links signifier and signified; the 'informational content' (Semetsky 2010: 105) which is anchored in a certain interpretation creates the meaning of a sign. In that respect the terrorist attack on the 'Twin Towers' signifies the fundamental(ist) rupture of

---

2	My emphasis.

the hegemonic US power, which in the shock aftermath nevertheless managed to create an affective bonding to its hegemony: you are either with me or against me. The multi-dimensional connotation of difference and the variety of cultural interpretations appear as empty signifiers now. Instead, the significance of 9/11 suggests that we live inside one cultural realm from then on. Hence Western hegemonic 'informational content' has gone global while claiming cultural space as its unit.

The altered spatial dimension implies, however, that 'in global war, conflict cannot discretely remain spatial, a fact that has enormous implications in terms of the imaginary landscape. Because the "enemy" does not inhabit a clear territorial space, there is nothing geopolitical to attack' (Buck-Morss 2003: 34). Further, Susan Buck-Morss (2003) contends that the US and allies' wars contradict this assumption of a new globally connected space. It is 'the new global immanence' (ibid.) that poses radical new questions about the function of communication (media), society or notions of domestic and international affairs. As Bauman (2002) emphasises, too, this stretching global space translates into 'extra-territorial frontierlands' (2002: 90). The consequences of this transformation are manifold. As far as my feminist perspective on cosmopolitanism and gender in Europe is concerned the tension between symbolic community boundaries and gender requires further analysis. The following section looks at the impact of shifting symbolic community boundaries on the notion of gendered belonging.

Gendered Frontiers and Racialised Boundaries: Difference and Alterity

Nira Yuval-Davis and Marcel Stoetzler (2002: 330) argue that boundaries are gendered 'limit-lines of collectivities'. Apart from the multiplicity of situated biographical experiences within and across state borders, 'national borders become a specific form, spatially bounded, of collectivity boundaries' (2002: 334). In reference to Fredrik Barth (1969), Maria Triandafyllidou (2002) claims that national identity like ethnic identity is formed through interaction with the Other. Further, she argues that 'it is socially relevant factors that determine which differences are important, not the "objective" character of such differences' (2002: 30). Historically most social groups have existed in the same territorial space, organising themselves socially while using different mechanisms to draw distinctive boundaries. Thus, a constant re-creation of boundaries is a strategy of identity formation and negotiation. In this way the boundary is the point of realisation of both identity and difference. Georg Simmel (in Frisby and Featherstone 1997: 143) wrote that 'the boundary is not a spatial fact with sociological consequences, but a sociological fact that forms itself spatially.' He highlighted the 'formative power of the social context', which proves that the 'consciousness of boundedness does not necessarily involve "natural boundaries" (mountains, rivers, oceans or deserts) but rather ... merely political boundaries' (1997: 141). Similar to the modern view of Simmel, Joel S. Migdal (2004: 5) underlines that contemporary researchers on trans-nationalism and globalisation processes agree that borders and boundaries are impermanent rather than permanent features of life and that 'the status of borders has been contingent on varying historical circumstances'. Also, boundaries indicate a turning point (Migdal 2004), in which an 'us' is differentiated from a 'them'. Boundaries include symbolic and social dimensions and are associated with the border divisions that appear on the maps or, in other cases, on other dividing lines that cannot be found on any map at all. Migdal (2004: 6) approaches this phenomenon as a matter of two 'checkpoints': 'actual and virtual practices are used by group members to identify insiders.' Actual checkpoints include surveillance techniques, checking visas and passports or even racial profiling. Virtual checkpoints detect members by dress codes, language and habit differences (Migdal 2004). Apart from these direct monitoring processes, mental maps deliver a range of rather subtle faith inherited and value laden ideas addressing loyalty, emotions and passions. Characteristically various social groupings, in particular minority communities, cultivate their checkpoints and mental maps while following their own spatial logic that is not the same as suggested by the traditional nation-state. Migdal (2004: 10) writes, '[t] he reassuring message people take with them on their forays into meetings with strangers in familiar places, such as a *city bus*,[3] is that by knowing the markers and checkpoints they can minimize risk and know what to expect from others.'

The idea of a safe city bus evokes nostalgic feelings of a bygone era, a feeling of relative safety within Western and European societies. As a condition of blurred boundaries the meaning of the familiar local space has shifted fundamentally in recent years, particularly in London post-2005 as a result of the July bombings. In 2004 the terror attacks on a commuter train in Spain evoked the sense that global terrorism had entered European territory. Today, the US global bonding effect via 9/11 resonates with a revived form of territorial-spatial anchoring; the European experiences with fundamentalist Islamic terrorism engender European Union managed security interests.

The response to the various terrorist attacks has been the implementation of a controlled, multifaceted, layered system of surveillance over the external, but also internal, movement of people (Rumford 2006, Bigo 2006). In contrast to diffused boundaries of belonging and identification, governments' intelligence services turn to biometric I.D. cards perpetuating the myths of the *visibility of danger* and further, continue to keep racial profiling as a means of detecting 'the enemy'. In line with Migdal's terms, the overlap of 'actual' and 'virtual' checkpoints remains unchallenged in current notions of symbolic boundaries. The problem of visibility, however, is linked to perceptions of difference and contingent boundaries to mark difference symbolically.

Perceptions have to be regarded as a contextualised common sense of 'seeing'. Hence, the texture of visibility, or the way of seeing, has to be discussed further in concordance with the power of representation. Ambiguous aspects of

---

3   My emphasis.

'representation' could hint at deeply gendered perspectives and the problem of *normalising/standardisation* strategies.[4] As Zillah Eisenstein (2004: 4) argues:

> [c]olor, and its cultural and political naming in terms of race, has no one (single) meaning.… Language is the only means we have to name what we see, and it also gets emptied of meaning. Each word is filtered through the concentrated power of our times which selfishly captures meaning for itself.

Massimo Lollini (2002: 65) emphasises that 'the notion of representation is a fundamental category of political discourse'. Modernity and the increasing need for representation are linked (Lollini 2002; see also Heller 1998). While looking at notions of the Other we refer to the problematic issue of 'authentic representation' (Heller 1998: 342); ideological disputes surround claims that only those belonging to a particular group could speak in representation of its specific group members. Gayatri Ch. Spivak (1988) argues that the condition of learning is not 'to represent' (*vertreten*) but instead 'to present ourselves' (*darstellen*). In this regard the single voice, and even the subaltern voice, can be trapped by its own limits 'to represent' the Other; everyone has to be aware that privileges, for example derived from the male gender and articulated through the upper or middle class, will shape any voice. 'Authenticity claims' have been called a 'fundamentalism of difference' (Heller 1998: 343) and have been labelled as 'advocating' particular interests (Anthias and Yuval-Davis 1992). Thus, any 'authenticity' claim needs to be assessed critically. Despite this problematic situation of representation, Agnes Heller (1998) also admits that 'multiple perspectives in representation enrich understanding and self-understanding in a hermeneutic sense' (1998: 348). Hence, it matters in what ways 'group difference' can be articulated within a (possible) democratic debate and whether this difference is something other than the duplicate of a hegemonic self. However, as made clear above, the capacity to see is linked to the possibility of Others to speak out and to create various representations. With regard to the binary of 'the Other and the self' a hegemonic discourse tends to reinstall difference as the second order: the woman has been placed as 'the second sex'; the black individual is positioned as 'the non-white'; the Muslim or Jew is demarcated as 'non-Christian'. The de-centring of the othering self for that reason is confronted with ideologies which position difference as biased order.

The acknowledgement of difference presents us with a dilemma: to acknowledge and confirm difference means that we are also acknowledging and confirming the existence of a dialectic; for there to be difference there must also be a composite 'I' or 'us' for it to make sense. According to Cheyney Ryan (2002: 15), Emmanuel Levinas tried to grasp the ontology of 'difference and otherness'. While both categories challenge totality, difference gives allusion to

---

4   I will come back later to the notion of standardisation as normalisation force in Chapter 2. At this stage it is important only to know that I use this terminology in a Foucauldian reading; see for details Link and Hall (2004).

plurality, and further, suggests critique from the inside while the latter, otherness, proposes 'that a totality can be disrupted ... by invasion from the outside' (2002: 16). This analytical differentiation suggests a dialectic and two-tiered outlook on the anti-totalitarian potential of difference. Diversity as a plural image suggests a cosmopolitan realm; however, it has to be tested whether 'inclusive' plurality as a signifier of cosmopolitan cultures and identities is able to grasp the notion of otherness. Returning to the theosophy of Levinas: the Other is addressed as fundamentally 'infinite'.

Levinas intended to grasp a site of transcendence inhabiting the exteriority of the western world. Following his logic we have to approach and see the Other not at the disposal of the self.[5] The political consequences of this theoretical perception are highly contested. Edith Wyschogrod (2003: 2) stresses that it is 'the presence of the other as a human face that binds me in fraternity'. She states that strangers are recognised in their alterity, as 'the other is absolutely other' (ibid.). Accordingly, the theme of otherness is close to the notion of the stranger though it is not 'reducible to the stranger' (Honig 2001: 194). For Jacques Derrida responsibility and hospitality are understood as a radical individual duty that we owe to any 'Other' (Derrida 2001). Christopher Farrands (2003: 30) interprets Levinas' proposal of 'a radical care for the Other' as a moral demand for an international 'Politics of Compassion'. This gives allusion to a more female gendered perspective on the Other. But in what ways would this approach challenge traditional roles of women actually? How could an 'international politics of care' be conceptualised? Should we equally challenge hegemonic and nationalistic gendered social, economic, cultural and political orders in order to create this global politics of care? Consequently, a separation of the political and the spiritual should be rejected, and to push its ambit even further, traditional boundaries that lay claim to a female position of care within national (territorial) borders should be overcome. In its essence the response to the Other should be transcendence towards global social justice rather than a dutiful wish for shared communality. And here we re-enter the political discourse of universal humanity, of particularity and the difficulties to see and to negotiate differences beyond a reductive view of idealism vs. realism.

Engaging with difference also could mean favouring what Seyla Benhabib (2002: 40) calls 'universally shared ideals of reasonable conversations between and among cultures.' She argues:

> [c]ultures permit varying degrees of differentiation between *the moral*, which concerns what is right or just for all insofar as we are considered simply as human beings; the ethical, which concerns what is appropriate for us insofar as we are members of a specific collectivity, with its unique history and tradition;

5	Levinas (1974, 1991) regards the Other as, '[o]therwise than being or beyond essence'.

and the evaluative, which concerns what we individually or collectively hold to
be valuable, worth striving for, and essential to human happiness. (ibid.)

Benhabib's terminology draws attention to culturalised connotations of values
that are relevant to a contextualising of particularity, universalism and difference.
The German noun *Moral* in a German understanding refers to temporarily bounded
community attitudes whereas the word *ethisch* is much more independent of a
Zeitgeist. It appears as if the English language uses quite similarly sounding terms
to express the opposite. Benhabib's third differentiation of 'the evaluative' as
the place of actual judgement links moral perspectives with ethical perceptions.
Hence, when looking at the ideological construction of symbolic boundaries, it is
the power to evaluate and to come to general conclusions about the meaning of
universal human conditions that needs to be challenged. Both a principal moral
claim and an *ethische Gesinnnung* (ethical faith) are embedded in nationalised
and culturalised models of social solidarity, imposing doctrines of obligations
and shaping codes of rights and participation. All these practices are *framed* by
particularities rather than universalism, defined by specific (national) community
boundaries and hermeneutic perceptions of the Other. Accordingly, the language
and speech acts of 'morality' and 'ethics' are shaped by situated knowledge
referring to particular hierarchical orders of social imagination (Stoetzler and
Yuval-Davis 2002).

Like the notion of the modern stranger, which evokes an image of coming and
going to different (urban) places, the ascription of 'rootlessness' and fluctuation
of cosmopolitan habits is prevalent when we look at the notion of the nomad
(Deleuze and Guattari 1987, Bradiotti 1994). The nomad inhabits a symbolic
space that is often linked to cosmopolitanism and which is also traditionally
connected with Roma culture. In contrast to connotations suggesting that nomads
are permanently wandering people, the nomadism of Roma implies following a
route of commercial interests and periodical returns, for example. Historically,
nation states have targeted nomadic minority ethnic groups in their cosmopolitan
habits. In contrast, the contemporary world of flux movements integrates nomadic
individualism as a substantial personal capacity to sustain 'liquid life' (Bauman
2000). Nonetheless, positioned against a more glamorous transnational traveller
class, particular sections of under classed migrants are ascribed as 'foreign' in a
sense that their 'uncanny presence' means 'backward, dependent, immobilized in
time past' (Saunders 2001: 91). In the age of globalisation, therefore, the meaning
of 'infinity' pronounces new dimensions as the notion of cosmopolitanism is
changing. Fernando Arenas (2003: 105) proposes:

> [t]he privileging of 'the other' as a primary ontological, ethical, and political
> horizon in the literature and philosophy ... points to its emergence as a major
> utopian frontier within contemporary global culture. We can describe this
> phenomenon as the appearance of the 'utopia of Alterity' or the 'utopia of
> otherness'.

The 'privileging' of the Other hints at a cosmopolitan vision of expanding political community to all-inclusiveness. In what ways does Eurocentric imagination impact on the notion of the Other and projects of inclusion? Beyond the biased and hierarchical spaces that are connected to specific national and Western cultural histories the context of the current anti-Muslim rhetoric refers to notions of *Orientalism*, which will be explored in the next section.

'We and the Rest': The Paradigm of the Inside/Outside Border-Land

In particular, the elementary construction of self/other binary was attacked by Edward Said (1978) as the characteristic structure to collective Western imagination framing cultural expressions. He unpacked the binary of Occident and Orient and deconstructed *Orientalism* as rooted in western images and fantasies of the Muslim/Arabic Other. Analysing novels, poetry and works of Western philosophy, he highlighted the internalised gaze of Orientalism as dominant in influential cultural and aesthetic productions.[6] Gerd Bauman (2004: 20) argues that Orientalism cannot be regarded as 'a simple binary opposition of "us=good" and "them=bad", but a very shrewd mirrored reversal of "what is good in us is (still) bad in them, but what got twisted in us (still) remains straight in them".' In what ways is Orientalism a 'cultural' code underlying Western perceptions of difference? Is this contemporary perception gendered, too?

John Rundell (2004: 92) argues that '[o]utsiders are those absolute strangers without legal entitlement to either arrive or settle within a given territory.' In contrast to this legally prescribed status of the *absolute stranger* Georg Schütz's (1890, 1967) notion of the modern stranger contained more ambivalent and powerful aspects. He argued that the stranger shows a more open-minded habit as he does not have the same fixed social commitments as the locals would have. Schütz's notion of the stranger is similar to Bonnie Honig's (2001) perspective on the foreigner: Honig points out that the 'foreigner', as a notion of difference, is twofold. The foreigner is both an intruder to and an outsider who improves the civil realm. We can give an illustration of this ambivalence: despite his/her salient contribution to local economies and national cultures the contemporary absolute stranger in our metropolitan cities resides in the invisible and socially deprived exterior of civil society (Puwar 2006).

As a consequence, we could argue that the *absolute stranger* has moved inside while at the same time s/he is left outside the privilege of an accepted legal status. The illegal space is regulated and defined legally. Rebecca Saunders (2001: 89) uses the term 'global foreigner'. Similarly, John Rundell (2004: 93) argues, 'in the contemporary context, the paradigmatic form of the outsider is the refugee

---

6   Baumann (2006: 19) acknowledges that it was Said, who 'recognized the binary grammar at work in the long historical process of Westerners representing "The Orient" to themselves'.

who is not only an absolute stranger. He or she is also the absolute foreigner, the absolutely alien.' We can make a connection between this notion of the absolute alien and what Giorgio Agamben (1998) calls 'bare life' in describing this as the human condition regulated by absolute legal control. While referring to Agamben, Yuval-Davis (2005: 167) takes up the argument of 'bare life' by saying that it is the non-legal status of 'people on the move' that makes them the most vulnerable outsiders. The 'vulnerable outsider' to our global world, however, is not without a particular gender; she is female.

Year by year the UNHCR *officially* counts the numbers or refugees.[7] As the numbers of illegalised people are rising steadily, the ideological tension of legal and symbolic boundaries has emerged as a new contested discursive ground. Hence, it is the symbolic boundary that matters in which otherness as a collective signifier of uncanny and 'dangerous' abnormality is defined as the outside of the internationally enclosed civil order.[8] The majority of millions of refugees, internally displaced and stateless persons remain in camps in Africa, Asia and the Middle East. The majority of these refugees are female, accompanied by children and other vulnerable relatives. The camp evokes the notion of a guarded and controlled place. Leaving these displaced people there means leaving them outside. Bauman (2002:114) remarks that 'the proliferation of refugee camps is as integral a product/manifestation of globalisation as is the dense archipelago of stopover nowherevilles through which the new globe-trotting elites move.' The indefinite temporary stay of people in camps and the enforcement of people to move in a boundless way have become contemporary signifiers of 'global foreignness'. The ways these characteristics are different to previous, modern notions of the Other and the ways these new layers of difference are formulated need to be discussed further. Heller (1998: 354) proposes that 'the alternative is not between difference and universality, between internal and external, but between closure and openness.' As discussed here, refugees on the move, illegalised migrants and minoritised (orthodox) Muslims are discursively positioned as the symbolic outside to current political orders in the West. Of these groups, the last, especially, is undergoing a recurrent route of being ideologically turned into the signifier of the *uncanny Other.* These notions of the Other expose the weakness of essentialism and power relations. We are confronted with categories such as Other and Same; differences and similarities work as a connected discursive space. The notions of the Other as *a stranger*, *a foreigner* and *a refugee* correspond to symbolic representations that mark specific contemporaneous contexts. Georgio Agamben (1994)[9] refers to Hannah Arendt, who published her essay 'We Refugees' in 1943, when Nazi Germany had *legally* made her home- and stateless. Being a Jewish refugee and stateless meant she was outside any legal protection and without any stable shelter at that time. In a post-World War II and post-Holocaust frame of institutionalised

---

7   http://www.unhcr.org/4ce532ff9.html.

8   Also see Balibar 2010.

9   Retrievable from http://www.egs.edu/faculty/giorgioagamben.html.

Human Rights the meaning of legal status has to be re-interpreted accordingly: 'So, the question is: … if [Hannah Ahrendt] were writing now … [w]ould she be any less likely now than then to ask not just "what can we accomplish through law on behalf of human rights?" but also "what new political formations are being advantaged and legitimated thereby?" Her example suggests not' (Honig 2008: 104).

Honig's critical assessment underscores the intellectual task of being careful not to mummify the past atrocities and also to reinterpret the messages of its intellectual heroines. As David T. Goldberg (2006: 337) reminds us '[e]ach catastrophe is unique. The Shoah, the Nakbah, Rwanda, Cambodia. Each – and unfortunately there are others – has its own conditions of possibility, its singularity, its uniquely tragic effects.' That means we have to review particular notions of otherness against a contemporary discourse that announces a programmatic concept of cosmopolitan inclusion and plural difference. Here, we have to ask in what ways difference and otherness ought to be the same or even two sides of a cosmopolitan coin? Do notions of the Other fit to gendered 'racial arrangements and engagements' (Goldberg 2006: 335) that continue to be salient to European racisms?

Samir Amin (1988: 89) argues that Eurocentric culture presents itself as 'particularly European, rationalist, and secular ideology, while claiming a worldwide scope'. For this reason a question arises as to whether a Eurocentric 'role modelling' of universalism is essentially part and parcel of contemporary discourses on cosmopolitanism that continue to carry the pitfalls of its hegemonic lenses. In his critique of Eurocentric cosmopolitanism Derrida (2001: 34) searches for a way beyond the 'tired, worn-out, wearisome opposition between Eurocentrism and anti-Eurocentrism', an opposition that, according to him, is itself a symptom of 'missionary and colonial cultures'. To his mind anti-Eurocentrism does not recognise that counter-appropriations and transformations of cultures over the centuries make even European thought 'hybrid, grafted, multilinear, polyglot' (2001: 33). However, Derrida's acclaimed polyglot and hybrid European cultures come with a legacy of ethnic cleansing processes (Mann 2005); this includes the Holocaust as the systematic extinction of collective otherness in continental Europe.

Ironically we could argue that the late modern notion of plurality and diversity cherishes what has to be regarded as the outcome of various historical stages of exclusionary practices, ethnic cleansings and the Shoa in continental Europe. More optimistically we could say it is also connected with the struggle of minorities to gain rights within the Enlightenment promise of equality and participation. Nonetheless, we have to take into account that while the ideology of modernity is 'progress', there are analytically two dimensions inhabiting the idea of progress related to the possibilities of difference.

Ryan (2002) measures the critical potential of 'plurality' and 'alterity' while referring to two asymmetric couples. The first pair, 'Master and Slave', suggests a moral understanding in which the 'liberation of the slave' will also 'save' the master; in this reading liberation suggests 'becoming equal'. However, if we have a look at the second pair, 'the Civilised and the Savage', there is a different story to tell. Here, the savage 'progresses' with his or her domestication. Having said that, the gender of the savage is female or a feminine male; the projection of an object conveys gendering processes as second ordering. Progress of 'civilisation' is identified with expansion, such as conquering, removing, 'liberating' the savage nation' (ibid.). Ryan (2002: 18) proposes instead:

> [t]he challenge is not one of multiplying voices but opening ears: the notion of 'opening' suggests why this form of postmodernism is associated with becoming more 'hospitable' – opening oneself and one's own to 'the stranger' at the door.

Thus, the claim of cosmopolitan openness towards diversity does not automatically coincide with openness towards the global Other. Indeed, it is debatable how and to what extent contemporary visions of cosmopolitanism reconceptualise 'imagined communities' while constructing a modified boundary of political, here European, belonging.

Mihran Dabag (2000: 62) detects the eradication of otherness within the ideological concept of *Weltbürgertum* (citizenship of the world); he argues that 'the idea of a general citizen' (*die Idee eines allgemeinen Bürgers*), in terms of a notion of specific 'civil' duties and rights, arose through the Genocide of European Jews. At a time when modern nation building took place, Jews, as the European ethnic minority par excellence, were referred to as 'interfering' in the European state order (ibid.). Dabag argues that the contemporary situation of migrants is different from the conditions European Jews have had to endure. He argues that migrants have largely had to adjust and integrate into the existing state system. While the first part of Dabag's analysis is convincing, his interpretation of the situation of contemporary migrants, settled communities and also nation states has to be revised in the more recent context: I suggest that at the current transition stage of 'national' communities in Europe, ancient and primordial Christian anxieties create the religious-ethno 'alter ego' minority at their border-lands.

Concluding Remarks

To summarise the point of departure: what I am suggesting is to approach contemporary notions of difference, gender and discourses on cosmopolitanism through a theoretical differentiation between 'diversity' as the accepted plurality of secular individuals and 'alterity' as a signifier of *collectively ascribed otherness* that is *still* beyond deliberation. At the present moment, in a world heavily influenced by post 9/11 anti-Muslim xenophobia e.g. anti-Islam rhetoric, and institutionalised racism, it becomes crucial to understand the shifting meaning of European civic boundary building. Particular notions of significant *otherness* are inscribed historically in different nation state practices and the conceptualisation of 'the political'. Those differing conceptualisations might shape contemporary discourses on cosmopolitanism in Europe, and in Britain and Germany more specifically. As far as current political agendas are concerned, otherness is increasingly understood in contrast to civic European values, democratic integration, social cohesion and cultural diversity. However, these different historical legacies surrounding the social, cultural and legal positioning of the Other are unresolved in the contemporary context of the political project of the European Union, which is legally advocating cohesion, harmonisation and comparable standards in its EU member states. We could assume that a matrix of 'selfing/othering' (Baumann 2004: 19) underscores cultural expressions in national discourses dealing with contemporary cosmopolitanism in Europe. And further we could add that the current discourses on new cosmopolitanism might argue in favour of larger regional patriotic systems rather than abandon territorially fixed allegiances. In opposition, the fundamental question of economic global justice that might come up when talking about a utopia of all-inclusive cosmopolitanism rather appeals to old-fashioned ideals of socialist internationalism. But those socialist visions of global justice do not match with the appraisal of enlarged (territorial) policy units.

Various diasporic communities in Europe, which retain links to their communities all over the world, are confronted with an ideological process of a *Europeanisation* that previously underwent totalitarian ethnic cleansings, the Holocaust, and are shaped by various periods of imperialism and colonialism.

To make the analytical differentiation more concrete it will be argued in the next chapter that the current situation in Europe has to be understood as a *state order in transition* that is being accompanied by ideological strategies to redefine the symbolic boundaries of political community and social inclusion. The gendering of contemporary political community boundaries entails that we have to look more closely at the cultural binding strategies with respect to current EU anti-discrimination law alongside anti-'extremist'/fundamentalist illegalising measures.

Chapter 2

Recognition, Social Equality and the Current EU Anti-discrimination Policy

As argued in Chapter 1, *difference* has to be understood analytically as welcomed 'plurality/diversity' and targeted alterity/otherness. This distinction helps to comprehend how gendered symbolic boundaries of political communities are reframed in the current 21st-century world and how they impact on mainstream debates of new cosmopolitanism and gender in Europe. What we observe is a strong tension between notions of late modern democracy, minority group representation and recognition as well as gender equality and multicultural difference. The accommodation of minority cultural interests, in particular, has resulted in political conflicts in how far the state and its legislation should accommodate those religious and ethnic group differences that cross the modern democratic state's secular division of a public and a private sphere in Europe.

The ideological fusion of nation and state has been analysed as constructed historically (Smith 2001, Breuilly 2000, 2001) and as gendered (Yuval-Davis 1997a, 1997b, 2000). The central claim of democracy and democratic law would be that the rule of power is defined in terms of control by the people (for example Baker 1989, Archibugi 1998). Diverse national histories indicate that the national community ('the people') addressed in a definition of the democratic body is a fluid rather than a fixed sovereign. Likewise, borders of a specific national democratic entity as well as the boundaries of the political community are charged with temporality - shifting and changing, too. Borders signify tension and relate to complex processes of metaphorical as well as doctrinal discourses. Hence, borders and boundaries could be regarded as 'historically specific social systems' (Davis and Moctezuma 1999)[1] as argued above.

The purpose of external EU borders is made very clear, for example, by Romano Prodi (2001, cited in Com 2002/ 233: 1) when he argues that 'effective common management of the external borders of the Member States of the Union will boost security and citizens' sense of belonging to a shared area and destiny.' In 2007, Amitai Etzioni made a plea for a 'normative-affective community' in the European Union by strengthening its 'shared values'. Further, he criticised the lack of EU policing and co-ordination when tackling 'illegal immigrants, criminals and terrorists' (2007: 20). In Etzioni's reading, unwanted immigrants become associated with criminals and terrorists as he conflates semantically different categories of outsiders. This rhetorical attempt to outlaw people who try to cross borders can be

---

1 http://www.colorlines.com/article.php?ID=98.

regarded as significant to contemporary modified border and boundary discourses. In a reflection of the history of slave trade routes and contemporary paths of African Diasporic immigrants heading by boat for Europe, Jayne O. Ifekwunigwe (2006) points to the very contradictory notions of mobility and to the gendered as well as racialised borderland space regarding the Mediterranean Sea. She writes (2006: 92), 'at least 3,000 African Boat People or *Pateras* as they are known in Spain, have drowned attempting the passage across the Straits, described as "the largest mass grave in Europe"' (Tremplett 2001b). Whereas 'Spain is the third-most popular holiday destination in the world' (Ifekwunigwe 2006: 92), the Straits of Gibraltar and the sea around the Canary Islands have become signifiers of systematic EU exterritorial border control and clandestine mass death. Though 'visible alterity' (Ifekwunigwe 2006: 94) is ascribed to black African migrants as well as Moroccans, it is the '"Moorish" anxiety' (ibid.) that prominently shapes the discourse by way of addressing Muslims in the racialised position of the 'suspicious and threatening' Other. Against the background of the Spanish and intra-European expulsion of Jews and Arabs in the 15th century, this specific singling out of North Africans, who have played a major role in the making of what counts as contemporary European 'civilisation', appears as an indication of how the 21st-century imagination of Europe is haunted.

Etienne Balibar (2001) argues that the 'the notions of interiority and exteriority, which form the basis of the representation of *bordering,* are undergoing a veritable earthquake.'[2] Further to the external EU bordering, which is orchestrated by the EU agency Frontex,[3] a broader process of control and technological policing of people's movement is de-centred and spread inside the EU Member States. Due to transformed notions of what counts as border-lands, metropolitan and multicultural cities as dense and crowded places of movement have become spaces of control. Since post 9/11 we recognise a candidly intensified state funding of academic studies that tackle terrorism and security issues in and beyond Europe. Didier Bigo et al. (2010, see also Bigo and Guild 2005) approach surveillance and 'frontiers' from a critical perspective. Their research confronts the 'free movement' paradigm that privileges us as EU citizens with a map of detention centres and cumulating death points of non-EU citizens and illegalised immigrants across Europe.[4]

Evy Varsamapoulou (2009: 25) proposes that 'Europe ceases to be a geographic term of clear or obvious significance and becomes interrogated for its content as an idea and, almost immediately, as an ideal.' Europe presented as a 'space of becoming' is also put forward by sociologists Gerald Delanty (1996, 2009), Chris Rumford (2000, 2002, 2007, 2009) or Ulrich Beck (2004a–c, 2006a and 2006b) for example, who all engage with the socio-cultural consequences that emerge from the expanding European Union as a transnational political-economic

---

2   http://www.makeworlds.org/node/80.

3   http://www.frontex.europa.eu/.

4   http://www.libertysecurity.org/module/pdfs/LoRezCamps.pdf;   http://www.liberty security.org/module/pdfs/LoRezDeath_Map.pdf.

entity. It is telling though that the policy space of the European Union is often used synonymously with the notion of Europe.

What has the policing of the European Union at large to do with the disciplining of orthodox Muslim women who dare to wear a *nijab* or the *burqa* in some continental EU Member States? And what does this tell us about the gendering of political community boundaries across Europe? In what ways is this policing of the female body/face linked to the cultural identity project of the European Union and how does it articulate a hegemonic claim of *modern* cosmopolitanism in Europe? And further, why should we be troubled that gay as well as women's rights are thrown into this debate on 'equality and difference' and here used as a token of an 'Enlightened' and 'universal' European agenda of liberation?

This chapter intends to explore these questions more closely as we are witnessing a dramatic rise in public debates and parliamentary decisions for national legislations intending to outlaw gendered and cultural difference of minority orthodoxy as it is visible in various continental European countries. Recent legislative motions to ban the facial veil in Belgium, France and, more recently, initiatives taken in the Netherlands are following previous governmental regulations regarding the headscarf in other EU Member States. (Fisher Onar 2011, Edmunds 2011, Lettinga 2011) All these new legislative initiatives which have been established subsequent to a rise in political mandates for right wing or extreme right wing populist parties and coalitions appear to be the tip of an iceberg.[5]

Going back to the cosmopolitan claim of 'openness towards the Other' we might ask: what is left to the imagination of *cosmopolitan all-inclusiveness* in a post-9/11, and post 7/7 2005 terror-trauma that stigmatises all Muslims and orthodox Islam?

In contrast, the symbolic 'inclusion' of lesbian and gay minorities could be addressed as a symptom of more open-minded and relaxed 21st-century European democracies.[6] We could argue that the public recognition of homosexual intimate relationships, e.g. legalising the access to marriage or registered civil partnerships, indeed underscores broader processes of 'normalisation' in different European

---

5   At the time of finishing this book a fascist right wing Norwegian, named Breivik, killed more than 60 young people on a small island close to Oslo and further people died in an attack on a government building in the city of Oslo. Breivik knew that a Labour party youth camp was taking place and also caused the death of further victims by planting a bomb in Oslo's government building. In the mainstream media Breivik's ideological proximity to the far extreme right wing English Defence League as well as his fundamentalist Christian views were made responsible for engendering his hatred towards Muslims and the 'multicultural' Left. Some of the young people were aspiring future leaders of the Norwegian Labour Party. Less is said, however, about Breivik's extremist anti-feminist hatred and misogynist perspective on women. (see for further info, coverage by Amy Goodman, (democracynow.org, 30 July 2011).

6   The Netherlands was the first country to open the traditional heterosexual marriage to same sex couples. Across Europe 22 nation states recognise same sex unions (marriage and partnerships) by now.

Union Member States. Given that the notion of the Other is at the core of any utopian *all-inclusive* vision of cosmopolitanism there is a need to tackle the paradox of an increasingly *democratic* consensus in anti-discrimination standards[7] on the one hand, and the criminalisation of *particular manifestations* of faith (religious, cultural and political) and gendered minority difference, on the other. It is this two tiered distinction and paradox of 'democratic civic reason' that encompasses hegemonic understandings concerning 'European' belonging and 'civic' loyalty in the 21st century. To anchor this paradox in European philosophical legacies and modern understandings of reasonable law, secularism and normality, first, I will go back to Immanuel Kant's thoughts on cosmopolitanism while tracing back some of the problematic normative aspects of contemporary discourses on cosmopolitanism in Europe. Then in a second part, more concrete emanations of shifting cultural-symbolic boundaries in some EU Member states are analysed with respect to gender equality, ethnic and religious group interests and anti-discrimination law. Further, the political tension produced by the group recognition/redistribution dilemma is reviewed in order to clarify how the modern discourse of difference is confused with alterity as distinguished analytically in Chapter 1.

The (Ir)rationales of Normative Cosmopolitanism in Europe

According to Rundell (1998: 323) the sovereignty of nation-states is either based on a 'personalization of power' or on the 'codification of law'. With regard to the latter 'codification' refers to the meaning of contract as the legally defined sphere where negotiation, consensus and arrangements take place.

We have to keep in mind this meaning of 'contract/law' as the codification of democratic consensus is crucial to the discussion of the relationship between inclusive late modern democracy and visions of an all-inclusive and the planet's (human) beings encompassing cosmopolitanism.

Francis Cheneval (2002) suggests that contemporary cosmopolitanism is rooted in the philosophy of modernity, in particular in Kant's philosophical considerations of the meaning of contract, proposing the individual's emancipation from Absolutism.[8] Kant's vision of 'perpetual peace' has become very prominent in the normative discourses of cosmopolitanism. For instance, advocates of liberal-normative cosmopolitanism such as Jürgen Habermas (1970, 1996) or David Held (1995, 2004) as well as feminist theorists Seyla Benhabib (2002, 2008) or Martha Nussbaum (1997, 2010) are all inspired by Kant's philosophy. Hence, I will briefly unwrap some terminological tensions central to Kant's writing that

---

7   The positive effect of EU-anti-discrimination directives meant that all 27 EU Members states had to implement this anti-discrimination policy into national legislation.

8   Absolutism refers to the power of the absolute monarchy; the French king Louis XIV with his famous phrase '*L'état, c'est moi*' embodies this claim most explicitly.

affect the contemporary interpretation of the rule of democratic law and notions of a cosmopolitan 'civic consensus'.

In his famous essay *Perpetual Peace: a Philosophical Sketch* (1795) and even earlier in the *Idea for a Universal History from a Cosmopolitan Point of View* (1784; also in Reiss 1970) Kant promoted a utopia of worldwide peace (Kleingeld 2005), which he understood as an absence of eternal war. His vision posits that states should be 'organized internally according to "republican" principles, when they are organized externally in a voluntary league for the sake of keeping peace, and when they respect the human rights not only of their citizens but also of foreigners' (cited in Kleingeld and Brown 2006).[9] Significantly, Kant published his essay during the French revolution and contemporaneously with the international reception of Thomas Hobbes' *Leviathan*. In contrast to Hobbes, who proposed 'a kind of fortress state that can overwhelm both internal and external enemies' (Williams 2003: 219), Kant's statement can be read as an alternative political version that has an optimistic vision of how international political stability could be guaranteed.

As the theme of 'the enemy' is central both to the archetypal political discourses and to the contemporary language of the global war on/of terrorism[10] across democratic nation states,[11] the philosophical logic used by Kant will be discussed briefly.

In his most frequently cited work *Die Metaphysischen Anfangsgründe der Rechtslehre* (1797)[12] Kant approaches philosophically the meaning of the 'unjust enemy'. Kant (1797: 225, 226, 1970) conceptualised the 'eternal' of a cosmopolitan peace while also acknowledging that there is an Other outside the civilisation consensus. However, this Other is merely addressed as a state agent. Kant is differentiating very clearly between *Volk* (people) and *Staat* (the state) and thus leaving political space for civil dissent between the people as a republic on the one hand, and oppressive and unjust state orders[13] on the other. Besides, Kant

---

9   http://plato.stanford.edu/archives/fall2002/entries/cosmopolitanism.

10   According to Susan Buck-Morss (2008: 145), 'A conceptual distinction can be made between normal enemies – those who act as enemies are expected to act, positioning themselves within the mental landscape of the existing political imaginary – and the absolute enemy whose attack threatens the imaginary landscape itself. The enemy action by 19 young men within the United States on 11 September 2001 was an attack on this second, metalevel.'

11   Prominently, Chantal Mouffe engages with the theme of 'the enemy' when bringing in Carl Schmitt's writing and her critique of liberal cosmopolitanism. I will come back to this later in Chapter 4.

12   The original text is published in *Fraktur*, an 18th-century lettering of German language that does not correspond to the modern spelling. In English the title would be translated to 'The Groundwork of the Metaphysics of Legal thought'; which is the first part of the *Metaphysics of the Morals*.

13   Which at the time of Kant's writing meant the aristocracy/absolutistic monarchy in continental Europe.

made clear that he regarded the possibility of an 'unjust enemy' as a pleonasm; he argued that there could be no 'unjust enemy' because this would entail that there could be a 'just enemy' and resisting the just enemy would be an act of injustice. He concluded that for this paradoxical reason a 'just enemy' could not be 'my enemy' (Kant 1797: 227). After all, Kant's philosophy was devoted to an idealistic vision: he insisted that the idea of eternal peace is a *'unausführbare Idee'* (1797: 227), a 'non-executable idea'. Hence Kant regarded his vision as a utopian outlook which was necessary to advance peace, constructed as non-enforceable and therefore as *consensual justice*. Consequently, cosmopolitan 'perpetual peace' is bound to the idea of republican principles, which are addressed as evolving as a bottom up principle of participatory democracy that cannot be imposed by militaristic interventions. From this it would be clear that any attempt to change regimes in order to 'bring democracy' ought to fail. In addition, it is worth reflecting on the notion of 'republic' Kant might have had in mind and anchoring any connotation of 'republic and democracy' in the revolutionary spirit of the late 18th and early 19th century. At the end of the day, the consideration that there might be an 'unjust enemy' outside 'civilisation' hints at an imaginative realm beyond inclusive boundaries of the modern (secular) civil society.

Pauline Kleingeld (1998: 72) emphasises that Kant's cosmopolitan law 'is concerned not with the interaction between states, but with the status of individuals in their dealings with states of which they are not citizens. Moreover, he is concerned with the status of individuals as human beings rather than as citizens of states.' Enrique Dussel (1995) disagrees with this interpretation, claiming that Kant's idealistic concept is enshrined in a boundary construction of 'superior' white European civilisations versus the uncivilised Other (Dussel 2000). Accordingly, we could argue that a 'white' dismissal of the colonial context and sub-text of Kant's philosophy might be also characteristic to normative aspirations of visions of cosmopolitan democracy and loaded with potentially racist implications of Kant's contractual vision. Eduardo Mendieta called this recently, 'Kantian imperial cosmopolitanism' (2009: 246). Further, Robin M. Schott (2000, 1998) makes clear that feminist critical engagement with Kant's 'misogyny and disdain of the body' (2000: 39) highlights that there are substantially hierarchical and dualistic positions of 'mind/body, reason/emotion, public/private' (2000: 45, referring to Klinger 1995) in Kant's epistemology. According to Schott (ibid.), 'Kim Hall examines Kant's examples and metaphors to show the Eurocentric assumptions of Kantian aesthetics, which celebrate the colonizer who "civilizes" the "savages"' (Hall 1997).

Against the background of these critical observations I argue that Kant's vision of 'eternal peace' could lead to arguments which develop *global civic law*, but also call for actions that favour *global war against the savages*. There is a paradigmatic normative 'outside' to Kant's concept of universal peace as in principal there could be an 'unjust enemy' outside (European) Western civilisation. Hence, Kant's vision could lead to an ideological reading of human rights as constituting particular institutional boundaries: the Other who undermines the civilisation consensus might be constructed as outside the nexus of global civilisation.

To summarise: Kant's philosophical considerations and ideals have travelled through time and translation; they might have met Hobbes's ideas in a transformed context of a 'global inside' declared as *cosmopolitan civilisation*. While giving a privileged meaning to citizenship and bounded political community on the one hand, democracy going global does claim to be the foundation of universal rights and global humanity, on the other.

Another crucial layer encompassing the idea of a 'republican' Western civic order is the notion of *secularism* in Europe. Secularism at the heart of the public/private space division and nation state politics in Europe is increasingly contested as the modern state's consensual boundary marker of national communities. This challenge has to be interpreted against the background of fundamentalist Islamist terror since 2001 in Western societies and a rise in global migration and the post-Holocaust re-emergence of race-ethnically and religiously diverse societies. Maria Pia Lara (2007, 2003) argues that 'the vertigo of secularization' (2003) only shows the way humans struggle to live without an idea of final judgement. Bringing in Christina Lafont's (2005) response to Habermas's (2005, 2008) announcement of a new stage of post-secularism in Western nation states, Lara further proposes to regard

> (s)ecularization not as an ultimate goal, but rather as a 'particular complex process of building up a political state. Secularization, then, is not a Western panacea, but rather one political example – a model – in which we Westerners continue to learn how to cope with our religious fears in an open society. If we are conscious that societies struggle against the growing complexity of pluralism, we need to be in permanent alarm. (2007: 238)

This thought is interesting as it suggests that modern Western societies have to fight their own religious demons though it leaves it open as to where these demons are coming from. We could contemplate how the renaissance of public interest in religion in the connotation of a 'post-secular' society might be come about: whether Christian societies are haunted by their hidden shrines, having forced the explicit religious practice of minorities into privacy for some time,[14] or whether this has only become an obstacle through the public disputes, demands and presence of another powerful monotheistic minority religion. Islam might have dismantled only the secular mask of the hidden faith in Western societies. Here, the 'hidden shrine' gives attention to a particular framing of secular democracy. Christian-value laden connotations of secular democracy in Europe are traditionally underlying a republican notion of the *citoyen*.

The ideology of a secular class of citizens being at the centre of liberal market state order is addressed by Talal Asad (2000: 19), who argues that Muslims could not be politically represented in liberal democracies 'because in theory the citizens

---

14　More precisely, since 1648; the so called Westphalian Peace ended the 30 years lasting intra-European Christian war between Protestants and Catholics.

who constitute a democratic state belong to a class that is defined by what is common to all its members and its members only.' Looking at the political agenda of the European Union we might agree that this is indeed a 'members' club', which defines selectively who is mature enough to enter its 'exquisite' space. The debate addressing the civil 'maturity' of Turkey as a potential member of the European Union, for example, underlines in what ways Muslim societies and Muslim communities are viewed as 'interfering' in a supra-state system basically claimed as Christian. Asad (2000: 12) contends:

> [t]he idea of European identity, I say, is not merely a matter of how a more inclusive name can be made to claim loyalties that are attached to national or local ones. It concerns exclusions and the desire that those excluded recognize what is included in the name. It is a symptom of anxieties.

The ideological effort to bring 'European identity' to the fore raises significant concerns about the role of contemporary European policy strategies which aim to 'outlaw' particular Others as *culturally* different and potentially 'threatening'.

In the next section, I will look more closely at public debates in Europe concerning the majority's claim to have a right to *see/look at* the female face and body, which matches with a compulsory female duty to make her skin (and smile) available to the male gaze in the public sphere. Beyond my feminist critique of *any authoritative* rule that obliges women to dress in a modest or sexy manner, and that therefore might work as an obstacle to individual wish and need of female liberation, the more interesting question relates to the emergence of a broader 'democratic' *consensus* in different (continental) European societies regarding the policing of the orthodox female Muslim garment.

The Mono-Cultural (Male) Gaze at the Female Veil: Multicultural Paradoxes of Difference and Equality

McGoldrick (2006: 298) argues that 'in Europe in particular, the headscarf-*hijab* debate has become a microcosm of the debate on multiculturalism'. This observation might not come as a surprise given that the notion of 'multiculturalism' and multicultural democracy became subverted in recent years: among others the phenomenon of 'home-grown' terrorists and Islamic violent extremists confronted the British as well as the Dutch national fabrics, in particular, with gaps in their national self-image of being tolerant and *multicultural* societies. With respect to the British national context Wemyss (2006, 2009) argues that tolerance is connected to power. Those who structurally and culturally define the rules of belonging and appropriate behaviour in society grant tolerance to others. Nonetheless, the Other has to play by the rules. This 'hierarchy of belonging' (2009: 133 ff.) keeps the dominant power in place while also defining non-whiteness and minority ethnic difference as a lower social status. This common-sense normativity continues as a colonial subtext in different European societies[15] which approve white normality as their mainstream standards (Vieten 2011).

Despite the social ruptures indicated by 'race riots',[16] social movements and de-colonialising cultural struggles in various European countries, the contemporary national narratives keep alive a hegemonic gendered class order encompassed by *the normality* of a rather submissive co-existence of diverse minority ethnic and religious communities. Multiculturalism appears to be

> [c]haracterized by a paradoxical injunction that limits, but doesn't completely negate the possibility for 'ethnic minorities' to withdraw from their circumscribed status. On the one hand, 'ethnic minority' groups are encouraged, within the multicultural paradigm, to make their cultures inclusive and accessible in order to contribute towards a liberal-pluralist celebration of 'cosmopolitan' diversity and cross-cultural citizenship; on the other, it is forbidden to threaten their ethnic particularism, as to do so would contradict their claim to resources as a distinct group. (Nagle 2009: 5)

This 'double bind' (ibid.) message shows some of the multicultural dilemmas exposing and insisting on *visible difference* in terms of gendered ethnicity and race minority communities. However, any 'sexing up' of visible group difference, for example as advertised in the multicultural images of 'global cities' such as London, Berlin or Amsterdam, is troubled by a hegemonic class claim. It evolves predominantly around attitudes of consumption towards exotic and entertaining (food, sex and music) difference for individual pleasures. Problematically, the rosy version of national harmony disguises the rather conflict ridden reality of shrinking social welfare, lack of solidarity and psycho-emotional *Vereinzelung* (isolation) that leaves members of different communities in envy (also Nagle 2009: 171) and fear (Bauman 2006). Further, the 'hypervisibility' (Ghorashi 2010) of migrant/minority women who stand out visibly has triggered populist cultural

---

15   The outbreak of violent urban 'arson and looting' disturbances of mostly young men and some women in London/Tottenham in August 2011 and also striking other poor and often black communities of London before spreading north to Birmingham and Liverpool, for example, provoked openly racist comments by some white journalists and politicians in mainstream news. 'Black' culture was blamed as being at the roots of this upheaval of an underclass of young people. It appears as if the denied existence of huge income and class gaps in English cities, gendered and racialised as they are, erupted to the surface.

16   In the 1970s and 1980s predominantly black Youth protested collectively in London (Notting Hill 1976, Brixton 1981), in Leeds (Chapeltown 1975) as well as in Liverpool (1985). More recently, in early 2001 the violent protest of South Asian British Youth in some Northern cities, such as Bradford and Oldham (Greater Manchester) tuned public attention in to the social fabric and regional ethno-racial and economic situation in the Northern cities. The Banlieu riots in Paris add another stream of social riots to this account underlining that spatial and social exclusion operate along ethno-racial class barriers (Vieten 2009, 2011).

outrage. It is the female self-confident and identifying act of consciously drawing a symbolic boundary of group difference that causes public dismay and anger in some European societies, apparently.

As argued elsewhere (Vieten 2011), orthodox femininity signifies a gendered boundary between predominantly Christian-secular shaped national societies in Europe and the emergence of Muslim orthodox minority identities. 'The non-veiled Western *modern* woman symbolizes the "positive" in contrast to the "negative" image of the veiled woman' (Vieten 2011: 69). Either way the secular modern nation state and the orthodox religious community are claiming the female body as a gendered symbol of 'their' community (*Gemeinschaft*). However, this indicates how *woman* in terms of a Foucaultian bio-politics is considered patriarchal property (ibid.). It is worth noting too, that the French debate on the headscarf was engendered by president Chirac in 2003, explicitly referring to a national identity crisis torn between the republican '*laïcité*' and 'the citizens' Europe' (cited in McGoldwick 2006: 295). Jacob T. Levy (2010: 61, 62) uses an example from an ultra-orthodox Jewish community to bring out the sexist substance of the (patriarchal) doubt of a female individual right to come to an independent[17] reasonable decision: Levy gives the example (case 1) of a group of orthodox Jewish men in Montreal, who want the gym in their neighbourhood to use curtains for their windows so 'they don't risk seeing women exercising in skimpy workout clothes' (2010: 61). As Levy argues with reference to Chirac's 'hysterical claim that the wearing of a *hijab* in a school was an "assault against the [French] Republic", what one person wears on her head does not harm anyone else. But case 1 isn't about adherents of religion with the modesty norm seeking to remove themselves from other people's view – it's about trying to remove *other* people from *their* view' (2010: 62).

Though Levy regards these conflicts rather as a matter of *manners* with respect to (group) recognition and multicultural accommodation[18] his argument adds a further twist to my argument challenging a gendered male right or an internalised male gaze to see (or in case 1 to claim the right that the object should be removed; not to be seen) and the gendered female obligation to be seen (or not) in a public realm. While referring to Berghahn (2009), Fehr (2011: 122) stresses that 'forceful de-veiling represents a superiority complex and "late colonial" fantasies contrasting the progressive West to the backward misogynistic Muslim ideology.' Nonetheless, as public debates in several European countries have also shown, individually, minority feminists[19] likewise might support the banning of the veil while very explicitly arguing against the 'cultural' oppression of women. They might even

---

17   According to Fehr (2011: 123) 'Proponents of the view that Muslim women who wear the headscarf are dominated by men, submissive and in need of liberation played a powerful role in the French and German debates.'

18   I will come back to this in this chapter later.

19   For instance, Necla Kelek in Germany; Ayaan Hirsi Ali in the Netherlands; Fatiha Amara in France.

buy into a national state rhetoric that links western military interventions with women's emancipation (Pitcher 2009). Pitcher (2009: 126) rightly exposes that '[t]he repeated return to a figuration of antifeminism as an aberration from the norms of a cultural majority highlights the extent to which the very idea of gender equality feeds off the threat of the betrayal by racialised others.'

However, as outlined above, gendered state politics and feminist claims have become more complicated as some minority women identify with the normative frame of what is passed on in *the democratic contract* of modern and Western 'gender equality'. The larger discursive picture of contemporary European societies hints at complex hierarchical intersectional[20] dimensions of class, status, ethnicity/race, sexuality, nationality, religion/*Weltanschauung,* for example, impacting on gender interests and the way they are conveyed . The current 'hyper' interest in visible minority women in Europe, however, is not in any way matched by public interest in positive actions which ought to address the continuing gap between economic, political and social opportunity structures regarding the two sexes across ethnic/race and religious divisions.

In her discussion of Iris Marion Young's (2000) work on social justice in the context of immigration and inclusion, Mariam Martinez (2009) differentiates four systems of structural injustice and declares that,

> From the liberal perspective, *issues of gender* are sometimes hidden by general problems of religion where women normally are treated as the objects of the debate (Young 2000, p. 62). In the case of the *affaire du foulard,* or affair of the veil, in France for instance, religion has displaced other relevant questions about gender discrimination such as the sexual division of labor, gendered processes of socialization, and the establishment of hegemonic norms that limit real opportunities of women. (Young 2005a, p.22)

A similar point has been made by Nancy Fraser,[21] stressing that the emphasis on Islamic dress code, e.g. the polarisation regarding the public debate on the *hijab* in Europe, is quite similar to the debate on abortion in the US. However, a media-orchestrated rhetorical focus on 'value issues' and cultural oppression of minority women distracts attention from the deeper concerns of social rights and health care for all women in society (ibid.).

Going back to Young's (2000; 2006) feminist interventions in theoretical debates on group recognition, gender difference and social justice, it is convincing

---

20 Contemporary feminist social analysis takes Kimberlé Williams Crenshaw's (1989) analytical model of 'intersectionality' applied to the distinctive situation of US American black women further while interrogating complex social structures of group oppression (Yuval-Davis 2005, 2006) and anti-discrimination issues (Verloo 2006, Vieten 2009) in Europe.

21   http://www.youtube.com/watch?v=0KHRfnUCcko.

to bring in the notion of 'oppression' and 'normalization' to the theme of multiculturalism and religious orthodoxy.

According to Young (2006), distributive justice is shaped by *normality* and processes of normalisation (producing 'stigmatization' and 'disadvantage', Young 2006: 97), which might result in a lack of group (minority) recognition. At stake is the axis of redistribution/recognition rather than the 'accommodation of one group's practices and forms of cultural expression' (Martinez 2009: 221); the latter, however, is taken as the majority's threshold case of tolerance in the multicultural debate. Fraser (2002) argues that distributive justice is linked to Kantian *Moralität* (morality) and recognition to Hegelian *Sittlichkeit* (ethics); the binding towards universal justice is distinctive to particular cultural claims. She proposes a 'status model' (2009: 24) instead of the problematic group identity politics that pushes for internal conformism. Fraser writes:

> (w)hat requires recognition is not group-specific identity but rather the status of group members as full partners in social interaction. Misrecognition, accordingly, does not mean the depreciation and deformation of group identity. Rather, it means *social subordination* in the sense of being prevented from *participating as a peer* in social life. (ibid.)

Clearly, Fraser's view resonates with the legacy of Western ideals of liberal individualism as her emphasis is on the potential of individuals to participate as an 'equal'. The impact of multidimensional discrimination (Schiek 2011) on the grounds of sex/gender, religion and ethnicity on 'social status' of orthodox Muslim women, for example, can be followed up concretely in the litigation brought by female teachers who are not permitted to pursue their careers in educational institutions and as a result are social-economically marginalised or girls who are dismissed from schools and in consequence prevented from gaining higher degrees.[22]

With respect to the European Union the outlook on gender equality and group minority difference is linked to legislative measures that unfold through a web of EU Anti-discrimination Directives (Schiek 2002, 2005). It is made obligatory for the 27 EU Member States to implement equality law that covers also anti-discrimination measures tackling racial, ethnic and religiously motivated discrimination.

In the remaining part of this chapter I therefore turn to an inspection of EU Non-discrimination law, discussing first the tension between hegemonic perceptions of homogenous minority group formation, normalisation dynamics in the context of homosexuality and the inadequacy of non-discrimination law when it comes to the racialised situation of Roma in Europe.

---

22   I will come back to some of these effects in the following chapters.

Hybridity and Diversity in the European Union: How to Accommodate Minority Difference and Achieve Equality?

If we look at contemporary approaches to the notion of diversity we can recognise that groups often are considered as forming ideological, biological or cultural units. Fred L. Pincus (2006), for example, names explicitly class, race, gender and sexual orientation. He refers to ethnicity as a subcategory of race but sometimes enmeshes this category with race (see for example 2006: 61-63). Further, Pincus (2006: 3) argues that diversity could be approached as a matter of counting, as a matter of culture, as a matter of 'Good-for-business diversity' or as 'an indicator of conflict' (ibid.). The latter refers to an *understanding how different groups exist in a hierarchy of inequality in terms of power, privilege, and wealth*' (2006: 4).[23] This observation matches the critical notion of tolerance as argued above, making another case for my argument that diversity encircles accepted difference, at least temporarily agreed, and that a notion of difference as Alterity has to be differentiated analytically, that is beyond hegemonic tolerance. Though Pinkus's approach attempts to look at group conflicts from a structural level, the conceptualising logic remains immanent to the dominant ideology that constructs groups as homogenised units which can be tamed and controlled, and at best, *integrated*. Roger Brubaker (2004) criticises this approach, calling it 'groupism' (2004: 50). He explains, '[t]his is what I call groupism: the tendency to take discrete, sharply differentiated, internally homogeneous and externally bounded groups as basic constituents of social life, chief protagonists of social conflicts' (ibid.).

A push for inside-homogeneity of minority groups is processed both through internal and external violence. However the foundational hierarchical system within and across existing societies has to be understood as shaped predominantly by 'normative' male gender regimes. A male gender regime – Young (2006: 98) characterises it as 'Masculinist normalization' – takes hegemonic male standards as norms; any 'deviant' Other has to adjust to these standards. If those standards are defined as 'impartial', 'neutral', 'objective' or 'gained through individual merit', the complexity of networks, institutions and resources providing 'masculine forms of comportment' (ibid.) are out of the picture.

In terms of the situation of gay men and lesbians, Young is very much straightforward in her judgement. She argues:

> Oppressions experienced by queer people are entirely a result of processes of normalization. In our societies heterosexual orientation and gender behaviour conformity do not simply function as norms in the sense of the way the majority of people are. The society holds up heterosexual desire as normative ... And if the norm should become expansive enough to include some of them, the process of normativity continues to position some people as deviant. Thus, for example, some gay couples may try to conform to the norms of respectability dominant

---

23   It is written in italics in the original text.

in straight society; monogamous coupling with one or two children, inviting straight friends to dinner parties, and so on. Queers who do not wish to live this way then become further stigmatized. (ibid.)

Fraser (2009: 34 and 35) urges a similar direction when also referring to the question of same sex marriage. She explains:

> [t]he institutionalization in marital law of a heterosexist cultural norm denies parity of participation to gays and lesbians. For the status model, therefore, this situation is patently unjust, and a recognition claim is in principle warranted. Such a claim seeks to remedy the injustice by de-institutionalizing the heteronormative value patterns and replacing it with an alternative that promotes parity. This, however, can be done in more than one way. One way would be to grant the same recognition to homosexual partnerships that heterosexual partnerships currently enjoy by legalizing same-sex marriage. Another would be to de-institutionalize heterosexual marriage, decoupling entitlements such as health insurance from marital status and assigning them on some other basis such as citizenship and/or territorial residency.

The crucial point regarding Young's critique and Fraser's second suggestion is that minoritised group difference (of gays and lesbians, for example; but also of [white] ethnic minority women) should not be claimed as a template of (queer) freedom automatically. Rather, it matters if individuals are adjusting to a hegemonic way of life, or what we might call hetero-normativity, white-normativity; or Protestant-Christian normativity; and leaving broader concepts of liberation and emancipation of Others aside. As Günther H. Lenz and Antje Dallmann (2007: 9) in their introductory comments on Young's earlier work, *Justice and the Politics of Difference* (1990), emphasise, Young argued for 'a vision of a "heterogeneous public that acknowledges and affirms group differences", a vision she finds expressed in the ideal of city life (as against the celebration of a homogeneous "community") as the "openness to unassimilated otherness".' I want to draw particular attention to the latter. Providing some contestations to hetero-normative lifestyles a critical discourse concerning 'homo-nationalism' emerged in recent years that challenges hetero-normative life style orientations and common sense complicity to the 'war on terror' of the gay community in concordance with a queer postcolonial political framework (Puar 2007; Haritaworn 2008).[24]

According to Avigail Eisenberg (2006: 17), 'recognition' of group difference is relevant 'when it is a source of oppression or when it intersects with and is used to entrench oppression' (ibid.). That means group difference comes into sight or into political existence at a point of conflict, and contestation about the way *normality* is framed and in what ways social status coincides with certain opportunities and choices. Feminists put the analysis of contradictory and more

---

24   http://www.darkmatter101.org/site/category/journal/issues/3-post-colonial-sexuality/.

multi-dimensional layers to individual identity and group positions at the centre of their critique of hegemonic societies. After engaging widely with concepts of gender mainstreaming (Squires 2005) and gender equality in the European Union (Walby 2004), also as an aspect of Europeanisation (Liebert 2003), feminist debates in Europe are embarking increasingly on the theoretical concept and methodological approach of *intersectionality*. This is being done in the context of Gender Studies (Brah and Phoenix 2004, Prins 2006, Yuval-Davis 2006, Lutz et. al. 2011), with respect to the political formation of the European Union (Verloo 2006, Walby 2007), arguing for a transnational space beyond the EU and Europe (Vieten 2009), looking at its impact more generally on Law (Grabham et al. 2009) and more explicitly referring to EU Non-Discrimination Law (Schiek and Chege 2009, Schiek and Lawson 2011).

To confront the outlined social complexities of a recognition/redistribution dilemma with more concrete legislative strategies that aim to accommodate minority group difference, as a final point, the potential of legal anti-discrimination tools and its limits will be discussed with a focus on the transnational situation of Roma. The nomadic legacy and particular ethnic identity of Roma transgresses the legally and socially regulated space of the European Union; however, political self-organisation is benefiting from international Human Rights discourses and struggles.

According to Thomas Acton (1999), the International Romani Movement 'jumped on the buzz-word "transnational"' (1999: 147), which informs its political strategies in and beyond Europe. Today, Roma constitute the only *genuinely* European transnational ethnic minority community with a majority that live overwhelmingly in Central and Eastern Europe. Kristina Koldinská (2011) argues that '[a]round 70 per cent of the European Gypsy population (some 8 million people) live in Central and Eastern Europe'. (2011: 242) The enlargement of the European Union in 2004 and 2007 formally integrated post-communist states such as the Czech Republic, Romania, Slovakia, Slovenia, Bulgaria and Hungary. It is debatable to which degree the rise in (again) freely moving Roma across Europe has triggered anti-Gypsy racism in all EU Member States; for example in Italy and Ireland with attacks of Roma in recent years as far as Western Europe is concerned, and also further attempts to ghettoise Roma in Hungary. The rise of extreme and far right parties across Europe also suggests that a populist anti-Gypsy racism is supported by large proportions of the majority (ethnic) population (Koldinská 2011).

With respect to the post-Holocaust international grassroots movement of Roma it is worthwhile recording that as early as 1948 a group called '*Aboli Faik's Phralipe*' (Brotherhood) was founded in Skopje (Puxon 2000). Their activities included Romani football clubs, and a Chair for Romani Studies at the University of Bratislava was even established temporarily between 1968 and 1971. The Communist Party of the then Yugoslavia banned the Romani organisation in 1973 as any particular and ethnic group interest was regarded as a threat to the state (Puxon 2000) In terms of its trans-European and global repercussions the fall of the Berlin Wall, and thus the 'Iron Curtain', was a turning point for the possibility of reviving Romani activity. Despite this liberating and positive change in 1989 which made possible the re-embracing of the Roma nomadic lifestyle across Europe the 100,000 Roma refugees who claimed asylum for example in Germany in the early 1990s were regarded as a threat to its high standards of Western social welfare.

Koldinská (2009; 2011), but also Morag Goodwin (2009), stress the particular vulnerability of Roma women at the intersections of gender/sex, ethnicity/race and class. Goodwin more explicitly argues on the 'nexus of race and poverty' (2009: 137 ff.) while substantiating that poor housing, poor health conditions, and lowest employment prospects add to an overall frame of deprivation and social marginalisation. Goodwin summarises the limits of juridical settlements according to the reach of the EU anti-discrimination law:

> Litigation on the basis of racial discrimination undoubtedly works well in a range of areas, for example in gaining individual justice for individual acts of conscious discrimination, and also has a place in the arsenal of measures to tackle systematic discrimination where wider society is unaware of the disproportionate impact of a given measure and can be shamed into forcing change; but what a litigation approach arguably cannot do is take into consideration the overlapping problems that Roma face. What it does, instead, is exclude all the other factors that interact to create a desperate situation that the majority of Roma are in; that is, denies the complexities of the situation and attempts to reduce to it a one-factor issue: race. (2009: 150)

In line with Costas Douzinas (2002), who discusses the Hegelian '*Sittlichkeit*' paradigm as 'interpersonal process of reciprocal recognition' (Goodwin 2009: 156), Goodwin asks for an approach that has to tackle 'redistribution and recognition' (ibid.) likewise. As majority prejudices, hostility and the racialisation of Roma work dialectically, different social layers create socio-economic structural disadvantages for Roma and for Roma women in particular.

What is clear from these considerations is that Fraser's term 'social status' and Young's critique of 'normality' are echoed in different ways in the feminist critique outlined here to structural marginalisation of orthodox Muslims, e.g. Muslim women wearing culturally defined garments, and those of Roma, e.g. particularly stigmatised Roma women. What makes the situation of Roma particularly striking regarding their socially excluded status in the 21st century is their group history of being almost extinct in the Holocaust. If we talk of cosmopolitans in the new Europe, historically it would be Roma who could truly lay claim to this name.

Concluding Remarks

It has been demonstrated in this chapter how a *superiority paradigm* is linked to Kantian philosophy, leaving a problematic normative legacy to discourses on cosmopolitanism and multiculturalism today. Whereas orthodox religion, for example fundamentalist Islam, confronts the West at large and Europe, in particular, with a hidden shrine of a Christian-secular formation of democracy the more recent political and legal developments in several European Union countries point at a paradoxical situation: on the one hand, minority sexual 'identities' become *normalised* in a sense that lesbians and gay men are offered the chance to legalise their personal intimate partnerships, to become 'publicly' acknowledged. On the other, the individual decision of orthodox Muslim women to wear specific cultural faith garments (headscarf; *hijab/nijab*) is publicly outlawed and the female personal choice is pushed into the private sphere. The political economic outcome of these individual liberties (homosexual freedom rights) or penalties (orthodox Muslim counter rights/criminalisation) is related to what Fraser termed 'social status'. Also, the stigmatisation of Roma, e.g. Roma women, in Europe made clear that the redistribution/recognition dilemma affects women, the female gender, in a more rigid way than men. With reference to the dialectic construction of difference as *plurality* and *alterity* it is remarkable that the cosmopolitan Roma are still the minority ethnic group which is the most extremely marginalised and deprived in all EU/European countries. Despite its structural efforts for change the gender equality framework, gender mainstreaming and multidimensional EU anti-discrimination law policy is limited as it can only address legally defined forms of discrimination. Individual claims of discrimination could be litigated, but asymmetric power relations creating social injustice within and across national societies do require a different sort of political agenda: an agenda that might be conveyed in cosmopolitan utopia.

It is necessary here to go back to the visionary project of cosmopolitanism and cosmopolitan thinking that might be capable to challenge the status quo of *Realpolitik* and existing hierarchies. The utopian and emancipatory potential of cosmopolitanism needs the exchange of *different memories* and standpoints in conversations (Young 2000). It is the inclusion of divergent voices that would allow us to understand multiple positions and alternative conditions of the future. For this project it is important to listen to various, even antagonistic, voices contributing to the discourses on cosmopolitanism. For that reason the contributions by *internationally* recognised advocates of a new cosmopolitanism are explored, while also looking at critical feminist interventions. It is crucial that cosmopolitan concepts willingly foster social equality and hybrid cultures (society); thus, it is important that there is a continual debate about what kind of affiliations could create social bonds, solidarity sand commitment in the contemporary global context. To anchor the contemporary debate on cosmopolitanism and gender in Europe more concretely I turn to the recurrence of debates on cosmopolitanism in Germany and Britain. These two countries with significantly different cultures and democratic legacies towards the Shoa and Continental European Totalitarianism are suitable for tracing back notions of difference and Otherness, more specifically. The biased historical discourse of *Weltbürger/Kosmopolit* leads to the question of how far the 'diversity/plurality and alterity' division is relevant to the contemporary debates on cosmopolitanism.

Having introduced Kant's importance to normative cosmopolitanism, the particularly precarious situation of racialised Roma and the ambivalence of EU anti-discrimination policy, I will look more closely at the topic of gender and cosmopolitanism in Germany in Chapter 3. It is important to keep in mind the controversies on the recognition/redistribution dilemma here as debates on cosmopolitanism and social justice unfold which deal with gender equality, ethnic and religious group difference and liberal notions of individualism and personal opportunity structures.

Chapter 3

Kulturnation and the Homogenised Notion of Community Belonging: Jürgen Habermas's and Ulrich Beck's Approaches to 'European' Cosmopolitanism

Zons (2000: 17) proposes two models of urban citizenship that emerged during the Enlightenment and the period of economic transformation: the trader (*der Händler*) and the intellectual (*der Gelehrte*). Idealistically, it is the latter (*der Gelehrte*) who, as the '*citoyen*', signifies the liberation struggle of 'the people' during the French Revolution and which Kant referred to, as discussed above. This notion of the '*citoyen*' defined the republican ideal of citizenship that emerged in the German states following Napoleon Bonaparte's reign in continental Europe. It conveyed an ideal of cultural sophistication detached from revolutionary violent acts. It goes without saying that this 'abstract' notion of citizenship imagines fellow citizens and others without a particular gender, taking for granted 'neutrality'. This has been largely criticised for privileging male gender and also more recently, for ignoring further intersecting asymmetric dimensions of social divisions. As we will see later, the notion of a non-revolutionary (male and white) *citoyen* as already advocated by Kant is central to Habermas's approach to a *European* cosmopolitanism. In what ways is this approach also relevant to Beck's take on cosmopolitanism and are there feminist interventions that challenge these mainstream perspectives? I will come back to these questions later on.

It is argued in this chapter that a particular understanding of *Kultur* in the sense of a cultural-social cohesion project which emerged in the German states at the end of the 19th century impacts on mainstream opinions concerning new cosmopolitanism. In defining 'culture' one possibility is to regard cultural activity as 'cultivating and improving' someone or something. This is important to take on board, as the German concept of *Bildung* historically transmitted a strategy for authoritarian control within a general human duty for perfection. Zons (2000: 23) calls this authoritarian element of education *Erziehungsdiktatur* (dictatorship of education). It means that a cultural undertaking came about which was willing to teach its 'own' people how to behave well and in an educated manner; further, it suggests that there is a connection with cosmopolitan visions which intend 'to civilise' Others according to European 'standards of civilisation'.[1]

The chapter unfolds as follows: first, some decisive aspects of historical discourses of cosmopolitanism in Germany are discussed while considering the intertwined ideological positions of anti-Semitism and an ethno-national and homogeneous German political community as its roots. In this context, there are two key terms that are contextualised: that is, the *Kosmopolit* (cosmopolite) and the *Weltbürger* (citizen of the world). Second, the transformation of the German national community into a secular democratic European Member State is reviewed against the murderous legacy of two world wars and the Holocaust. As it is argued here, the legacy of a conflictive nationalistic history strengthens a framework of *culturalist*[2] *cosmopolitanism* that combines some elements of normative cosmopolitanism and prioritises an institutional form of political federalism.

In the second part of this chapter, the work of both Habermas and Beck on cosmopolitanism will be read against a feminist intervention, e.g. by the socialist-feminist and critical voice of Hanna Behrend. The contributions of German intellectuals to the framing of new cosmopolitanism have to be understood in concordance with contemporary processes of globalisation and Europeanisation. I will analyse their interventions according to the signifiers of community boundary mappings post-1989/1990 and post-2001, as explained in Chapters 1 and 2.

In the following section, first, the peculiar tension between *cultural federalism, anti-Semitism* and (Christian) *faith conformity* that framed German nationalism and state integration since the 19th century is explored with respect to the place of the Other in the imagination of cosmopolitanism.

The Legacy of Cultural(ist) Cosmopolitanism: The German Vision of European 'Civilisation'

During the pre-1848 revolutionary period cosmopolitanism became the prominent element of the German imagination wishing for a united German nation, but also for a *European* identity. In parallel to the founding years (*Gründerjahre*) of the First German Reich a public fascination with anthropological thinking led to a number of privately founded ethnographic museums and societies in different major cities

---

1   In 1805 Johann Gottlieb Fichte argued, for example, that '*Kosmopolitismus*' could be understood as the determination (*Wille*) to achieve the purpose of mankind in humankind (Fichte 1806, cited in Steinbeck 1941: 226). He contrasted this world view with patriotism, understood as the willpower to achieve this purpose, by giving attention primarily to the nation we belong to. After achieving nationhood Germany should reach out for humanity. Fichte's idea was a homogenised German nation that aimed at a broader 'mankind' perspective leading eventually to a culturally united Europe.

2   I use the term 'culturalist' to stress racialising dynamics of a hegemonic culturalising discourse.

(Weindling 1993).[3] As H.G. Penny (2003: 83, 86) argues, it was middle class confidence and cosmopolitan visions rather than interest in nation and *Reich* that motivated local directors of museums in Hamburg, Leipzig, Munich or Stuttgart to compete with the Prussian attempt to found a 'national ethnographic museum' in Berlin: '*das nationale ethnographische Museum – das nie gebaut wurde.*'[4] Though these early modes of culture-civic cosmopolitanism suggest an open minded attitude we have to take into account the terminological and *value* driven split into two different notions of cosmopolitan subjectivity: whereas *Weltbürgertum* (middle classes of the world) connoted an idealised perspective which addressed the potential of citizens of the *civilised world* as belonging to a European culture, the term '*Kosmopoliten*' (cosmopolites)[5] became a negative idiom condemning Jews as unpatriotic and as not belonging to the German national fatherland. In the hegemonic nationalistic imagination Jews were outsiders to the male capacity to obey the patriotic cause by performing military duty. The stigma of 'the people without land' who were criticised as being 'rootless', however, does not tell the story of national anti-Semitic laws: Michaela Wirtz (2006: 24) argues that the love for the fatherland was perceived as dependent on the relationship to the own acre (field). This right to have an acre of land was actually giving what we understand to be 'freehold'. But Jews were forbidden to acquire property and thus they were legally excluded from the status of free land owning citizens (ibid.).

Despite their structural legal, political and social exclusion, many German Jews identified with the idealised notion of *Kultur* as an enlightened cosmopolitan mission of 'starting with the national, but aiming at all humanity'[6] (Wirtz 2006: 28). Prominent German Jewish intellectuals such as Heinrich Heine and Johann Jacoby, for example, were engaged with the democratic movement of the pre-March period of 1848 (*Vormärz*). Jacoby, in particular, moved from an earlier support for a German liberation to a notion of universalism and an ideal of social humanity (Wirtz 2006: 136). Likewise, Heine associated cosmopolitanism with European belonging and civil spirit.[7]

At the beginning of the 20th century Friedrich Meinecke's book *Weltbürgertum und Nationalstaat* (1906, 1928)[8] intended to bridge the ideological rift between

---

3   Weindling (1993: 52–53) mentions the Ethnographic Museum in Munich (1868), an anthropological section in the Zoological Museum in Dresden and several local societies for German anthropology in Freiburg, Göttingen, Würzburg, Munich and Vienna.

4   It reads: 'the national ethnographic museum that was never built.'

5   This term is another expression for 'cosmopolitan'.

6   The enlightened slogan *vom Nationalen zum Allmenschlichen*' (cited in Wirtz 2006: 28) could be translated as 'starting with the national but aiming at the all human'.

7   Heinrich Heine (cited in Thielking 1999: 69) characterised the declining of a broader European spirit as an outcome of the destroyed revolutionary movement in 1848. He connected this larger European horizon with cosmopolitan spirits. For an interpretation of the cosmopolitanism in Heine's literary work, see Cusack 2010.

8   Originally it should be translated as *The middle classes of the world and the national state*, but was published in English as *Cosmopolitanism and the National State*.

German traditions of an early cultural cosmopolitanism in the 18th century and the increasingly *völkisch* nationalistic ideology based on ethnic homogenisation since the end of the 19th century. In opposition to an increasingly nationalistic and anti-Semitic mainstream discourse Meinecke emphasised that the German national identity could also include the cosmopolitan ideal of humanity beyond nationality. In retrospect this was only a marginal voice, one of only a few critical speeches. On the brink of two nationalistic wars that the German nation inflicted on other countries in the 20th century, only the socialists Rosa Luxemburg and Karl Liebknecht voted against military aggression and World War I respectively in the *Reichstag* and further condemned the racist colonial war against the Herero in German occupied South West Africa.[9] Luxemburg and Liebknecht were murdered by paramilitary *Freikorps*[10] later in 1919. Notwithstanding these murders and a salience of nationalistic and rising fascistic orientations during the subsequent Weimar Republic, the end of World War I also led to a renaissance of interest in cosmopolitanism. German sociologists such as Leopold von Wiese and the anthropologist Max Scheler revived cosmopolitan ideas, though concentrating on *'Europäität'* (Thielking 2000: 87).

Next, I will discuss Scheler's ideas in greater detail as his arguments offer insights into some persistent themes that shape contemporary discourses on cosmopolitanism in Europe.[11] Scheler interpreted internationalism and cosmopolitanism as socially classed world views. He regarded the notion of internationalism as rooted in the industrial sphere of work and capital conflict, and cosmopolitanism as linked to rather spiritual, even trans-generational, cultural connections prominently found among different national elites. In order to encourage thinking beyond this classed dichotomy he proposed the concept of a genuine European cultural bond (*Europäität*). According to Scheler (1915: 253), it is the strict division between either nationalism or internationalism and cosmopolitanism that oppresses a more realistic perspective addressing the facts and ideas of a European cultural community. Further, Scheler argued that 'we would be torn apart between a narrow minded chauvinistic nationalism or

---

9   On the 11th of August in 1904 at the Waterberg, Lothar von Trotta and his troops hunted 25,000 Herero tribe including women and children and left them in the desert to die. Between 1904 until 1908 camps, deportation and slave labour were systematically introduced i.e. with the co-operation of the protestant Rhineland mission (Zimmerer 2004).

10   The *Freikorps* are said to have been soldiers, who fought in World War I and were sympathetic to the fascist-nationalist movement.

11   Also, we can detect a *dynamic of travelling ideas* concerning a specific Germanic discourse that imprinted also on the political theorist Carl Schmitt. Importantly, Schmitt's ideas influence the British contemporary discourse on new cosmopolitanism as we will learn in the following chapter. Chantal Mouffe, for example, argues explicitly with a Schmittian inspired terminology of a 'multipolar world order' against liberal cosmopolitanism (Vieten 2010).

imperialism and an empty, standardizing internationalism or cosmopolitanism.'
('*German to English' translations by the author if not stated otherwise.*)[12]

Rooted in what I call a 'culturalist' perspective, he was in favour of different *geographical regions* as he believed each region to have different histories, cultures and outlooks. Despite his argument to transcend the binary of 'nationalism' on the one hand and 'internationalism and cosmopolitanism' on the other we can see that Scheler's point of view conveys an essentialist and dualistic *Weltanschauung* that regards culture, region and nations as 'naturally' different. Scheler opted for a 'multiversum',[13] arguing that the ideal of a universe should be regarded as the idealistic projection of European philosophers.

Another stream of early 20th-century authors, for example Hayman (1924) and Francke (1928), who published in the years of the Weimar Republic, approached cosmopolitanism by tracing its ideals back to philosophers and writers such as Immanuel Kant, Johann Gottfried Herder, Friedrich Schleiermacher, Gottlieb Jacob Fichte and Alexander von Humboldt. With reference to Fichte's notion of state,[14] the German national aspiration was ideologically set apart from English (for example, John Locke) and French (for example, Jean-Jacques Rousseau) perspectives. A broader academic discourse aimed at establishing an ideological vision of German nationhood as a *cultural feeling*, a feeling of being predestined for higher things within humanity.[15] This discourse of 'superiority' persisted and extended throughout the short democratic period of Weimar.

---

12   'Denn durch das ausschließliche Denken in diesen Gegensätzen wird die Tatsache und Idee einer europäischen Kulturgemeinschaft völlig unterdrückt, und wir werden zwischen einem engen chauvinistischen Nationalismus oder "Imperialismus" und einem leeren, nivellierenden Internationalismus oder Kosmopolitanismus geistig hin und her gerissen: Ideen, die beide die innere Lage nicht auszudrücken vermögen, welche wir innerhalb der Gliederung der Erdbevölkerung faktisch einnehmen.'

13   Thielking (2000: 90) stresses that the term 'Multiversum' was actually introduced by William James (1909). I will come back to a discussion of this term later when I discuss Mouffe's approach to cosmopolitanism and when I look at some of the ideological transgressions between and beyond contemporary German-British academic discourses on cosmopolitanism.

14   According to Friedrich Hayman (1924: 104) 'Der Fichtesche Staat will nicht wie der Lockes und Rousseaus vorhandene irdische Güter und Eigenschaften seiner Glieder bewachen und bewahren, sondern in unendlichem Fortgang zum "Reich", das rein Menschliche in dieser Nation (VII, 392) ausbilden.' (The state as conceptualised by Fichte, unlike that of Locke and Rousseau, is not content with guarding and maintaining such earthly goods and features of its members, but rather intends, while steadily progressing towards the Empire, to foster the pure human nature within its nation).

15   Francke (1928: 41) describes the peculiar faith of the German nation as 'So handelt es sich dann auch für Schleiermacher ebenso wie für Fichte und Humboldt nicht so sehr um die nächstliegenden Bedürfnisse der nationalen Wirklichkeit (national facts) als um die unsichtbare Kirche des deutschen Geistes (the invisible church of the German spirit), deren Grenzen mit dem weiten Reiche menschlicher Ideale aller Zeiten und Völker zusammenfallen (whose borders overlap with the realm of the ideal of humanity for all times and all people).' Both Francke and Haymann use the term 'Weltbürgertum' explicitly.

The Weimar Republic ended with the beginning of the institutional project of systematic mass murder in Europe: Hitler's and the National Socialist Party's political triumph in 1933[16] was a 'democratic mandate' to rebuild the German nation as a racially pure ethnic entity (Winkler 1993).[17] Erich von Kahler (1967), a contemporary of Thomas Mann, predicted in 1935 the anti-universal essence of German National Socialism, its decline from any kind of '*Weltverflochtenheit*' (being interwoven with the world), and its anti-human mission (cited in Thielking, 2000: 159). According to Sigrid Thielking (2000), the radical extinction of Jews, Sinti and Roma, disabled people and otherwise declared 'unworthy life' (*unwertes Leben*) and the will to rule the world (*Griff nach der Weltmacht*) demonstrate the total perversion of universal ideals (2000: 160).

Her interpretation stresses the murderous mission of a Germanic defined European civilisation: while identifying as belonging to the 'higher order' of human beings, the feeling of 'superiority' unfolded into the most extreme terror. Actual cosmopolitans were mass murdered in Auschwitz and in other death camps in Poland.

The nationally enshrined German institutionalised anti-Semitism had labelled Jews as 'journeymen without fatherland' (*Vaterlandslose Gesellen*) since the 19th century, and uprooted later actual cosmopolitan communities who were European or German. The refugees who escaped the concentration and death camps had to cope with the devastating contradiction between a cultural meaning of a 'citizenship of the world'/*Weltbürgertum,* and the cruel reality of damaged and outlawed cosmopolitan lives. Whereas the cultural image of the citizen of the world suggests the freedom to choose abode freely, exiled intellectuals, such as Thomas Mann, Stefan Zweig or Hannah Arendt, struggled very differently with their gendered and classed accommodation to the English and American language and the diffusion of their original cultural belonging. Mann called the state of mind of those enforced cosmopolitans '*Kosmopoliten aus Instinkt und Notwendigkeit*'[18] (cited in Thielking 200: 161). European exiles who found refuge in the United States were impressed by the openness of Americans; Thielking (2000), for example, quotes Hans Sahl, who states that 'cosmopolitanism was regarded as a substantial aspect of the American way of life' (cited in Thielking 2000: 162). The life abroad often merged with a new self-understanding of being explicitly cosmopolitan (ibid.). The existential threat of being 'stateless', left without passport and thrown into an illegalised life caused many Jews to commit suicide.[19]

---

16   In the 1932 election the Nazi Party won 33% of the vote and held a 'relative majority'; it was Franz von Papen who convinced president Paul von Hindenburg to hand over power and appoint Hitler as chancellor on 30 January 1933 (Canfora 2006: 145).

17   'Rückführung der Nation auf die rassisch "artgleiche" Abstammungsgemeinschaft' (Winkler 1993: 15).

18   It says, 'Cosmopolitans of Instinct and Imperative'.

19   In Jewish cemeteries in Berlin, for example, we can find testimonies of an increase of death by suicide of whole families during the 1930s.

Stefan Zweig (1990: 468), one of the most prominent suicides, had expressed his desperation and the paradox of the *Weltbürger*-cosmopolitan:[20]

> [i]t did not help me that I trained my heart to sound 'weltbürgerlich' according to the rhythm of a 'citoyen du monde' for nearly half a century. No, the day when I lost my passport at the age of fifty eight I discovered that losing one's 'Heimat' means more than simply losing a piece of bordered soil.[21]

The Shoa is the end of European Jewry and marks the extinction of ethnic minority otherness in continental Europe. The systematic mass murder of European Sinti and Roma, which is less commemorated in the context of the Holocaust, is most relevant to current forms of racialised boundary drawing in Europe as discussed in Chapter 2.

In the aftermath of World War II and Auschwitz only a small circle of pacifists engaged with the topic of cosmopolitanism and peace building (Becker 1947, Berl 1947, Lehmann-Russbueldt 1950). The 'cold war' as the dominating ideological frame for *Realpolitik,* but also the repression of guilt for the Holocaust and the lack of any open confrontation with the nationalistic totalitarian past, had an impact on the public silence on cosmopolitanism, too. As Thielking (2000: 254) underlines, political cosmopolitanism became somewhat taboo and a return to Eurocentric cultural concepts of Occidentalism was prevalent. The ideological division between West and East Germany framed a political and academic discourse concentrating on nation state building, federal democracy and economic integration into the Western Bloc[22] as far as the FRG is concerned; and communist state building, anti-capitalism and socialist centralism in dependence on the USSR as far as the GDR is concerned. The geographical proximity of two antagonistic ideologies undermined any ideals of transcending political community borders. In addition, the ethnic dimension of the signifier 'German nation' remained salient to the political 'unification' agenda in West Germany.

Despite the *moral* legacy of the Holocaust as the reference point for the democratic efforts of what the 21st-century German nation state aspires to stand for, German citizenship continues to be bound to ancestry (Brubaker 1992: 165,

---

20   Zweig and his second wife Charlotte Elisabeth Altmann committed suicide in Brazil in 1942.

21   'Es hat mir nicht geholfen, daß ich fast durch ein halbes Jahrhundert mein Herz erzogen, weltbürgerlich als das eines 'citoyen du monde' zu schlagen. Nein, am Tage, da ich meinen Paß verlor, entdeckte ich mit achtundfünfzig Jahren, dass man mit seiner Heimat mehr verliert als einen Fleck umgrenzter Erde.'

22   With France, the Netherlands, Italy, Luxembourg, Belgium, the FRG was one of the founding members of the European Coal and Steel Community (ECSC), set up in the *Treaty of Paris* 1951. This meeting of nations contributed to the 1957 *Treaties of Rome* which established the European Atomic Energy Community (Euratom) and the European Economic Community (EEC). The EEC was the institutional predecessor of the EU. I will come back to other relevant aspects of Germany's commitment to the EU later.

Fulbrook 1999: 179, Boes 2007).[23] Turks and other Germans with mixed or non-white background are labelled as *Ausländer* (foreigner) or with respect to the vernacular presence of 'new' Germans are still addressed as second or even third generation *migrants*.[24] In this regard, the dominant consensus of ethno-cultural symbolic boundaries is crucial for an understanding of gendered discourses of new cosmopolitanism.

The outbreak of racist violence against refugees and immigrants in the early 1990s was ideologically used to launch the revision of asylum law in Article 16 GG (German Constitutional Law). In the East German city *Rostock – Lichtenhagen* refugees were targeted in an arson attack[25] and most of the victims of these attacks of New Germany's racism in the West, in *Mölln* and *Solingen* for example, were settled female Turkish immigrants. Given that traditionally women and children stay at home, these maliciously calculating arson attacks at night show a clearly gendered dimension of violence. Turks represent the largest group of immigrants in Germany, with an estimated number of between 2.1 and 2.5 million people (Green 2001; 2004), and thus have been the public focus of anti-immigration arguments.[26] This powerful discursive speech constructs a symbolic outside to the national collective and therefore is discursively reifying the notion of the '*Ausländer*' as the Other (Erel 2003). Negative stereotypes of Islamic religion and culture are drawn upon to construct Turks as essentially different; it is claimed that they cannot be integrated into the defined Christian-European German society and culture. It has been argued that the discursive establishment of a 'Turkish question' (Seidel-Pielen 1995: 18) provides an outlet for repressed anti-Semitism. Ruth Mandel (2008) in her book *Cosmopolitan Anxieties – Turkish Challenges to Citizenship and Belonging in Europe* illustrates how this legacy of ethno-national

---

23 The *Staatsangehörigkeit* reform, introduced by the Social Democrats Green coalition in 1999/2000, allows dual citizenship for children born in Germany until the age of eighteen, when they have to choose either German citizenship or that of their non-German parents. Despite being introduced as a paradigm shift in the 'blood' ancestry logic the new citizenship law does not provide the redefinition of German citizenship as promised. Since 2005 the *Zuwanderungsgesetz* (act regulating immigration) defines the legal conditions of entry, stay and naturalisation in Germany. See also http://www.ces.fas. harvard.edu/publications/docs/pdfs/Boes.pdf.

24 I agree with Umut Erel (2003) that it is highly problematic that media and academic discourse constantly 'refer to second or third "immigrant generations", calling them 'hyphenated "Turkish-Germans"' (2003: 169).

25 This attack was screened on television (a team of reporters was equally trapped in a burning building) and showed cheering crowds of onlookers and a police passively observing the crime.

26 Thilo Sarrazin, Social Democrat and until recently working for the Bundesbank, published his book *Deutschland Schafft Sich Ab: Wie wir unser Land aufs Spiel setzen* (*Germany does away with itself: How We Are Putting Our Country at Risk*) in July 2010. While using biologically and culturally shaped racist prejudices he blamed Muslims and Turks, in particular, for undermining German society.

belonging in contemporary Germany influences a contradictory experience with vernacular multiculturalism and biased claims of new cosmopolitanism.

The *visibility of difference* as an ascribed spiritual strangeness is the key issue linking martial racist violence and ideological processes of *othering difference* in Germany. Visibility of difference has to be understood in a broader discursive sense: apart from skin colour, identifiable signs include orthodox clothes of minority faith communities (Vieten 2009, 2011). In the contemporary debate the wearing of the headscarf, for example, as discussed in Chapter 2, is ideologically laden and, as far as a mainstream discourse is concerned, understood in terms of a political fundamentalist statement[27] rather than as the legitimate expression of Muslim faith.

In stark contrast to xenophobic and racist attitudes to Otherness several crucial EU directives,[28] as made clear in the previous chapter, ask for a broader implementation of multi-dimensional equality and anti-discrimination practices across all EU Member States, including Germany.

To summarise: historically, the potential of cosmopolitan subjectivity was split ideologically: Jews and Roma were constructed as rootless *Kosmopoliten* in opposition to a culturally shaped ideal of the *Weltbürger.* Paradoxically, the negative connotation of a 'rootless cosmopolitan'[29] evolved along with a positive connotation of Eurocentric *Weltbürgertum*[30] as a cultural commitment to be educated and to educate others. In the late 19th and early 20th century Germany's thinking and acting on nationalism and *Weltbürgertum* are strongly embedded in an ideological project of federal cultural integration, linked to *Bildung* and European visions of 'superior' civilisation and further, fostering social cohesion in society. The latter has evolved in various processes of territorial changes since then, including the late establishment of a 'united' German nation state in the 19th century as a top down autocratic decision; the war-colonial extension of the 'Third Reich' in continental Europe; the post-World War II separation of two German states; and the most recent transformation of Germany into a confident and economically leading Member State of the European Union.

The Holocaust and other colonial crimes against humanity have to be regarded as decisive to an understanding of contemporary mainstream approaches to new

---

27　In January 2005 Germany announced its first ever *Zuwanderungsgesetz* (Immigration Act). Different statutes address residence and working permits as well as mobility issues (EU internal migrant movement); these were later combined into a single immigration act. In this act the naturalisation of extremists is totally excluded (*Extremistenklausel*).

28　Directives establish Community objectives but Member States have to apply these objectives nationally. It is obligation of Member States to transfer the content of directives into domestic law, although the way it is achieved is matter or the national parliament.

29　This term was used in Russia targeting Jews as part of the critical elite during the Great Purges of the late 1930s (see for details Slezkine 2004).

30　The middle classes of the world are in turn equated with citizenship of the world.

cosmopolitanism and counter discourses on national identity and nationalism in Germany. Accordingly, an awkward relationship to national identity signals problematic tensions: typical tropes that correlate to the historical frames outlined above are (a) social cohesion, (b) territorial integration, and (c) convergence of difference. Given the biased, racist and male gendered connotations of a *Weltbürger* and the *Kosmopolit* that were central to the Germanic approach to cosmopolitanism and nationalism, it is relevant to follow up how prominent male mainstream advocates of cosmopolitanism in Germany, e.g. Habermas and Beck, refer in their writings to similarly sounding tropes. In what ways are these themes even present in critical and feminist approaches to cosmopolitanism? What does this mean for the ideological projection of a Europe and a global society beyond policy borders of the European Union?

Of particular relevance to a German discourse on gender and cosmopolitanism is the first decade following the fall of the Berlin Wall in 1989. The post 1989 area initiated a contradictory process of re-unification while at the same time constructing new racialised boundaries within Germany, as made clear above. I will now turn to the two most prominent German sociologists, who have both engaged with the notion of cosmopolitanism since the 1990s. I will also draw attention to a marginalised Marxist–feminist and East German perspective challenging some of the narrowly defined European connotations of cosmopolitan practices and normative associations. Before looking more closely at their arguments and bringing in the critical feminist intervention, I will give a brief overview of Habermas's and Beck's earlier work.

Habermas's and Beck's Interventions on Cosmopolitanism in the 1990s Read Against a Socialist-Feminist Minority Perspective

Jürgen Habermas

Robert C. Holub (1991) acknowledges that Habermas developed a unique voice which engaged intellectually with contemporary philosophy and equally importantly with the present-day political debates in Germany. Habermas's criticism of the neo-conservative *Historikerstreit* (historians' quarrel)[31] in the 1980s, for example, has to be regarded as his personal stand to challenge the revision of German history which intended to 'normalise' the federal republic. First and foremost, Habermas asked Germans to accept responsibility for the deeds of the National Socialism period as a 'filter through which we can evaluate the very substance of an ambivalent tradition' (ibid.). Welcoming the student protest in 1968 initially, Habermas condemned the students' turn to violence later on. Holub (1991: 98) suggests that Habermas's harsh response to violent street protest has to

---

31 Conservative historians such as Ernst Nolte used historiography to constitute a conventional national identity (Holub 1991: 185).

be understood as a sign of his 'inability to credit non-rational actions with political value.' This evaluation points at a strong tension inherent to Habermas' normative thinking that affects his writing on cosmopolitanism as well, as we will see later. He privileges 'rationality' over 'irrationality' and while doing so underestimates the ambivalent dimensions of what a reasonable action and human subjectivity might mean to individuals, lacking communicative power and, perhaps, positioned lower in a gendered social hierarchy.

By keeping a strong distance from any radical political protests during the 1968 student revolt, but also later in the 1970s when the German *Red Army Fraction* (R.A.F.) killed some prominent representatives of the German state and economy, Habermas sided with the Western German social democracy and expressed disapproval of extreme political visions and criminal violence. Habermas's systematic distinction of communicative spheres as 'system' and 'life world' further echoes assumptions of gendered life and classed spheres that underestimate multi-layered and intersected social divisions overlapping in different cultural and social spaces. According to Alan How (1995), Habermas constructs a clear-cut opposition between authority and tradition on the one hand and autonomy and reason on the other. In contrast to the critical approach of Max Horkheimer and Theodor Adorno (1947, 1979) to the dialectics of the Enlightenment, Habermas (1962, 1985: 490) defends its 'dismissed possibilities' insisting on the positive meaning of 'rationality' (1962, 1985: 490–491). The dispute between the different generations of intellectuals at the *Frankfurt School* clings to the dissimilar understanding and biographical experiences of 'instrumental reason' (*'instrumentelle Vernunft'*; Habermas 1962, 1985: 490) as either driven by 'totalitarian purpose rationality' (*totalisierte Zweckrationalität*), which threatened the life of Jewish Germans and forced them into exile, or by 'communicative rationality' (*kommunikative Rationalität*), which the non-Jewish ex-*Wehrmacht* soldier wishes for in a post-Holocaust German society.

Michael Roberts and Nick Crossley (2004: 11) propose that 'the bourgeois public sphere arose as a response to the ambivalent, expressive and effectual practices of the Other.' Nick Crossley (2004: 92) points out that Pierre Bourdieu similarly criticised Habermas for his equation of universal (transcendental) values with the particular interest of the middle classes and their (power) means to generalise their particular perspectives. And further, Franck Poupeau (2005) refers to the ideological tension between domination and legitimacy that is also relevant to this debate. He (2005: 95) argues that Habermas focuses on 'the order of the factual' presuming that 'system' as the realm of technology and regulation is encircled in a separate normative sphere, idealistically opposed to a non- or less regulated private realm ('life world').

Feminist intellectuals (Benhabib 1986, 1992, Young 1987, Fraser 1992, 1995, Fleming 1995) have largely criticised Habermas's failure to acknowledge the fundamentally gendered bias shaping the bourgeois dichotomy of the public and private sphere. Enclosed in a pre-civil state of nature, lacking self-autonomy and mutually oriented abstract reason, *woman* is conceptually excluded from the politically ascribed realm of public law and civil regulation. Iris M. Young, for example, underlines that middle classed and predominantly male (habitual) standards dominate communication in the democratic public sphere. This is in line with the considerations given in Chapter 2 regarding 'processes of normalisation'. According to Laura McLaughlin (2004: 160):

> [f]eminists have underscored the extent to which the liberal-bourgeois model's abstract principle of generality acted in fact as an exclusionary mechanism, such that the discussion of 'common concerns' tended to preclude debate that was disassociated from the interests of white, male, educated property-owners.

Nonetheless, in his role as one of the leading public intellectuals Habermas had criticised the increase of xenophobic public discourses in the early 1990s when racist violence targeted Turkish families and black refugees. He (1994: 126 and 127) pointed out that politicians[32] '[s]ucceeded in getting the point across to even the dimmest of wits: the problem with the hatred of foreigners is the foreigners themselves, which diverted attention from the real problems of a badly engineered unification process.' Against the background of his critical interventions during those years it is interesting to see how his public advocacy for the Other as 'foreigner' and victim of racist attacks is consistent with his writings on new cosmopolitanism.

To summarise: Habermas was born in 1929. He belongs to a generation that grew up during the German National Socialist regime. As a boy soldier he fought in the Second World War; his later work and personal standpoint have to be measured against this biographical background. One of the most significant characteristics of Habermas's social philosophy is his focus on the meaning of rationality, morality and law as the prominent angles for developing social integration. In contrast to the legacy of the *Frankfurt School* whose Jewish German founding members, such as Adorno, Horkheimer and Marcuse, kept a Marxist critical position towards society despite being in US American exile, Habermas's approach is influenced much more strongly by Anglo-American pragmatism. His ideological adjustment to 'liberalism and social democracy' as the substantial face of democracy[33] has to be read in concordance with these diverse intellectual, moral and political influences.

When discussing his interventions in discourses on cosmopolitanism in the following sections I am concentrating on the epistemological limits of his notion of impartial dialogue, the notion of the Other with respect to multiculturalism

---

32   The CDU politician Heckelmann, state minister of the interior for Berlin, responded to the attack in Rostock by saying '[i]t was not right wing extremism, xenophobia or even racism (that voiced itself) in the displays of approval, but rather the completely justified indignation ... (about) the massive misuse of the asylum laws' (quoted in Mattson 1995: 3).

33   Unlike the Jewish German founding fathers of the original institute, Habermas is a protestant Christian. This different cultural and religious background might have an impact on his 'value' perspectives on rationality, ethics and morality.

and the purpose of social inclusion. The latter in particular, with reference to his proposals of 'institutional patriotism' and 'post-national' Europe, is important to the critical discussion of different discourse streams of cosmopolitanism and Europeanism that emerged in the 1990s.

In his publications *The Postnational Constellation* (1998b, 2001a) and *The Inclusion of the Other: Studies in Political Theory* (1997, 1998a) Habermas focuses on the tension between new forms of political allegiance, i.e. cosmopolitan belonging and the construction of symbolic boundaries. Thus, these publications give insight into the ways Habermas enmeshes hegemonic notions of the 'national' with the 'nation state'; this in turn affects his reading of notions of the Other. Somewhat sceptical of the legitimacy of a cosmopolitan political order and its ability to guarantee rights, Habermas (2001a: 119) remarks:

> [i]n the transition from nation-states to a cosmopolitan order it is hard to say which poses the greater danger: the disappearing world of sovereign subjects of international law, who lost their innocence long ago, or the ambiguous mish-mash of supranational institutions and conferences, which can grant a dubious legitimation but which depend as always on the good will of powerful states ... In this volatile situation, human rights provide the sole recognized basis of legitimation [*sic*] for the politics of the international community ...

Further in this text Habermas admits that 'only after tough struggles ... workers, women, Jews, Romanies, gays, and political refugees' (ibid.) were recognised as human beings with (formal) equal opportunity. When discussing human rights he takes into account the ambivalent political function of its discourse and suggests that the wish to include the Other could lead to its opposite (Habermas 2001a: 120). Hence, Habermas is aware of the potential of powerful states to misuse the human rights discourse for their own purpose.[34] In Habermas's view individual rights conferred by law do not pose a principal contradiction to rather 'multicultural' community interests (2001a: 126). According to Habermas (2001a: 126) there needs to be a balance between individual and collectivist approaches as 'only the dialectical unity of individuation and socialization processes' could deliver the 'integrity of individual persons'.

During the 1990s, the international academic debate regarding multiculturalism increased and Habermas joined the debate in 1994 when he challenged Charles Taylor's ideas.[35] Though Habermas recognised that individuals are formed in an inter-subjective communicative space, i.e. in a dialogue with the significant Other, he kept his *discursive approach*, arguing for the need to find mutually agreed

---

34   Habermas (2001a: 124) argues, '[r]ather, the question is whether the traditional forms of political and societal integration can be reasserted against – or must instead be adapted to – the hard-to-resist imperatives of an economic modernization that has won approval on the whole.'

35   For details see Taylor et al. 1994.

solutions to conflicts. While both scholars stressed the importance of language to communicate group differences, Taylor called for a 'politics of recognition' that would treat people differently rather than individually (Munro 1997).[36] In contrast to this position, Habermas's ideal of a liberal and individual universalism insisted on the possibility of individuals to say either 'yes' or 'no' to normative claims.

At the core of Habermas's uneasiness with the criticism of individual rights is an understanding that collective perspectives tend to threaten the individual point of view. Foremost, this strong reservation appears as enshrined in his biographical experiences with totalitarian collectivism, namely National Socialism. Whereas Taylor (1994) proposed the 'fusion of horizons', Habermas advocated a neutral sphere necessary to mediate those horizons.

In *The Inclusion of the Other* (1998a), for example, Habermas discusses in depth the claims of various minority and interests groups, stressing that:

> [t]oday we live in pluralistic societies that are moving further and further away
> from the model of a nation-state based on a culturally homogeneous population.
> The diversity of cultural forms of life, ethnic groups, religions, and worldviews
> is constantly growing. (1998a: 117)

Despite taking feminist and postcolonial interventions of the 1990s into consideration Habermas leans on the Kantian and the classic vision of 'the political' as a rational and idealistic realm. It could be argued that the ideal of a one-dimensional political (democratic) space actually is not appropriate for post-industrial global societies and their communication networks which indicate a 'multiplicity of comparing publics according to a positive notion of egalitarian multicultural societies' (Postone 1992: 23).

In the 1990s Habermas (1998b: 88) talked explicitly about a 'cosmopolitan compulsive solidarity' ('*kosmopolitische Zwangssolidarisierung*'), which would connect single states via civil societies and political public spheres. He assumed that inherent to this kind of global solidarity would be a thinner idea of belonging than exercised in nation states (1998b: 89). His idea of a *thin* cosmopolitan vs. a *thick* national belonging has to be understood in relation to his situated outlook on the political content of any collective belonging. We are confronted with one of Habermas's core assumptions, i.e. that national civil societies as collective national identities coincide with the borders of given nation states. As Will Kymlicka and Christine Straehle (1999) argue, the hegemonic agenda of the nation-state should be identified rather as that of a 'nationalizing state' (1999: 70). They propose a dialectical structure of nation state building, basically arguing that the modern state building process destroyed and therefore potentially could (again) destroy minority nations. This critical view, however, is not present in Habermas's outlook on the role of the nation state.

---

36   http://www.collectionscanada.gc.ca/obj/s4/f2/dsk2/ftp01/MQ28625.pdf.

In what ways does Habermas refer to the tropes differentiated above, e.g. territoriality/the spatial borders of the EU, and social cohesion/here the notion of social solidarity? Before discussing this in greater detail it is interesting to bring in an intervention by the Marxist-feminist and East German intellectual Hanna Behrend, who was[37] a marginalised voice in Germany. Born, like Habermas, in the 1920s,[38] she illustrates an alternative reading of German nationality situated biographically differently to the period of German National Socialism as well as to the FRG/GDR anachronism. Her approach offers a different outlook on inclusion as well as social solidarity feeding rather a critical cosmopolitanism in and beyond Europe.

In February 2001 and before the Twin Tower attacks happened on 9/11, Behrend gave a lecture at the international conference *Strategien neoliberaler Hegemonie – Kritische Erneuerung emanzipatorischer Standpunkte*[39] in Hamburg. The editors of the conference collection refused Behrend's revised article for publication later on. According to Behrend,[40] the editors were uncomfortable with her approach concerning 'the national'. They expressed fundamental doubts about the need to use the concept of 'nation' while simultaneously interrogating its meaning as a concept of emotional belonging ('*gefühlsmäßige Verbundenheit*') and its strength in delivering a strong alternative angle for future socialist politics. They also regarded it as extremely problematic to differentiate a socialist reading from the right wing claim of 'nation' which had dominated the public discourse in Germany up to then. Further, the editors argued that the notion of '*Weltbürgertum*' would not automatically coincide with a lack of belonging ('*nicht ohne weiteres bindungslos*'). And, last but not least, the contemporary situation would also require a critical discussion of the 'cultural reference to Europe' ('*Frage des kulturellen*

---

37   1922–2010; Dr Hanna Behrend passed away in Berlin last year.

38   Behrend was involved with the Hamburg based Journal *Argument* in the 1990s and set up a series of publications called 'In search of the future lost' (*Auf der Suche nach der verlorenen Zukunft*). Following the '*Anschluss*' ('annexation') (Behrend 1996a), of the GDR in 1990, Behrend was one of only a small number of critically socialist and feminist East German intellectuals who challenged the total economic, civil and cultural demolition of their ex-communist state and society (1995, 1996a). In the 1990s she published several essays on the pre and post-*Wende* situation of East German women and their loss of economic independence due to the Western 'colonial' mentality and legal deregulation of equal rights (1992a, 1992b; 1994a, 1994b, 1996b, 1997). Furthermore, Hanna Behrend was a founding member of both INKRIT (*Institut für Kritische Theorie i.e. Institute for Critical Theory*), a registered private association, and UFV (*Unabhängiger Frauenverband*, i.e. Independent Women Federation), the East German women coalition, founded in December 1989 and dissolved in 1998 (Humpel-Ulrich 2000).

39   Strategies of Neo-Liberal Hegemony – Towards a critical reformation of Liberating Standpoints.

40   http://www.glasnost.de/autoren/habehrend/nenner.html.

Bezugs auf Europa').[41] Behrend's provocative perspective on the possibilities of cosmopolitanism unfolds against the background of a differing experience as an exiled Austrian Jew in the 1930s, and as a female communist who decided to immigrate to the socialist GDR and who became citizen of the post 1990 Germany by virtue of history, but not by conviction. In her lecture Behrend (ibid.) argues:

> [b]oth nationalism and racism are discourses of exclusion. These discourses are used to gain power or to sustain power. But even when reducing structures of hierarchy and power neither the nation, the people or other forms of community will disappear; furthermore these forms of community have to develop alternative forms of integration while abandon their mechanisms of exclusion. This would mean that they would get a *menschengerechte Gestalt* that is suitable for all human beings) for the first time ever. To achieve this, the people marginalized have to make their voice heard and those who belong to privileged groups have to become conscious of their structural privileges and the injustice created by their privileges.[42]

In this lecture she also recalls prominent 19th- and 20th-century German (Jewish) exiles and refugees such as Marx, Friedrich Engels, Anna Seghers as well as August Bebel and Clara Zetkin (2001b, 2001c), who vehemently struggled to liberate the German nation from its nationalism. In her view this struggle was an essential part of German socialist and Marxist feminist counter hegemonic political discourses. Behrend's lecture ends with the following questions:

> [s]hould our future depend on a detached *Weltbürgertum* rather than on the internationalism of anti-fascist and feminist traditions? Anti-nationalism as expressed in some statements of younger left and feminist critics is, in Tucholsky's words, the other side of the Janus-faced German nationalism which is no less excluding. Someone who does not belong to somewhere, only can

---

41   I took the information from the letter of one of the organisers and editors sent to Behrend. Despite the above-mentioned arguments explaining their rejection, the author appreciated Behrend's perspective which demanded a more complex confrontation with the ambivalence of the term 'nation'. Nevertheless, the author of the letter also admitted surrendering to the difficulties to communicate Behrend's 'marginal' point of view as there would not be accompanying follow-up articles focussing on a similar frame. I am grateful to Behrend for sharing this information with me in the interview I did with her in 2005.

42   'Nationalismus und Rassismus sind Ausgrenzungsdiskurse zum Zweck der Machtbeschaffung oder -erhaltung. Mit dem Abbau hierarchischer und Machtstrukturen werden weder die Nation, das Volk oder andere Gemeinschaftsformen verschwinden; vielmehr könnten alle diese Gemeinschaftsformen beginnen, sich zu öffnen, Ausschließungsmechanismen zu eliminieren und damit erstmals menschengerechte Gestalt annehmen. Dazu müssten sich die heute Marginalisierten zu Wort melden und diejenigen, die zu den privilegierten Gruppen gehören, sich ihrer strukturellen Vorrechte und der damit verbundenen Ungerechtigkeit bewusst werden.'

attend to his [*sic*] affairs; he or she who has no attachments to others to share collective experiences of labour, culture, language and social life with will not fight for the good fortune of humanity.[43]

What is striking in Behrend's texts, as well as in the editor's reluctance to include her paper in the publication, is the reference to the German notion of cosmopolitanism as *Weltbürgertum*. As introduced above, *Weltbürgertum* connotes the image of privileged, sophisticated, and principally nation state based middle classes of the world (citizens of the world). Conversely, the notion of 'cosmopolitans' connotes ascribed 'rootlessness' though 'collective detachment' means something different. Behrend accentuates the essential need to belong and as far as her point of view is concerned this collective belonging depends on shared social, cultural and political experiences. Given the complicated tension between civic *Weltbürgertum* intertwined with German cultural nationalism, Behrend's reference to the term 'nation' needs more attention and clarification. In reference to Anna Seghers (1942) Behrend defines *Volk* (people) as a '(c)reated community, based on mutually shared social processes, through its work, *Kultur* (sophistication and traditions) and language.' Examining her overall statements more closely, we can discern two lines in her argument concerning the tension between political community, citizenship and notions of the Other. Firstly, she identifies with other German and Jewish anti-fascist exiles who advocated for a socialist vision of a German nation. Secondly, she states that there is a need to deepen national inclusion through a feminist theory of difference (*Feministische Differenztheorie*).

For Behrend, the 'deepening of inclusion' is another central aspect of her emancipatory outlook on the German nation. In what ways do we find some of her perspectives also in Habermas's approach? Or is the outlook of the mainstream male writer, although her contemporary in terms of generation, bound to his particular individual belonging to the hegemonic majority group?

Habermas regards 'new modes of belonging' (1998b: 116; 2001a: 75) and the 'individualization and the emergence of "cosmopolitan identities"' (1998b: 116; 2001: 76) as the expressions of a post-national constellation in Europe. He argues that it was the 'cultural interpretation of political membership rights' (ibid.) that pushed a more 'abstract level of social integration' (ibid.). As Robert

---

43   'Liegt unser aller Zukunft in einem bindungslosen "Weltbürgertum" oder nicht vielmehr in einem Internationalismus in der hier skizzierten antifaschistischen und feministischen Tradition? Der Antinationalismus, der aus einigen Aussagen neuerer linker und feministischer KritikerInnen spricht, ist, wie Tucholsky sagte, die andere Hälfte des janusköpfigen deutschen Nationalismus, nicht minder ausgrenzend als dieser. Wer nirgends dazugehört, kann sich nur noch um sich selbst kümmern, wer keine Bindung zu denjenigen hat, mit denen er oder sie "durch gemeinsam erlebte gesellschaftliche Vorgänge, durch seine Arbeit, seine Kultur, seine Sprache" verknüpft ist, der wird auch für das Glück der Menschheit nicht kämpfen.'

Fine and Will Smith (2003: 475) contend, Habermas does not differentiate the notion of 'transnational' and 'postnational' communities in relation to his concept of deliberate democracy. Apparently, here we come across a rather hegemonic (Germanic) notion of an ethnically homogenised nation state in Habermas's approach, which has strong consequences for his idea of cosmopolitan belonging and the transformation of national democracies. Whereas Habermas (1998b: 81) talks in this 1990s publication about the 'achievements' of the nation-state on the one hand, he also recognises growing social conflicts on the other. He is aware of the decline of the sovereignty of nation states in terms of their social, economic and political functions. Further, he argues that the post war European welfare state delivered a broadly integrated population guaranteeing both social peace and democratic stability. Thus, in his view, economic and cultural globalisation is jeopardising the consensus of the nation-state, i.e. citizens who were socially integrated before are increasingly deprived of resources. In another publication (1996, 2000) he explicitly talks about the 'European nation state' when considering the transformation of nation states[44] in general (Habermas 1996: 286).

Habermas (2001a: 72) argues that the 'social consensus' is vanishing and stresses the rising 'ethno-centric reactions' of 'our own prosperous societies' when confronted with 'anything foreign'. He identifies '[f]oreigners, other faiths and races; marginalised groups, the handicapped and – once again – Jews' (ibid.). Significantly, the notion of 'foreign' intrinsic to the syntax of his sentence refers to various group differences. Difference is generally connoted with 'otherness'; here it is defined as 'foreign'. Ethnic, religious people and those who are socially identified as having a disability and Jews are named as those targeted. Habermas refers to the brutal eruptions of racist violence against minorities in Germany in the early 1990s as mentioned above.

Despite his critical intentions, however, Habermas uses a semantically problematic language of drawing a symbolic boundary according to hegemonic historical lines when talking about 'our prosperous societies' against the otherness of the 'foreign'. Another pre-conceived notion of territorial as symbolic 'inside' and 'outside' can be detected in two other examples he gives. He refers to Italy (Northern League) and to Germany (financial redistribution within the sixteen federal states), stressing the shrinking idea of 'solidarity' (ibid.). Both examples of EU countries refer to *territorially* ascribed interests, which propose that regional location determines allegiance and (financial) support. Further, we find an emphasis on the political meaning of regional vs. supra-regional bonds of solidarity. This again underlines that Habermas identifies with territorialised

---

44　In his previous publication on *The Structural Transformation of the Public Sphere – An Inquiry into a Category of Bourgeois Society*, (1989, 1992) Habermas discussed and compared in detail the ways public spheres developed in Britain, France, the United States of America and Germany quite distinctively. Thus, the equation of the German model of social cohesion with an overall model of social cohesion in Europe and elsewhere is somehow not consistent with this earlier work.

notions of community belonging and enmeshes the boundaries of the nation with those of the nation state. As he argues:

> [t]he form of civil solidarity that has been limited to the nation-state until now has to expand to include all citizens, so that, for example, Swedes and Portuguese are willing to take responsibility for one another. (Habermas 2001a: 99)

From these statements we can detect that Habermas addresses other European citizens in an overlap of territorial notions of political community and social solidarity. Besides, he applies this concept explicitly when talking about the European Union. According to Habermas (1999), the debate about the post-national political constellation is crucial to any 'straightforward statement' (*offensive Stellungnahme*) concerning the European Union. He explicitly addresses the citizens of 'our region' (1999: 426) urging them to support a federal deepening of the European Union. This extension should be enacted with 'cosmopolitan intent' (*weltbürgerliche Absicht*), aiming also to include other countries and continents in perspective. He argues:

> This debate, finally, is decisive for a supportive position to the future of the EU. If the citizens of our region, privileged as they are, would at the same time consider perspectives of other countries and continents they must pursue the federal deepening of the EU with cosmopolitan intent. This would create the condition of global domestic politics. (ibid.)

It has to be emphasised that Habermas, in his German diction, uses the phrase '*Weltbürger*' to stress the engagement of 'citizens of the world'. This is different to his 1998 use of '*kosmopolitische Zwangssolidarisierung*', which echoes Thomas Mann's remarks of an 'enforced and compulsive cosmopolitan existence', introduced above in this chapter. Apparently Habermas's outlook on cosmopolitan solidarity considers the two dimensional terminology applying *Weltbürger* when addressing citizens, but also using *kosmopolitisch* to characterise an enforced situation as common fate. Further to this, Habermas wishes to establish a strong European Union as an essential first step to advance global domestic politics.[45] He accentuates the need to close a 'disintegrated life world' (*desintegrierte Lebenswelt*) according to expanded moral and cultural horizons[46] (1998b: 127; similar in 2001a: 108). Profoundly, Habermas identifies with a territorial notion of democracy

---

45 'Diese Debatte stellt schliesslich die Weichen für eine offensive Stellungnahme zur Zukunft der Europäischen Union. Wenn die insgesamt privilegierten Bürger unserer Region dabei gleichzeitig die Perspektive anderer Länder und Kontinente berücksichtigen wollen, müssen sie die föderative Vertiefung der Europäischen Union in der *weltbürgerlichen Absicht* betreiben, die notwendigen Voraussetzungen für eine Weltinnenpolitik zu schaffen.'

46 Habermas (1998b:126) claims 'Bei jedem neuen Modernisierungsschub öffnen sich die intersubjectiv geteilten Lebenswelten, um sich zu reorganisieren und erneut zu

that relies on a particular 'demos'. In his view federal governance in Europe, i.e. the EU could respond adequately to the increasing weakness of nation state sovereignty. However, he still constructs demos within specific modified territorial borders without considering the paradigm shift that might demand *a cosmopolitan belonging beyond Europe* transcending geopolitical pragmatism. The tension between democracy, federalism and 'cosmopolitan intent' (*weltbürgerliche Absicht*) is most relevant to Habermas's proposal of cosmopolitan belonging. In particular, Habermas's approach to a cosmopolitan world community is based on a strong and positive notion of impartial law and democratic formal processes. Pablo de Greiff (2002) refers to Habermas's 'institutional proposal' (2002: 426 ff.) as a pragmatic orientation to develop existing supranational institutions. In spite of Habermas's (1997) acknowledgement of an essential democracy deficit as far as the European Union is concerned, he nevertheless holds in high esteem the EU's transnational bureaucratic institutions and its agents. To make this contradiction more apparent I will discuss his proposal of 'constitutional patriotism' in greater detail.

Habermas's proposal for a 'constitutional patriotism' symbolises a fusion of two conflicting angles: law and morality. 'Constitution' refers to something that is agreed by law, and 'patriotism' refers to a form of political allegiance. However, the synthesis of these two terms in 'constitutional patriotism' is problematic as far as the political frame of the European constitution is concerned. Jan-Werner Müller (2005: 18), for example, considers 'constitutional patriotism' as rooted in 'constitutional identity'. Further he suggests that the upholding of constitutional democracy is strongly linked to 'morality, memory and militancy'. Müller (2005) argues that in post-war West Germany a defensive idea of constitution was established. On the one hand radical parties and individuals were banned and democracy 'secured'; on the other this constitution as delivering freedom and citizen rights was set apart as a legal practice from the totalitarian non–constitutional period between 1933 and 1945. We saw above that Habermas kept a strong distance from any form of militant political action. In 1977, Habermas, like the academic Peter Brückner (1980) and the writer and Nobel laureate in literature Heinrich Böll (1972), criticised the then Social Democratic government about the 'German Autumn' (*Deutscher Herbst*).[47] Despite the protest of different public intellectuals, left wing resistance was banned and isolated and the FRG restricted some essential rights of lawyers and the freedom of information rights. Against this background the notion of 'constitution' offers problematic readings. Rile Hayward (2004) criticises Habermas's mantra of 'constitutional patriotism'

---

schließen.' ('With each new push towards modernization life environments that are shared subjectively open for a reorganisation and ensuing closure.')

47   This is a metaphor for Helmut Schmidt's anti-terrorism politics at the end of the 1970s, targeting all left wing people who might be sympathetic to the militant resistance, i.e. the RAF or simply disagreeing with the way the government handled it, i.e. humiliated imprisoned terrorists of the Red Army Faction (RAF).

on a very sensitive issue; she mistrusts his proposal of (democratic) constitution loyalty, and argues that:

> [c]onstitutional patriotic identification not unlike thicker republican forms of civil identity can legitimise intolerance and aggressiveness towards their others: a capacity that creates a strategic incentive for political elites to manipulate and exploit such principle based identities. (Hayward 2004: n.p.)[48]

To conclude: Habermas (2001a: 100) claims that the 'European civil society' might transform itself into a 'Europe-wide political arena'. He recommends the EU as the power in Europe that could integrate and transform the different nationalised state spheres. According to Neil Walker (2005), Habermas advocates the establishment of 'continental regimes' (2005: 7), in particular the European Union, in line with a generally territorial perception of social solidarity. John Elliott (2003: 111, 112) regards Habermas's (2001a: 103) idea of a 'pan-European political public sphere' as grounded in his earlier work on the structural transformation of the bourgeois public sphere. In contrast, Behrend's perspective is nurtured by a strong internationalist orientation that survived different political totalitarian German regimes. What is interesting to the contemporary debate is the complete neglect or even denial of an alternative reading to German national identity. Behrend's argument as a contestation of liberal-capitalistic *Weltbürgertum* reminds us that the bourgeois meaning of the *Weltbürger*-cosmopolitanism does not add up to a broader inclusive vision of global social justice and emancipation. Nonetheless both German intellectuals refer to a strong notion of territoriality and social cohesion though with different purpose.

Habermas's reductive take on cosmopolitan subjectivity for European cultural-social belonging, in other words a citizenship of the 'European Union', the meaning of violence and war in that respect, and possible alternative feminist perspectives will be followed up later, tackling the theme of cosmopolitanism in a post-9/11 context.

Ulrich Beck

Unlike Habermas, who was born in the Rhineland (*Düsseldorf*) in West Germany, Beck was born in the Pomeranian town of Słupsk (Stolp) in 1944. At the end of World War II the town and its population returned to Poland. Beck's family then became German *Heimatvertriebene* (refugees of 'homeland') and re-settled in the city of Hanover in the former FRG.

Beck started publishing academically at the end of the 1970s and co-published[49] several books (1977, 1978, 1980), that focussed on the social meaning, structure

---

48   http://psweb.sbs.ohio-state.edu/intranet/poltheory/Constitutional_Patriotism.pdf.

49   Ulrich Beck predominantly published with Michael Brater who is still working in the research field of vocational and higher education.

and change of professional work. His books were very much in line with the then sociological debate in West Germany that addressed concerns regarding the 'future of professional work'.[50] In 1986, he published *Risk Society* (*'Risikogesellschaft'*)[51] a volume that became an academic bestseller in Germany[52] and which was translated into English in 1992, capturing the *Zeitgeist* and going on to become an international bestseller in the field of sociology for years to come.

Beck's more recent approaches concerning the global risk society, cosmopolitanisation and the term 'Second Modernity' (*'Zweite Moderne'*) are grounded in his earlier approach to the phenomenon of socially engendered risks. In introducing the catchphrase 'Hardship is hierarchical; smog is democratic' (Beck 1986: 48),[53] Beck argues that ecological risks do have an equal impact on everyone. Hence, environmental risks would harm people independently of the social differentiation and social divisions within society. In reference to the overall theme of 'risk', Beck (ibid.) claims that the political agenda shifted from 'class societies' to 'risk societies' at the end of the 20th century.

In reference to Mary Douglas and Aaron Wildavsky (1983), Birgit Kleinwellfonder (1996: 131) analyses the problematic rooting of risk definition in cultural prejudices. In principle 'we' are confronted with a selective perspective on reality: 'the construction of risks cannot be detached from social and cultural practices' (ibid.). She regards Beck's approach as the 'stage design for the social production of risk'[54] (1996: 126). In contrast to Beck's 'specifically German (or

---

50   Less recognised are German feminist publications by Maria Mies and Claudia von Werlhof. The latter, in particular, wrote about the 'Hausfrauisierung' the female gendered 'private' condition of the housewife as the blueprint of future work condition; this meant that the typically gendered (invisible) work, ascribed as housewife work, would become the general framework for lower paid working class people. For further details see also http://emanzipationhumanum.de/downloads/LasVegas.pdf (checked 11 September 2011).

51   The term 'risk' signifies the threats and insecurities that are considered typical to our late modern societies (Beck 1986; 1992). Beck claims that the 'risk society' is fundamentally different to former societies, i.e. the modern society of the 20th century. Further he regards radical individualisation as an outcome of structural modernisation processes that challenge fundamental social concepts, for example, family (gender 'arrangements'), class (social collective awareness) or nation-state (representative, social or liberal democracy).

52   In 2006, the 18th German edition was published.

53   'Not ist hierarchisch, Smog ist demokratisch' (Beck 1986: 48); the German term *'Not'* refers to an emergency situation where people lack essential goods such as shelter, food or a healthy environment.

54   'Der Entwurf der Risikogesellschaft ... läßt sich in der benutzten Theatermetapher als *ein Bühnenbild der gesellschaftlichen Inszenierung von Risiko* ansprechen ...' ('The concept of the risk society is capable of being addressed as a stage design for societal production of risk, using the metaphor of theatre ...').

even Bavarian)' (Scott 2000: 34) perception of complex modernity,[55] Douglas and Wildavsky (1983) outline the notion of risk while shedding light on its hypothetical and thus constructed elements. They focus on the importance of cultural traditions and argue for the need to *situate knowledge* more clearly; in doing so they state that our perception of 'risk' is dependent on a definition of 'risk'. As Barbara Adam and Joost van Loon (2004) also argue, it is important to situate academic research and the notion of a 'risk society' more concretely in order to generate critical knowledge. If this is not seriously taken on board, any academic 'risk and security discourse' can be used easily to manipulate people and their fears.[56] And here we can think again about the 'civic binding/bonding logic' exposed in Chapter 1 that supports specific risk and security discourses.

In the late-1990s Beck shifted his research focus explicitly towards an analysis of processes of individualisation. In reference to Giddens (1990), Beck (1997: 95) clarifies the term 'individualization':

> [i]ndividualization' means, *first*, the disembedding of industrial-society ways of life, and, *second*, the re-embedding of new ones, in which the individuals must produce, stage and cobble together their biographies themselves. This 'individualization' is connected to the 'conditions of the *welfare state* in advanced industrial labour societies.

In this quote he connects processes of individualisation with the rather collective and politically relevant question of national welfare systems. Like Habermas, Beck turns to the topic of solidarity systems when interrogating the problem of global transformations.

Scott Lash (2002: IX) emphasises that Beck's advocacy for a more fundamental paradigm shift in contemporary society relates to the theme of a radically individualised reflex to a 'world of speed and quick decision making'. This kind of immediate reflex would be different to the modern notion of 'reflection', which considers biographical choices beyond, for example, ethnic heritage or original class status (ibid.). As an effect of globalisation processes that have created an

---

55   In his response to his critics, in particular to Scott (2000), Beck argues predictably, '[m]ay be [*sic*] there is a German background to risk society theory. Being "green" is undoubtly [*sic*] part of the German national identity. Many Germans want Germany to be a greater, greener Switzerland. Testing atomic weapons may be part of the French national identity – I don't know. And the cultural significance of "British (Sunday lunch) beef" may be an important backdrop to the BSE crisis' (Beck 2000a: 223).

56   According to Adam and van Loon (2004: 4), '[t]he socio-cultural study of risk thus exposes disembodied information as a farce and reveals instead (a) that knowledge is principally embodied, contextual and positional ... it places those in charge of theory and analysis in the position of having to insist that there are no unambiguous, objective, scientific facts to be presented.'

increased time-space compression, social life and its decisions confront individuals with new requirements to respond to it.

Further, between 1995 and 1997 Beck was a member of the 'commission for future concerns' (*Kommission für Zukunftsfragen*) of Bavaria and Saxony, two German federal lands governed by Christian Democrats at that time. The commission was set up to develop strategies to tackle the increasing numbers of unemployed. Beck suggested the concept of 'citizen engagement' (*Bürgerarbeit*) as an alternative scheme of working 'voluntarily' for the public good to avoid disproportionate increases of tax based costs of unemployment benefits.[57] Beck's experience in policy research and his proximity to mainstream politics indicates that he could be regarded as a public academic who supports (governance) policy with his sociological research. Further, Beck's sociological research addressing problematic social issues of national, European and global transformations has to be interpreted with reference to wider social policy interests in risk management and liberal ideals of individual choices and opportunity structure. Consequently, it is important to relate Beck's 'risk' terminology to notions of the Other when later analysing his contributions to the contemporary discourses on new cosmopolitanism.

To conclude: Beck, who grew up in the FRG, belongs to the so called post-Holocaust generation. His sociological themes of the 1970s and 1980s echo futuristic aspects of society i.e. professional work, social structure and social risks, rather than dealing with the legacy of history. At the end of the day, Beck's sociological 'risk' discourse correlates to both an emerging global debate of solid ecological and military risks, and to local and varying governance projects that mediate 'reflexively' global change and social transformations as 'cultural' security issues. Beck's frequent publications on cosmopolitanism are particularly relevant to a discourse of gender and cosmopolitanism in Europe through his close academic links with David Held and the London School of Economics (LSE) which provides space to circulate his approach to European cosmopolitanism internationally.

I now turn to Beck's contributions to discourses on new cosmopolitanism in the 1990s, concentrating on the ways in which his concept of a 'risk society' influences his approach to discourses on cosmopolitanism and the notions of the Other. In parallel with the theme of reflexive modernisation, Beck explicitly points to questions of difference and otherness in his 1990s publications, in common with some of Habermas's topics. Beck is very specific in defining what is relevant to the global transformation of 'the social', the role of citizenship and the notion of

---

57   In recent years German governments, both the Schröder led Social Democrats and Green coalition as well as the Merkel led Christian and Social Democrats as well her Liberal Democrats coalitions, changed regulations regarding social welfare incomes. The shorthand '*Hartz I*' to '*Hartz IV*' gained significance when introducing limited social freedom to unemployed persons. These 'reforms' force people who cannot find regularly paid work to do '1€ jobs' (per hour) to 'compensate' society for paying social benefits to them.

the Other, respectively. Above all, he discusses the notion of the 'stranger' in his essay 'How Neighbours Become Jews: the Political Construction of the Stranger in the Age of Reflexive Modernity' (1998a). In his analysis of the ideological construction of enemy stereotypes Beck writes:

> [s]trangers are, in this way, a living refutation of the apparently clear borders and natural foundations through which affiliations and identities are expressed in the nation-state. … [T]here are natives and foreigners, friends and enemies – and there are strangers, who do not categorically fit into this model, who dodge, obstruct, and irritate oppositions. (1998a: 127)

Here, Beck proposes that a situation of in-between or beyond is characteristic to the notion of the stranger, who remains trapped in an 'ambivalence of existence' that is beyond a clear-cut identification of a 'friend-enemy' scheme (1998a: 130). In his broader approach to 'reflexive modernization' (Beck 1998a: 131) Beck links increased mobility, globalisation and its impact on the structure of boundaries and borders to the notion of the stranger. Further, he poses the question, 'how does the category and condition of the stranger shift when it is universalised?' (1998a: 133) In this interpretation *becoming a stranger* is turned into a general and mutually shared social condition of second modernity (human) life. As the world of flux disturbs fixed orientations Beck proposes that the culturally constructed stranger is formed bureaucratically (1998a: 135). Beck differentiates between 'stereotypes of the stranger' (1998a: 137) and 'enemy stereotypes' (ibid.) and further elaborates more thoroughly on the notion of the 'enemy' (1997: 82 ff., 1998b: 141ff.). What is also relevant is that Beck accentuates the anti-democratic purpose of the ideological construction of an enemy. Beck (1997: 83) argues:

> [s]ince consensus has become a chronically scarce commodity in all democracies one can say that democratic states are particularly dependent on a second, para-democratic source, the enemy stereotype, from which consent bubbles up. Enemy stereotypes, turned domestic, open up sources of extra-democratic and anti-democratic consent. Cultivating these makes it possible to become independent of consensus by consensus.

Thus, Beck lucidly perceives an ideological vacuum within the political transformation of the contemporary order of states, a legitimacy vacuum that can incite the state to take recourse to *enemy stereotypes* that declare a particular difference, a particular strangeness as its Other. As Beck (1997: 82) writes, '[t] he concept of the "enemy" is the strongest possible antithesis to the concept of "security".' What is persistent in Beck's social analysis is the way he identifies topics of political relevance for the next century. For example, he depicts the following scenario (1998b: 150–151):

> [l]ack of an enemy does not mean lack of an enemy stereotype. ... [T]he trend runs from the concrete to the interchangeable enemy: First, there is the *mobile* enemy; the grand enemy is replaced by interchangeable enemies of the moment (Islamic fundamentalism; the Third World, Iraq, Serbia and so on). Second, while governments or religions may be the point of focus here, as *abstract* enemies they are replaced by diffuse collective groups (asylum-seekers, foreigners, migrants).

This is, indeed, an important insight arguing back to the way 'the stranger' acquires an institutionalised meaning as the enemy of 'Western' societies.

In 2000, Beck began to focus on the theme of 'cosmopolitanization' as far as the global transformation of nation states is concerned and also to look at the role of humanitarian military interventions. He observed very sharply that '[m]ilitary humanism which the West has taken up by embracing human rights fills the vacuum perfectly by providing institutions which have been deprived of an enemy with a cosmopolitan mission' (Beck 2000c: 86). And further, while bringing in directly the topic of 'risk', Beck (2000c: 101) argues:

> [c]haracteristic of the global threats is that they can develop a society changing power precisely in places where they have not appeared and put into action the underlying political meaning of risk dramaturgy.

Here, he addresses the imminent 'problem of risk regimes' (2000c: 95) by outlining problematic political dimensions inherent to a global risk definition. Obviously, Beck identifies the ideological connection between a 'risk discourse', security, cosmopolitanism and the construction of 'the enemy' already at the beginning of the 21st century. Further, he (2000c: 98) exposes different agents of transnationalism, for example, '(n)ot only privileged capitalists and the intellectual professions but also various ethnic groups, women, immigrants, all those who are marginalized in the national space.'

Beck constructs particular notions of difference, but he approaches difference as a one-dimensional ascription of identity groups: the elite is connoted implicitly as male, non-ethnic and settled in nation states. In this statement women, for example, can be neither intellectuals nor capitalists. Accordingly, Beck refers to a mono-dimensional methodological social analysis that constructs social groupings along classic hierarchies of gender, ethnicity, 'race' and class while not reflecting on feminist approaches to social complexity which look at overlapping aspects of social locations. Clearly, Beck's perception is related to the late 20th-century agenda of politicised group differences (feminist movements; postcolonial discourse and so forth) and its public demand to be acknowledged as different or discriminated.

To end this section, I will refer again to the feminist socialist voice of Behrend (1999),[58] who was influenced by the work of black feminists, in particular the

---

58   http://www.glasnost.de/autoren/habehrend/hirar.html.

writings of Mae G. Henderson (1989). Henderson suggests, not unlike Crenshaw, that we have to take into account the 'simultaneity' of oppressive discourses when evaluating social phenomena. Taking this approach seriously and in contrast to a hegemonic discourse of social 'individualization', Behrend focuses on material social differences by looking at contradictions and their potential to foster emancipation. She does so while going beyond an orthodox Marxist view. As Behrend (2000: 1161) puts it, '[e]quality is a condition for the possibility of non-hierarchical difference; to make it work it needs both Marxist as well as poststructuralist understandings of the partial. Also, theory and practice will always be guided by interests and rooted in specific historical circumstances.'

To conclude: in his 1990s work Beck focuses throughout on social changes and the transformations of national societies in a global age; this is very much in line with his previous interest in risk analysis and the futurity of social practices. Also, the two main angles of his research, 'reflexive modernity' and 'individualization', echo his academic proximity to Giddens' thoughts of the 1990s. In his attempt to define minoritised groups as Others, Beck refers to significant group classifications that respond to the political protest of minority groups of the time. Unlike Beck, Behrend catches up with international postcolonial and black feminist thoughts. She tries to combine Marxist class analysis with the social and cultural protest movements going on elsewhere. Most importantly, Beck grasped some of the ideological effects of the political power order in transition. He detected some crucial dilemmas of an emerging discourse of human rights interventions in 2000 and proposed that this discourse could be misused for 'cosmopolitan' military missions. Finally, Beck's global 'risk society' approach turned more directly to discourses of cosmopolitanism at the beginning of the new millennium; it is therefore most relevant to follow up his arguments after 9/11. What kind of consequences does he draw from the ambivalent potential of cosmopolitanisation, risk dramaturgy and the ideological function of constructing the Other as 'enemy' in this context?

In the remaining part of this chapter I assess Habermas's and Beck's writings while considering Hanna Behrend's critical interventions in a post-9/11 political climate.

'United We Stand': The 'Cosmopolitan' Turn to European Realpolitik in Response to Global Terrorism and Uncertainty

Though 9/11, unlike the fall of the Berlin Wall in 1989, took place in the United States and therefore territorially speaking outside Europe, the commemoration of the victims of the New York attack has been effectively orchestrated worldwide and inaugurates what I described in Chapter 1 as a phenomenon of 'civic bonding'.

In 2002 Daniel Levy and Sznaider (2002: 87 and 92) argued that the 'abstract nature of good and evil' and the 'identification with distant others' generates a de-territorialised memory. In their analysis they show that the local though distinctive memory of the Holocaust is globally transformed and changing commemoration into an unbound 'morality' paradigm. Accordingly, '[t]ransnational memory cultures ...have the potential to become the cultural formation for global rights politics' (Levy and Sznaider 2002: 88). In this text Levy and Sznaider (2002: 100) also critically discuss the Stockholm Forum[59] while stating that '"culture" offered "politics" a template for how a unified Europe, the site of the historical Holocaust, could imagine itself as a community of shared values.' During this forum the Holocaust was officially declared a European memory and identified as a 'founding moment of European civilization' (2002: 102).

But what does this mean to us given that there are different and contradictory memories and cultural identifications in Germany and abroad? The theme of 'European civilisation' and an anti-militaristic stance are highly contested grounds that overlap with considerations about the notion of the Other, terrorist and militaristic violence and discourses of new cosmopolitanism.

According to these considerations concerning the symbolic significance of 9/11 and the Holocaust the different writings on new cosmopolitanism will be explored in the following sections. I am going to start with Habermas's post 9/11 writings, but will bring in various interventions made by Beck and Behrend later on.

In 2004, Habermas (2004: 229) wrote about the increasingly abstract character of political community and proposed that supra national populations will be drawn to an idea of shared 'universal content' (*'denselben universellen Gehalt'*). In consequence, the identification with universal content would lead to a form of 'rational' and social integration: (1) it would encompass a growing consensus on legal principles; (2) it would foster the enlargement of supra-national organisations; and (3) it would diminish criticism of the judiciary of international courts of justice (ibid.).[60]

In his proposal, Habermas presumes that as a consequence of an increased awareness of the regulatory power of law, abstract and legally mediated transnational governance will eventually be established. According to Habermas, the mutually shared idea of 'universal values' should be at the core of a supra- or transnational system that substitutes state regulation of a bounded community and coherent terms

----

59   A European Intergovernmental Conference on the Holocaust that took place in January 2000.

60   'Indem sich der Akzent von der Staatszentrierung auf die Verfassungsorientierung verlagert, gewinnen die universalistischen Verfassungsgrundsätze gewissermassen Vorrang vor den partikularen Einbettungskontexten der jeweils eigenen nationalen Geschichte. Diese Struktur einer schon von Haus aus abstrakten und rechtlich vermittelten "Solidarität unter Fremden" kommt einer transnationalen Erweiterung der national-staatlichen Solidarität über nationale Grenzen hinaus entgegen. Je mehr sich die Aufmerksamkeit auf *denselben universalistischen Gehalt* richtet, umso weniger kontrovers sind die Rechtsprinzipien, die den Ausbau supranationaler Organisationen und die Rechtssprechung internationaler Gerichtshöfe schon längst bestimmen' (2004: 229).

of group solidarity.[61] As argued above in this chapter, Habermas's key concepts of *rational* free speech, autonomy and consensual morality define any other themes he is engaging with. In principal he cherishes modern rationality as the driving force that enables *cultural strangers* to communicate with each other.[62]

As mentioned above, Hayward (2004: n.p.) points out that while '[t]he Habermasian might say although indeed it [constitutional patriotism] excludes, [it] excludes in a way that is legitimate'.

This evaluation has resonances, for example, with the ways the German Constitutional Court decided on the case of Fereshta Ludin: the German teacher of Afghan background wore a headscarf and was banned from teaching and hindered to pursue her career. The Court argued that the decision of the federal state's educational government department to stop her from teaching was *unlawful* as there was no legal basis enshrined in positive law of the federal state of Baden-Württemberg at that time.[63] What happened next was that this federal state issued new legislation banning the headscarf. (Fehr 2011, Lettinga 2011) In effect, this means that those individuals that are declared as 'illiberal' and 'anti-democratic' can be ruled out of solid society, as are those such as women dressed in a manner not accepted by the majority. Consequently, a hegemonic discourse of majority values could convey *totalitarian tendencies* if it is unconscious of its own particular normative perceptions and remains unchallenged.

Currently, we are confronted with a political project that re-defines 'bounded people' though in abstract terms, *normatively*, and by doing so it is actively producing exclusion. Hence, we need to assess further the ways in which the 'constitutional' establishment of regional regimes fixes the established line between 'citizens and non-citizens' and to what extend Others, as illegalised immigrants, orthodox Muslims and female refugees, might be removed from a constitutional agenda that co-opts cosmopolitan belonging for established hegemonic interests and elite purposes. Again, as argued here, the intermingling discourses of a specific European (secular) cosmopolitanism and European Union policy could give insights into the rhetorical strategies employed to organise new symbolic boundaries, accordingly. An angle to explore this in greater detail is the tension between human rights, war rhetoric and institutional visions of cosmopolitan global democracy.

In 2005, Habermas published an essay in a German law journal. Here, he argued that future politics ask for the establishment of a global and multi-layered

---

61   Habermas refers to '"Kommunikative Verflüssigung" fixer Werte' (Habermas 2004: 231).

62   Habermas addresses a more sophisticated level of morality which is different to concrete ethics. He stresses the importance of '*höherstufige Intersubjektivität*' (Habermas 1991: 113), (higher levels of inter-subjectivity) allowing a '*Verschränkung der Perspektive eines jeden mit den Perspektiven aller*' (ibid.), (the interrelation of each perspective with the perspectives of all).

63   http://www.migration-info.de/mub_artikel.php?Id=030801.

state system. To make this global system work it would require transferring established functions of the state to transnational world organisations, for example the UN. Due to their special qualifications regarding peace actions and the global enforcement of human rights, multi-layered governance could guarantee security, law and freedom (2005: 235). He differentiates these governance structures of global politics from the challenging tasks of coping with the 'discrepancies in wealth' ('*Wohlstandsgefälle*'), and 'ecological imbalances' ('*ökologische Ungleichgewichte*') and the goal 'to create an intercultural understanding as part of a dialogue of world civilisations that aims to achieve effective equality' ('*eine interkulturelle Verständigung mit dem Ziel einer effektiven Gleichberechtigung im Dialog der Weltzivilisationen herbeizuführen*'). Habermas categorises the social-political dimensions of global inequity as 'domestic world policy' ('Weltinnenpolitik') (ibid.).[64]

In this text Habermas carries on with the classic frame of territorial nation state politics in which the domestic vs. international politics is actually transferred to a virtual inside/outside binary of world domestic and world 'foreign' affairs. In another text he suggests that the 'functional organisation of the world at a global level' ('*funktionierende Weltorganisation*') requires a thin base of integration (Habermas 2004). This echoes his previous perception of a thin cosmopolitan bond as outlined above and also implies that for pragmatic reasons 'sovereignty' is transferred to global institutional bodies. Further, he argues explicitly that global peace keeping actions would echo a mutually shared 'moral stance' ('Empörung') towards the violations of human rights. However, unlike this kind of weak bond the European Union should establish a stronger connection (Habermas 2004: 231).[65] Though Habermas's academic discipline is sociology, or alternatively social philosophy, his proposal here is close to David Held's vision of democratic cosmopolitan institutions as we will learn in more detail in Chapter 4. Apparently, we are confronted with an indicator of intertextuality that crosses specific boundaries of national academic disciplines and is international in its outlook. It seems as if the question of building governance institutions globally and regionally (i.e. the EU) transverses different fields of academic inquiry.

---

64   Beck comes up with this terminology in a co-authored publication (Beck and Grande 2010) without referring to Habermas.

65   'Dieses Potential genügt allerdings nicht für den Integrationsbedarf einer Europäischen Union, die nach außen mit einer Stimme zu sprechen lernt und im Inneren weitere Kompetenzen für eine gestaltende Politik an sich zieht. Die Solidarität einer politischen Gemeinschaft, und sei sie noch so groß und heterogen zusammengesetzt, kann nicht allein über starke negative Pflichten einer universalistischen Gerechtigkeitsmoral ... hergestellt werden. Bürger, die sich gegenseitig als Mitglieder einer bestimmten politischen Gemeinschaft identifizieren, handeln in dem Bewußtsein, dass sich "ihre" Gemeinschaft von anderen durch eine kollektiv bevorzugte, jedenfalls stillschweigend akzeptierte Lebensweise auszeichnet' (Habermas 2004: 231).

Also, Beck crosses the disciplinary boundary of his sociological inquiry into cosmopolitanisation[66] when he enters the discourse field of international politics and political theory. He (2002d) advocates formal negotiations, institutional agreements and proposes that only 'one principle', namely the principle of law, can be the adequate political response to transnational terrorism.

In a text called *Kleine Grabrede an der Wiege des kosmopolitischen Zeitalters* ('Minutes of a funeral address at the cradle of the cosmopolitan epoch') Beck (2002a: 441) develops, nonetheless, an insightful argument towards a totalitarian scenario of a cosmopolitan doctrine of humanist interventions. While rhetorically exaggerating a dictatorial scenario, he predicts a kind of 'holy cosmopolitan alliance' that would act on behalf of an empirical self-rationale (*'empirische Selbstbegründung'*). By claiming a 'cosmopolitan mission' that would bring democracy, liberation, and 'human rights', this 'alliance' would be regarded as a legitimate agent. Beck denounces this kind of cosmopolitan project as timeless or never ending (*'endlos'*).

He calls this encapsulated totalitarian risk a (Western) 'anti-democracy fundamentalism of good intentions' (*'Entdemokratisierungsfundamentalismus der guten Absichten'*) (Beck 2002a: 444). Alternatively he advocates a synthesis of democracy and human rights whose tools should be (re-)negotiated while taking reform to institutions such as the IMF and the World Bank. Further, he proposes the establishment of institutional conflict mediation, a world parliament and global, transnational organisations (2002a: 445–446).

As argued above, Beck takes up the political issues of the day, here related to the aftermath of 9/11 and the US-British war alliance against Iraq. Beck takes the 'legal' philosophy of global governance institutions even further. He distinguishes two models of conflict resolutions. He related the first one to a US-American concept of globalism and the second one to an UN approach of cosmopolitanisation (Beck 2004a). Also, he suggests (Beck 2005)[67] a soft hegemony of a European Empire. Conceptually this cosmopolitan Empire would oppose the US-American unilateralism. According to Beck (2005: 11) 'the cosmopolitan Empire Europe operates openly and co-operatively with reference to its inside and outside. Therefore, it is positioned in a significant opposition to the imperial supremacy of the USA.' For Beck, Europe's actual power (*'reale Macht'*) would derive from its model character, demonstrating how militant history can be changed into a co-operative future (ibid.). He also claims that gentle world power and the term 'empire' would put Europe on the same eye level with the different (*'andersartiges'*)[68] US-American Empire (ibid.). In another publication,

---

66   I will come back to this later.

67   Beck and Grande (2004) developed the concept of a European cosmopolitan Empire in Chapter III of their co-edited book *Das Kosmopolitsche Europa*.

68   Here, the German term *'andersartig'* needs attention. It echoes an anti-Semitic and National Socialist terminology that Beck certainly did not want to apply deliberately. But even a Freudian slip tells a story about problematic legacies.

co-authored with Edward Grande (2004) Beck recommends a tamed version of 'empire' as a multi-layered institutional response to global transformations. The 'European Empire' likewise should compensate for the jeopardised system of the European 'nation-state' and respond to a unilaterally defined global war on terror. Beck and Grande (2004: 98) admit that Michael Hardt and Antonio Negri (2000) inspired this approach. We could ask, is there another reading available to this mainstream European anti-war pretext and civilisation discourse?

Behrend devoted two essays to the subject of the new 21st-century wars (2001d, 2002c). Despite different styles of presentation,[69] the content and diction remain largely the same. In her writings Behrend addresses the split of the German Left and criticises their surrender to the Western military logic that was initiated by Bush's declaration of the total war against terrorism and rogue states. The ways in which Behrend organises her argument is significant. Foremost, in terms of references, she works throughout the texts with material taken from 'private' public discussions on this issue (local, personal conversations; international email chats; alternative internet media resources such as the British 'indymedia';[70] lectures) or from left wing, predominantly ex-East German newspapers and magazines (*Das Blättchen,*[71] *Neues Deutschland,*[72] *Freitag,*[73] *Konkret*[74]). In her essays Behrend pays attention to the widespread protests and peaceful interventions of local, national and international grass root movements all over the world.

According to her testimonies, resistance to Bush's declared and demanded 'Campaign Against Terrorism' (*Feldzug gegen den Terrorismus*, 2002c: n.p.) developed inside and outside the US. 'Ordinary' citizens and prominent individuals[75] opposed different stages of the USA administrative power as it established its role as 'world policeman'. To Behrend's mind there is neither a specific national, European or Western response to this US approach, nor any kind of homogeneous group of East or Muslim countries that 'welcome' or 'support' terrorist attacks. Clearly, she condemns terrorist murder, viewing terrorists as targeting the 'comforts of freedom gained in modern civil societies' (2002c: n.p.).[76] Also she remarks that violent acts do not possess any kind of emancipatory character (ibid.).

---

69   The text, published in 2002, introduces Behrend's statements as numbered hypotheses. In an academic context hypotheses are open to challenge and thus she is inviting discussion.

70   http://www.indymedia.org.uk.

71   http://www.dasblaettchen.de/GANZE.htm.

72   http://www.nd-online.de/.

73   http://www.freitag.de/.

74   http://www.konkret-verlage.de/kvv/kvv.php.

75   She mentions well known intellectuals, such as Noam Chomsky, Susan Sontag, Arundhati Roy, Edward Said, Tariq Ali and Gyorgy Konrad, by referring to their national background but then also adds less internationally known East (Daniela Dahn, Lothar Baier, Friedrich Schorlemmer) and West Germans (Günter Gaus, Elmar Altvater) separately.

76   'Errungenschaften … der modernen Zivilgesellschaft' (2002c, n.p.).

Her tenor in judgement echoes a general attitude which keeps its distance from individual and collective acts of militant aggression. However, a look at the sample of phrases she uses shows that Behrend's approach to 'responsibility' is arguably different. According to her Marxist-Feminist standpoint the place of resistance is multi-vocal and above all female[77] (Behrend 2001d) as the war alliance is specified as an imperial strategy of 'powerful white men' (2001d: n.p.). Criticising the split among the Left (Germans) and the missing analytical link between war politics and peace politics, she (2001d, n.d.) writes:

> [t]he war schedule of the powerful white men will not take place in Europe but largely in Asia. It will increase not prevent the likelihood of more terrorist attacks, for example, targeting nuclear power stations or US American army sites within NATO states. Predominantly, this connection is masked in the media and therefore could not reach the majority of people. Similarly, the link between billions of dollars invested in direct and indirect war purposes as well as in secret intelligence operations and as a result, steep cuts in social, health, culture and education budgets, are not presented as a public issue.

Hence she disputes the messages of hegemonic media that do not challenge the immense costs and also the causes of the rise of Islam fundamentalism. In opposition to the mainstream discourse she uses the label 'fundamentalist' while also talking about 'home-grown right wing -nationalistic fundamentalism' (2001d: n.p.). As will be shown next, here she comes close to the view of Habermas, who similarly argues that in principle all religions could nurture fundamentalism and that Muslim terrorists identified previously with nationalism.

In his pre-9/11 writings Habermas had claimed that fundamentalist ideology would not be compatible with a society that demands equality among all citizens; ultimately, for Habermas (2001a: 127) all three monotheistic religions could be fundamentalist, in principal.[78] Also in 2004, Habermas (2004: 40 and 55) regarded global acting terrorism as a modern phenomenon, mentioning that several terrorists identified as secular nationalists before engaging with violent religious fundamentalism (Habermas 2004: 59).

However, Behrend is closer to home when assuming that the danger of fundamentalism and extreme violence is produced in society: according to Behrend, no community 'has a natural tendency to become fundamentalist or terrorist' but any kind of nation and people might become vulnerable and

---

77   She mentions in particular, various international groups of 'Women in Black', the federal women council of the 'League 90/Green party', but also the declarations of 'Churchwomen', namely female Christian theologians, based in Austria, Switzerland and Germany.

78   'In the view of Islam, Christian, or Jewish fundamentalists, their own truth claim is absolute in the sense that it deserves to be enforced even by means of political power, if necessary' (Habermas 2001a: 127).

attracted to fundamentalism' (ibid.). In addition, she blames the US's installation of oppressive, sexist and totalitarian regimes as responsible for a broader push towards religious fundamentalist movements in non-Western countries. In this sense Behrend challenges the comfort of the enlightened West, arguing that we all have to be aware of the rhetorical strategies being used by governments, often in the name of community interests, to manipulate public opinion.[79]

Coming back to the mainstream push to narrow down cosmopolitanism to European cosmopolitanism and, in particular, European Union policy, it is of further interest to examine Beck's contributions in greater depth as he has published prominently on cosmopolitanism in the last decade.

To gather more information about the extent to which he has been working with different and biased connotations of the Other (alterity and plurality) in the context of his vision of cosmopolitanism, I focus on his British publication *The Cosmopolitan Society and its Enemies* (2002c) and the German publication *Der kosmopolitische Blick: Krieg ist Frieden* (2004c), published as *The Cosmopolitan Vision* (2006b). I look at the ways Beck's ambitious claim to recognise the otherness of the Other fails to capture the different meanings of 'difference' and 'otherness'. In picturing a 'cosmopolitan' fusion of national borders and boundaries Beck (2002c: 3) points to the fall of familiar, 'old' borders and 'plausible ways of drawing new borders'. He refers to Daniel Levy's and Natan Sznaider's (2002) essay about the cosmopolitanisation of the memory of the Holocaust introduced above, while accentuating that cosmopolitan societies, not unlike national societies, will operate along ethical lines (Beck 2002c: 4). While comparing universalism and cosmopolitanism Beck argues in the German publication that cosmopolitanism shows a stronger potential as it 'accepts that the Other is different but of equal worth'.[80] Further, in his German publication he elaborates on a 'realistic cosmopolitanism' (2004c: 77) taking for granted a minimum of universalism ('*universalistisches Minimum*') as a body of binding moral rules (ibid.). He refers to a mutually shared understanding 'not to sell women and children or to use them as slaves' (2004c: 77), and 'the possibility of allowing free speech as judgements about government and God without being threatened with death' (2004c: 78). Here, his rhetoric hints to prejudices that other (minority) ethnic and religious orthodox groups might break the normative rules of a 'minimum of universalism' and also would commit criminal acts against women such as trafficking, for example. In his English publication '*The Cosmopolitan Vision*' (2006b) he writes 'Cosmopolitanism without universalism – this much is clear – is in danger of slipping into this kind of multicultural randomness' (2006b: 59). It is somehow inappropriate that the German here scandalises 'multiculturalism' that, in contrast to Britain for example, never received an official dictum and appreciation in post-

---

79   'Even people who claim to be Left ignore that the US government and NATO states are lobbying high-tech globalism and this does not mean that it is in the same interest of the people of those states' (Behrend 2001e).

80   'Dass das Andere anders ist und trotzdem gleichwertig' (Beck 2003: 36).

Holocaust Germany. In addition, Beck introduces the idea of a collective right to cosmopolitan defence in this section of his German publication (ibid.).

For this reason there is a delicate tension between Beck's assumption of minimum standards of cosmopolitan enlightened societies and a non-cosmopolitan collective orthodox Other. In Beck's (2002c: 21) view it is 'multiculturalism' that responds to the cosmopolitanisation of reality with a 'collective image of humanity in which the individual remains dependent on his cultural space' (similarly 2006b: 62). Also he argues that both multiculturalism and universalism would represent closed-minded approaches to the tension of equality, alterity and individuality (ibid.). He criticises 'universalism' as Eurocentric, but proposes 'realistic cosmopolitanism'. In 2010 it is called '*Cosmopolitical Realpolitik*', though (Beck and Grande 2010: 436).

Another interesting contribution by Beck refers to the question of widening the scope of research methodologies. Beck (2004a) differentiates between a normative (philosophical) cosmopolitanism concerning the 'citizen of the world' and 'a descriptive-analytical social science' perspective focusing on the 'growing interdependence and interconnection of social actors across national boundaries'. In his perception this actual existing cosmopolitanism has to be researched within an alternative methodological framework. In common with his British colleague, John Urry (2000: 18), who asks for a sociology that goes further than examining national societies and 'new rules of method' Beck argues in favour of a new sociological understanding of social-spatial concepts. Programmatically, Beck (2002, 2003a; 2004a, 2004b) asks to replace the national with a cosmopolitan methodology (see also Wimmer and Glick-Schiller 2002). It is cosmopolitan methodology, on a theoretical and also empirical level, that became central to Beck's approach in recent years. Daniel Chernilo (2006) suggests that both logical and historical layers need to be distinguished when criticising the national (nation-state) grounding of social theory. This is important as I will show next how the reductive view of a single 'internal' European modernity is enmeshed with the particular narrative of modernity in the perception of Beck. He writes explicitly in 2004:

> [t]he normative and political meaning of cosmopolitanism have wandered through world history completely entangled in the enemy image drawn up by its national opponents...[I]n the age of national modernity, cosmopolitan reality could sway only in people's heads, it could only be conceptualised not experienced. (2004b:133)

Contrary to this view it is argued here that the metropolitan urban cosmopolitan space provided ambivalent experiences with the Other. Cosmopolitan Berlin of the 1920s symbolises, for example, ambivalence, exotic world culture and tolerance towards cosmopolitan difference although in a dissimilar way. While referring to Eleonore Kofman (2005), Mary O'Reilly (2006: 7) says about the image of the 'new (Berlin) woman', '[i]f the figure of the Wandering Jew represented the second, dangerous meaning of cosmopolitan, the figure of the Berlin woman represented the first meaning – a pleasurable, privileged mobility.'

This suggests the need to establish a two-dimensional reading of cosmopolitanism inside modernity, above all as an element of the modern German nation state the ambivalent legacy of modern cosmopolitanism signifies different spatial positions. Hence, the notion of *mobility* signifies inclusion; *migration*, within the nexus of illegitimate migration, however, refers to a context of marginalised and subaltern existence. We have to bear this in mind since in the context of contemporary discourses of new cosmopolitanism in Britain and Germany the freedom rights of movement across the EU states support cross border migration in the sense of a 'late modern mobility'. Accordingly, equally biased connotations inherent to the *Weltbürger/Kosmopolit* bias surround mobility/migration with respect to the current European perspectives as argued in Chapter 2.

Coming back to Beck's approach, we can note that he rather simplifies the alongside existence of various intra-European modernities creating different positions for minorities against specific national ethnic majorities. In the next chapter we will see how more complex materially and symbolically layered social realities encompass the theme of cosmopolitanism and the plurality/ alterity nexus in Britain. Thus, he ignores the variety of modernist cultures in and across different national spaces and places in Europe and beyond. Despite his situated and particular German outlook he claims, nevertheless, that 'analytical-empirical cosmopolitanization' would be 'value free' in contrast to normative cosmopolitanism (Beck 2004b: 139). However, this is a claim that he cannot sustain, as argued here.

As made clear above, since 2004 Beck has devoted several publications to the topic of European cosmopolitanism (Beck 2004a, Beck and Grande 2004, Beck 2005, 2006). In these books the European Union occupies a central position. In contrast to Beck's (2000c) previously expressed criticism of the strict legal demarcation of 'mobility' and 'migration' by nation states and also of Habermas's advocacy for European people,[81] most of his post 9/11 publications indicate an ideological shift. There is a proximity to power and institution building along social cohesion and federal integration themes that comes up when linking Beck's current research focus and the overall 'integration' project of the European Union. More recently, Beck also acts as the promoter of professional knowledge elites, who represent more positive images of European mobility and the potential of individual 'citizen of the world–cosmopolitan' competences (for further details see Nowicka and Ravisco 2008).

In several of his post 9/11 publications (2002b, 2002c, 2004a, 2004b, 2009, Beck and Grande 2010) Beck states that risks are rooted in 'ecological, economical and terrorist' threats. In his view the 'enemy' could be rooted in 'nationalism', 'globalism', and 'ethnic fundamentalism'. Inherent to the use of the term 'enemy'

---

81   Back in 2000 Beck (2000c: 91) had criticised Habermas's focus on 'European people' and his in-depth arguments of 'closure'.

is the conceptual language of otherness as alterity; imagined as a 'threatening other'. Beck's reference to Mohit Randeria's (1999) term 'divergent or entangled modernities' (cited in Beck 2002c, Beck and Grande 2010) to show his open minded attitude towards 'other' cultures does not contradict this interpretation as it only refers to a positive reception of 'hybrid' *secular modernity* in other continents. Though Beck (2009; see also Beck and Grande 2010) has partly 'redefined' his Europeanising perspective of cosmopolitanism more recently (Beck and Grande 2010: 420 ff.) this effort takes place while considering 'Asian' and other non-European geo-political views. He even speaks of 'self-provincialization of social theory' (Beck and Grande 2010: 412), without, however, referring to Chakrabarty (1999) whose book *Provincializing Europe* became synonymous with this critique. Apparently, Beck is attempting to de-centre the Eurocentric and male hegemonic voice. The appreciation of other 'hybrid secularities', however, captures a self-projecting idea of what a 'entangled modernity' should look like. Hence, there is a moment of 'selfing/othering' (Baumann 2004) in Beck's approach to cosmopolitanism which is at the core of Orientalism.

It should have become clear by now that the contemporary discourse of new cosmopolitanism is crossing national academic fields and in particular Beck's close academic relationship with Britain, e.g. David Held and the LSE, significantly shapes his sociological outlook on cosmopolitanism. So, as already anticipated in 2007,[82] it does not come as a surprise that Beck is broadening the scope of his cosmopolitan inquiry by now, even mentioning the possibility of *cosmopolitanism in the plural* and alternative feminist perspectives (Beck and Grande 2010: 433).

Concluding Remarks

In the aftermath of the Nazi horrors and as a consequence of Germany's liberation by the allies after World War II, the country was split into the GDR and the FRG; the latter became integrated step by step into the Western Bloc. Due to multilateral agreements the (West-) German nation state later became a member state of the European Union, in fact one of its keenest supporters. Thus, a multi-governmental political system continuously shaped and reconstructed the notion of the 'nation' through its legal top down processes since its beginning in the 19th century. Through the European Union federal system, the construction of national citizenship and national identity is shaped by new layers of EU fundamental freedoms (*Grundfreiheiten*) that construct new and more complex angles of belonging that supersede territorial allegiance to single nation states.

---

82   'Held's approach concerning global democracy institutions of the late 1990s and the early 21st century shifted more recently to a friendly support of Fraser's theoretical approach that acknowledges the fusion of the Westphalian state and democracy paradigm. We can have a guess how this will affect Beck's future publications' (Vieten 2007: 196).

Already in the 1990s Habermas started to advocate '*weltbürgerliche*'/global citizen aspirations to engender a European public sphere. He addressed the social, political, and economic transition of the German nation state as anchored in a hegemonic notion of the one nation state. While engaging increasingly with the European Union and an emerging European public sphere he refers structurally to familiar social forms of territorial allegiance and the need to achieve social cohesion. In contrast to an ethno-nationalistic identification this cohesion has to develop normatively. Habermas's focus on legal frames and formal standards of contractual negotiations echo his Kantian inspired philosophy and the post-Holocaust morality and democracy debate in the FRG, but also his acknowledgement of US American liberalism and pragmatism.

Beck engaged with modernisation theory while turning to a concept of flexible modernity in the mid-1990s. In contrast to Habermas and Behrend, who ground their alternative social visions in historical accounts, he gives priority to policy issues concerning global transformations and their impact on social structures in the future.

We find rather biased notions of *otherness* in Habermas's and Beck's outlook: drawing a line between an ethical-legal (civic) ideal of a cosmopolitan (continental) Europe – including plurality – on the one hand, and on the other, the virulent and threatening violence of state and non-state actors on the other, which also partially includes the unilateral war politics of the US. There is a claim that 'Europe' is plural in terms of its amount of different states and nations, but also as far as themes of hybrid individuality and the mixture of collective and individual identities are concerned. Further, we can detect that cosmopolitan visions, particularly in the new millennium, are increasingly reduced to a matter of European *Realpolitik*. However, it has to be emphasised that Habermas, unlike Beck, had already conceptualised his vision of '*weltbürgerliche Absicht*' (cosmopolitan intent) against the background of classic nation state based political notions of a democratic 'opening and closure' in the 1990s. Thus, his advocacy of the EU is somehow consistent with his earlier perspective.

In opposition to a celebration of European cosmopolitanism we find in Behrend a marginalised voice, critical to the German notion of *Weltbürgertum*. Behrend's perspective makes a difference to the public international debate on cosmopolitanism as she articulates a tabooed point of view by rejecting new European cosmopolitanism as the universal notion of the older *Weltbürgertum cosmopolitanism*.

History is particularly important when looking at Behrend's and Habermas's approach: their biographies, their differentiation of the terms '*Weltbürger*', cosmopolitan and their passionate political engagement with social justice and public concerns give evidence of a commonly shared generational link despite differently rooted gendered, social, cultural and ethno-religious locations. Beck can be seen as introducing a different (younger) generation of German academics trying to come to terms with the history of German National Socialism/totalitarianism(s) but in a much more detached and pragmatic way.

What is striking when comparing the German interventions in discourses on cosmopolitanism is that all relate to a 'territorial understanding' of a thick, political community in spite of their huge ideological differences. Behrend turns to a Marxist interpretation of the 'nation' keeping the idea that 'working class people' who live in geographically close relationships are best equipped to struggle for their emancipatory goals. Habermas is in favour of the European Union as the relevant and most capable regional body to create and regulate bounded solidarity interests. He keeps the hegemonic perspective that the territorial space works in line with the social space. Beck's suggestion of a 'European Empire' echoes cultural legacies of Eurocentric superiority as well as '*weltbürgerliche*' intent; this intent underlines his adjustments to *Realpolitik* and more recent state or supra-state policy matters. He shifted his broader understanding of social processes in the 1990s to a strategically narrowed down Europeanism in the new millennium. Beck and Habermas, while different in their accentuation of normative constitutional aspects (Habermas) and cultural and methodological phenomena (Beck) circulate dominant knowledge according to an ideological Europeanisation process. Their prominence as international 'public intellectuals' also indicates a male gendered institutional frame leaving out largely minoritised feminist and, ultimately, alternative utopian socialist interventions such as Behrend's, for example.

Back in 1999 Scott (1999: n.p.) criticised British academics for not taking a clear and outstandingly public stance regarding the Kosovo War and contrasted this 'relative' silence' (ibid.) with the debate taking place in the German press. At that time Habermas supported NATO's intervention as a 'cosmopolitan case' and 'legal pacifism' (ibid.), while Beck called it 'militaristic pacifism', linking its mission to the danger of misusing notions of cosmopolitan civilisation (cited in Scott 1999). Scott, not by chance, referred to Beck and Habermas as two academics who dominate the image of the public and male German intellectual. However, this perception is connected to a larger international hegemonic discourse that is mediated through national media which give space to particular opinions and disregard others. Behrend's feminist and Marxist counter voice did not make it to the mainstream national and international media when the 'new wars' topic emerged, but she gives an example of an *outsider intellectual* who resisted academic adjustment and found her way to alternative media. She gives a testimony of critical Marxist, feminist and utopian perspectives that could offer some hope to an emerging *transnational global public sphere*. I will come back to this in the final chapter of this book.

The next step is to look more closely how cosmopolitanism or discourses of cosmopolitanism engendered in Britain and whether we could trace some typical elements that are prevalent in the contemporary British based interventions in discourses on new cosmopolitanism.

Chapter 4

Global Trade, the City and Commercial Cosmopolitanism: David Held's and Homi K. Bhabha's Approaches to New Cosmopolitanism

Britain's history of Empire, its Commonwealth legacies and ample experiences with multiculturalism and liberal individualism set the background to contemporary discourses on gender and cosmopolitanism in Britain. According to Derek McGhee (2005: 163) the presumed cultural agenda of 'differentiated universalism' (Lister 1997a) is currently being broadened to a generally 'other-friendly citizenship grounded in difference' in Britain. Problematically this enlarged inclusive citizenship agenda is activated by 'cosmopolitanization' (Beck 2004a, 2004b, Beck and Grande 2010) as a 'compulsory' (McGhee 2005: 175) instruction project that aims to 'educate' citizens towards a more flexible and engaging attitude. In contrast to traditional notions of collective allegiance the new cosmopolitan citizen has to obey hegemonic British values and cultures and, at the same time, sustain a flexible membership in different communities. This top down imposed project of 'cosmopolitan practice' aims to overcome the group 'indifference' of a multi-cultural society that wishes to encourage the members of different communities to engage more with multiplicity and diversity. It means that Britain is prepared to adopt an ideal of plurality that connotes cultural and hybrid variety 'inside' the nation state and across its divergent communities. In what ways could this push for 'cosmopolitanization' override existing asymmetric social imbalances with respect to class, ethnicity and gender/sex? It is arguable whether a normative individualisation at the core of contemporary societies rather feeds a cosmopolitan subjectivity that ignores global social-economic injustice (lack of redistribution) and for that reason, does not reach out for a cosmopolitan connection in a sense of a global human bonding. The shortcomings of this idea of individual inter-cultural cosmopolitanism might correlate to the inadequacy of a liberal-capitalist society offering 'recognition' only in terms of individual hybridity and incorporated middle-class identities. We will see later in what ways advocates of liberal cosmopolitanism, such as Held and Bhabha, respond to these problems and how far the post-Marxist and feminist critique by Chantal Mouffe is equipped to tackle these issues.

The theme of the first part of this chapter is the emergence and transformation of *historical discourses* of cosmopolitanism in Britain. The main topical angles of the analysis are notions of individualism and community, the economic, cultural, social and political role of centralism, i.e. London in the south of England, and the question to what degree the English ideal of 'tolerance' in terms of a *laissez faire* recognition of group differences changed over time and influenced the understanding of the boundaries of the national community. It is argued that *significant* notions of otherness evolved in the 19th and 20th centuries in Britain, mapping out symbolic boundaries according to an English hegemonic *Weltanschauung*.

Images and cultural practices of cosmopolitanism today are linked to metropolitan and multicultural urban spaces.[1] Hence urbanity easily becomes connected with cultural images of modern citizenship and, beyond that, links it to frequent experiences with strangers and the presence of migrants (Vieten 2010). The resident of the urban city has been described in a number of ways before. Yet as introduced in the beginning of Chapter 3, Zons (2000) differentiated two 'cultural' models of the citizen. We saw the republican ideal of the *citoyen* that dominated the emergence of nationalistic societies in continental Europe, e.g. Germany in the 19th century. The trader (*der Händler*), in contrast, refers to a male individual who is primarily engaged with building property (*Besitzbürger*). Further, this privileged position echoes the liberal idea of fair play and free market. The figurative differentiation of the two divergent role models of *the citizen* is important as it gives us a lead to the argument that the imagination of difference and the Other evolved historically and specifically in line with hegemonic national ideals corresponding to commercially (Britain) and culturally (Germany) shaped and situated discourses of cosmopolitanism in the plural (Vieten 2007).

In the second part of this chapter I turn to some of the prominent and internationally recognised advocates of cosmopolitanism in Britain, David Held and Homi K. Bhabha. In February 2011, Held hit the headlines when it became clear that he had 'informally advised' Saif Al-Islam Gaddafi, who obtained a Ph.D. from the London School of Economics (LSE).[2] Some of us might remember the news coverage showing Muammar Gaddafi's son siding with the brutal violence of his father's regime against the democratic movement in Libya. Beyond the question of what this might tell us about the sustainability of power and the close link between *ideology* and *education* it is common knowledge that leading British universities such as the LSE or Oxford/Cambridge have a historical record in training the 'beautiful' and the rich next generation of the world's elite.

Does it matter whether the money for university fees might come from dictator families across the world and not only from the hard working middle class? Apparently, the *ethics* of international business demands us to rethink the framework of power and gender against a solid project of globalising just democracy. Hence, academic calls for change, social justice and cosmopolitan

---

1 With reference to London, see Nava 2002; 2006; 2007; with regard to Los Angeles and Mexico City, see Jérôme Monnet 2005.

2 http://www.guardian.co.uk/world/2011/feb/21/saif-al-islam-gaddafi.

democracy should be scrutinised against a sometimes very much *mundane* and temporary morality.

But first I will review historical manifestations of cosmopolitanism in the British context while considering the prominent role that *commercial cosmopolitanism* played in the growth and development of the British Empire, also in connection with the cultural, economic and political centralism surrounding London. Metropolitan London gives a specific example of how an urban city can create and offer cosmopolitan spaces in which multi-cultural and multi-racial differences can be encountered. Nonetheless, its centralism has to be contextualised against social and cultural conflicts that have occurred in Britain since the 1950s. These social conflicts received new attention in the most recent urban riots of August 2011. Despite the prevalence of racism, i.e. against black people as the significant 'colonial' Other and a very much classed social fabric, the acculturation of different minority communities has transformed modern Britain, as we will see. Finally, I will discuss the tension between spatial and social allegiances of diverse communities that have sent Britain in new transnational and *Euro-bureaucratic* directions since it became a Member State of the European Union (EU).

The Melancholy of a Classed as well as Raced Empire[3]: Multicultural London, Colonial Others and Social Spaces of Difference

Cosmopolitanism as a broader cultural theme emerged in the English language in the early 19th century, which was characterised by expanding nationalism and imperialism (van der Veer 2002).[4] The concept of free international trade had developed in the 18th century, most famously advocated by the political economist Adam Smith and the School of the Scottish Enlightenment.

According to Kleingeld (1999: 518), the idea 'that the economic market should become a single global sphere of trade' conveyed what we refer to as 'economic cosmopolitanism' or 'commercial cosmopolitanism'. In *An Inquiry into the Nature and Causes of the Wealth of Nations* (1776) Smith outlined his vision of commerce as the tool to sustain peace between different nations. Fonna Forman-Barzilai (2002: 417) argues that 'Smith thought international commerce could produce cosmopolitan ends without cosmopolitan intentions'. Similarly, Georg Cavallar (2005) regards Smith's perspective as a hope that free global trade would

---

3   This is, of course, an allusion to Paul Gilroy's (2004) book *After Empire: Melancholia or Convivial Culture?*

4   Peter van der Veer (2002: 171) for example, points out that John Stuart Mill's advocacy of the 'liberty of speech' and the meaning of secular freedom were intertwined and rooted in colonial thinking. Mill's tolerance *of otherness* took for granted that those belonging to 'modern civilization' adhere to the 'moral principle of progress' (ibid.). Similarly, Immanuel Kant and other contemporaries advocated Eurocentric philosophical models; I will come back to this later.

substitute the conquering and colonial exploitation of other nations. Further, Forman-Barzilai (2002) points to a particular tension between Smith's main work regarding the rise of the wealth of nations and his earlier publication *The Theory of Moral Sentiments* (1759). The latter approaches the theme of 'sympathy' while stating that 'sympathy seems to be constrained by geographical limits' (Forman-Barzilai 2002: 391). Hence, she argues that Smith's view about an 'unbounded' cosmopolitanism seemed to be implausible (ibid.). In a more recent publication she also brings in the term 'self-centred cosmopolitanism' (Forman- Barzilai 2010: 198). Forman-Barzilai's comment is important as it displays a problematic tension between spatial and social responsibility that is decisive for the perspective on a cosmopolitan subject and generally to the question of the social position of the Other. Thus, the concept of 'proximate interaction' (Forman-Barzilai 2010: 189) is discussed further. Also, I will look at some emanations of liberal cosmopolitanism, and social and cultural encounters with otherness in the metropolitan space of London and in colonial India.

According to James Sturgis (1984), conscious imperialism[5] (1892–1902) established the peculiar colonial consumerism that became apparent in major cities like London or Liverpool. The accessibility of exotic goods and an increasing cosmopolitan awareness were essential to a broader cultural consent creating 'an appetite and interest in overseas activity' (Johnson 2003: 43). The metropolitan city of London with its spatial crossing of gendered, classed and racialised boundaries, introduced cosmopolitan movements as diverse efforts to leave contemporary restrictions to social differences behind. Although whiteness, as well as middle and upper class standards, has to be regarded as the salient subtext to British 'nationality', an increasing tension between mainstream Englishness and the actual diversity of society in terms of gender, race and ethnic communities became decisive. Nava's research (2002, 2006, 2007), illustrates the complex, contradictory and gendered aspects of commercial cosmopolitanism in metropolitan London before World War I.

Gordon Selfridge, the founder of the Selfridges department store, was a '[s]upporter of women's suffrage, a promoter of equal opportunities for women shop workers ... [and] an ardent cosmopolitan' (Nava 2002: 86). While crossing rigid social group boundaries, Selfridge's cosmopolitanism became a field of symbolic contestation between 'modern outlook' and 'social prejudices of conservative mainstream English culture' (Nava 2002: 89). Another example outlining the links between female emancipatory movements, such as the fight of political suffragettes, and the spread of consumerism is given by Barbara Green (2003). Green argues

---

5   Sturgis (1984) differentiates three significant periods of British imperialism. The transitional stage between 1870 and 1888 gave way to a hesitant phase between 1882 and 1892 whilst awareness of competing European nation states influenced the international strategies of the British Isles. Predominantly, commercial and political alliances were built to protect British interests in the colonies. The 'Imperial British East Africa Company' represents this kind of politically instructed commercial companies.

that Rebecca Young, a socialist feminist journalist, 'stood at the intersection of feminist movements, women's experiences of modernity, and socialist and feminist deliberations about the practices of everyday life' (Green 2003: 222). These dynamics of a gendered modernity suggest a more complex outlook on British metropolitan cosmopolitanism. In line with this social and political transition Stuart Hall (1984: 15) proposes that '[b]etween 1880 and 1920, Britain became a "mass democracy"'.[6] Despite a general notion of a classed, raced and gendered English society, London and its vibrant cultural mixture of urban modernity also became the signifier of black metropolitan presence (Schwarz 2003).[7]

A further expression of cosmopolitan encounters can be seen in the crossing of social classes in critical consumer movements and broader concerns of international peace and socialist cosmopolitan thinking that became also relevant in the 1930s. With regard to Virginia Woolf's[8] affiliations with the Women's Co-operative Guild (WCG), Jessica Berman (2001) outlines the overall socialist principles of the co-operation movements. In favour of internationalism, the co-operations generally were critical to the nation as 'the primary locus of community affiliation' (Berman 2001: 127). Hence, the specific vernacular and 'visceral' (Nava 2007) cosmopolitanism of London (Nava 2002, 2005, 2006) has to be regarded as an outcome of global commercial trade and a specific metropolitan culture of openness and indifferent tolerance. This form of tolerance encouraged spontaneous encounters of people who had migrated to England and London in particular from places all over the world. However, this local cosmopolitanism co-existed with racist institutions in and beyond Britain. Alongside metropolitan London, imperial rule formed particular cosmopolitan communities in the Empire 'abroad', who lived in-between and at the margins of local hierarchies. British commercial interests, for example, could rely on a sophisticated system of utilised differences in its colonies. Yuri Slezkine (2004) differentiates 'Mercurian' and 'Apollonian' communities. Whereas he characterises the first group as providing services, the latter refers to settled communities associated with peasants and food delivery. This division echoes some nomadic images of 'cosmopolitan' versus 'locally rooted' communities. While talking about 'Mercurian' communities such as Jews, Romani or Armenians, Slezkine also refers to the Parsis in colonial India (2004: 4).

---

6   The backbone of this process was the successive, contested extensions to the suffrage which took place across the period.' Nonetheless, still in 1914 only '[a]bout seven million men were entitled to vote by virtue of the household occupation qualification … just under 60 per cent of the adult male population had the vote, while no women at all had the vote' (Marwick 1977: 22). Though suffrage was gained after World War I the issues of social class remained on the agenda for decades.

7   Despite a structurally racist society a particularly gendered and erotic dimension of cosmopolitan encounters emerged in the city of London as white women dated Black GIs (Nava 2002; 2006).

8   It is beyond the scope of this section to discuss Woolf's particular role as a feminist writer, her literary work and her political stance. For details see Walkowitz 2006a.

The resistance of the *colonial Other* also had a significant impact on the reception of colonialism in Britain. According to Bernard Porter (1968) western ideals of civilising non-Europeans had already been challenged by the mid-19th century.

Looking at the social positions of *significant Others* abroad, the Indian Mutiny (1857–58) and British rule in India embody and transmit complex racialised meanings of colonial armed conflicts and cosmopolitan encounters. According to Victor Kiernan (1995:48) '[T]he revolt was the first massive revolt of Asia against Europe.' Jan Nederveen Pieterse (1985: 124) notes that the rebellion of Muslims and Hindus, who were offended by Western-British ignorance about Indian ethnicity, caste and religious customs, was a turning point in racial relations 'uniting resistance against cultural imperialism.'

The English Crown and its hegemony were contested not only abroad, but also closer to home. The struggle for independence by indigenous nations such as the Scots and the Welsh (Colley 1994), but above all the situation of the Irish in Ireland and in Britain, highlight the violent and symbolic contestation regarding the dominance of Englishness. In addition, Kearns makes clear that the particular alliance between Irish nationalism and Catholicism has to be understood as a response to England's attempt to 'extirpate the Catholic religion' (2003: 205). Thus, an ethnic-cultural rift between different Christian faiths and their institutional structures to sustain power also underlay 'national' domestic conflicts.

Whereas in 1913 Viscount Hythe compared the government of the United Kingdom with a 'great business concern such as Messrs. Vickers or Messrs. Armstrong, with three or four great departments' (1913: 8), the Earl of Dunraven (1920) approached the possible devolution of the Empire while depicting the Irish famine and a lack of satisfying jurisdiction as central to the evolving 'anarchy' in Ireland. The social tension was fostered by unsatisfying English legislation. In this respect Adam Smith's perspective, introduced above, of an intrinsic link between sympathy and geographical proximity indicates a principal dilemma between the *visual* and the *emphatic recognition* of the Other. There remains a moral contradiction between the political claim to rule the Other and the actual indifference when it comes to the recognition of autonomous needs of the Other.

Apart from the indigenous Celtic people,[9] Jews were 'the first distinct minority ethnic-religious group in Britain' (Bloch 2002: 21), settling since the 12th century and after their expulsion by Queen Elizabeth I returning during the time of Cromwell.[10] Jewish mass immigration between 1882 and 1905, which was caused by Pogroms in Russia and East Europe 'coincided also with periodic economic depressions and phases of high unemployment' (Cesarini 1997: 61). As a draconic

---

9   Cohen (1994: 12) differentiates the Celtic fringe (Scots; Welsh; Irish) from the English as an internal ethnic boundary.

10   As Cohen (1994: 38) underlines 'the entire Jewish population, some 15,660, were deported' on behalf of Queen Elizabeth I, but allowed to return '367 years later during the Cromwellian period.'

policy response to the 20-year campaign against Jewish-Russian newcomers the first official legislation, the *Aliens Act*, was introduced and restricted immigration into Britain in 1905.[11] Similarly in 1914, the *Aliens Restricting Act*[12] was also 'passed just before the First World War to extend immigration control' (Sondhi 1987: 8).[13]

As a sign of a significant *racialising boundary* Randall Hansen (2000: 4) points to the hegemonic perception of a 'white' and European society before 1945:

> [b]efore 1945, The United Kingdom was ... [a] mélange of Anglo-Saxon, Jewish, Irish, Welsh, Scottish and Huguenots and other European refugees. This patchwork was, however, European and, more importantly, perceived, since 1945 (but not before), to be largely undifferentiated in terms of culture. By contrast, non-white immigrants were viewed as qualitatively different, as alien.

Thus a 'homogenized' perspective of a *united white* British national community unfolds in opposition to the historical tensions and various racialising dynamics that targeted indigenous minority groups and religious ethno-minorities (Anthias 1990; 2001b; Anthias and Yuval-Davis 1992; Hickman 1998). The hegemonic narrative of an assimilated cultural melange of 'whiteness', however, is relevant as it illustrates in what ways the meaning of foreign and alienated otherness shifted historically to the current and dominant discourse of *black otherness* after World War II. This is the case although the slave trade had been officially banned in Britain since 1807 and black people had settled in England since the early 19th century.[14] Between the 15th and 19th centuries Britain was one of the leading nations involved with the Trans-Atlantic trade of black people as slaves. An estimate says that more than 10 million people were shipped from Africa across the Atlantic mainly to North and South America. The 'ship' also is used by Paul Gilroy (1993) in his book *The Black Atlantic – Modernity and Double Consciousness* as a metaphor for the boundary crossing and remapping of the racial formation of the modern nation state which involved this enforced and brutal migration/movement. Though rather underestimated in European historiography, the Haitian Revolution

---

11   According to Bhabha and Shutter (1994: 20) the 1905 Aliens Act explicitly aimed 'to reduce Jewish immigration to Britain from Eastern Europe.'

12   These restrictions continued during peacetime by yearly renewals until the Aliens Order of 1958 was passed (Sondhi 1987).

13   The 1919 Aliens Restriction (Amendment) Act, additionally, was intended to restrict further immigration to Britain as an outcome of the upheaval caused by the revolution in Bolshevik Russia.

14   More than hundred years later, Eric Eustace Williams gives a rare example of a black scholar who was awarded a PhD at Oxford University at the end of the 1930s, but could not find an adequate academic position in England and therefore had to emigrate overseas. He finally succeeded and got a Professorship at Howard University in Washington in 1939 (Gaspar 2003).

in 1804 and the Emancipation in the British West Indies in 1838 urged European, e.g. English, businessmen to reconcile their interests (Wong 2010).

In the 1950s, there was a fundamental shift in the legal construction of civic inclusion, and as a result the position of being a British subject. According to John Solomos and Les Back (1998: 46), research on the period of the 1940s and 1950s emphasises that 'control on immigration and social integration was part of a wider political discourse which constructed "coloured immigration" into Britain as a problem.'[15] Whereas a settlement of around 200 000 Eastern Europeans between 1947 and 1952 was fairly accepted as 'adding whiteness to the British stock', 500 Jamaicans who landed at Tilbury in 1948 were considered as 'problematic' (Cesarini 1997: 64).

World War II had changed the political landscape internationally: in 1947, for example, India won independence; in 1948 the Israeli war of independence succeeded and the British Mandate in Palestine ended. In Britain 'over the next twenty years the empire disappeared' (Sinfield 1983: 15). In this period the legal links between Britain and the European Community evolved in a cultural re-centring of (white) Europeanisms as the settlement of the monarchy's black subjects was increasingly restricted.

As Eleonore Kofman et al. (2000: 52) emphasise, '[u]nder the 1948 British Nationality Act, Commonwealth subjects from the Caribbean and Indian sub-continent were able to enter Britain, to settle and bring their families.' That meant that about 800 million British subjects had the right to enter Britain, in principal. This shifted dramatically when the 'Commonwealth Immigration Act' (1962) restricted and controlled the right of black Commonwealth citizens to travel to and settle in the United Kingdom. In 1971, Parliament, with its Conservative majority, passed the Immigration Act, which replaced former legislation and based the right to enter and settle in the United Kingdom on 'patriality' and restricted immigration from the New Commonwealth to family reunification (Sondhi 1987, Mason 1995). The 1981 Nationality Act created three distinguishing categories of citizenship[16] and perpetuated the tendency to reserve genuine citizenship rights for the 'patrials' (Mason 1995).

Marc Joseph (1999: 91) makes clear that the 1970s also 'marked a shift away from Blacks as immigrants to the realization that a generation of young Black Britons were now old enough to demand rights in Britain as Brits.' Paul Gilroy's book *There Ain't no Black in the Union Jack* (1987) discusses the black contribution to British culture, arguing that it was generally *invisible* to the British nation. The 'Race Riots' that shook London and Liverpool in 1981 and Bradford as well as Oldham in 2001 have to be regarded as violent eruptions of youth anger in socially deprived city areas. In addition, the Brixton and the Bradford riots

---

15   As Hansen also clarifies (2001:69) the development of British citizenship 'is also a story of a gradual but ultimate merging of nationality and territory.'

16   Firstly, British Citizenship, secondly, British Dependent Territories citizenship and thirdly, British Overseas citizenship.

have to be interpreted as classed, gendered and generational responses to the local presence of fascist groups[17] and racist actions of police.[18] Yet back in 1997, Peter Lewis also pointed to the impact of religion on ethnic positions within a racialising frame. As he (1997: 129) argues:

> [T]he Irish Catholic experiences in Britain is significant in that it highlights a continuing failure of progressive thought to anticipate the importance and tenacity of religion as a component in ethnic identity and the possibility of maintaining multiple identities … [t]he supposed unitary identity generated by class solidarity did not obliterate other loyalties and commitments.

His main argument here is about the religious diversity within particular national groups of immigrants to Britain. In a hegemonic discourse perspective, complexities of diverse faith and racialised groups are enmeshed statistically in a blurred frame of 'ethnic and racial minority communities' (Vieten 2011).

The recent riots of August 2011 which hit several poor boroughs in London and also some northern cities such as Manchester, Liverpool and Birmingham appear as more opaque youth riots. Predominantly male street fighters expressed their social detachment as well as criminal intent. As it happened, three young Pakistani British citizens were killed in Birmingham, some arson attacks and looting took place in Turkish/Kurdish local neighbourhoods as well as small shops run by English owners were affected in London. These more random attacks underline that inter-ethnic conflicts are classed and further cross the white ethnicity/black ethnicity race line.

Further attention is needed to the tension between a secular cosmopolitan view on religion and the political encounter with faith orthodoxy that can be detected in the 1980s fatwa and the discursive crisis surrounding the poet Salman Rushdie. Jeremy Waldron (1995) connects *The Satanic Verses* and its author to cosmopolitanism. Rebecca Walkowitz (2006b: 132) argues that 'Rushdie uses the mix-up [of Sisodia's[19] and British colonialism] to introduce new experiences of contemporary immigration and also to distinguish between the cosmopolitanism of exploitative fusion, on the one hand, and the cosmopolitanism of tactical syncretism, on the other.' This remark reflects the two dimensions of cosmopolitanism as a mode of exploitative consumption and as an open encounter of new beginnings. Whereas *secularism* in Britain, for example, claims to be religiously neutral, it nevertheless maintains particular Christian values (Anglican High Church) as the public face of society. In recent times, we can recognise a modified state policy of *inclusive differentialism* that intersects with institutional

---

17   In Bradford, National Front sympathisers gathered in a pub provoking protest and resistance among Asian youth.

18   In London (Brixton) the protest of young black people arose as a response to the death of black men on remand in the local prisons.

19   The main character of *The Satanic Verses* is an Indian film producer living in London.

state racism (Goldberg 2002). As this shift correlates with the transformation of Britain in response to globalisation but also to its membership in the European Union, I turn finally to a discussion of the wider social-political implications of this membership and previous engagements with the idea of Europe. As it is argued here, the European Union and its supranational legal regulations do shake the social fabric of the British nation and reshape its hegemonic tradition of a commercial cosmopolitanism and multiculturalism.

Not unlike in Germany of the peacetime years of the early 20th century, and in particular during the years following World War I, peace and democratic movements began to form a broader outlook while focusing on Europe in terms of international democratic movements. Apart from British Quaker pacifists, who supported the idea of a 'United States of Europe' by 1910, several other British organisations such as 'the National Peace League' (1911) and 'the European Unity League' (1913) subscribed to pan-European efforts backing international peace movements (ibid.). By 1914 the 'Union of Democratic Control' was founded in order to advocate world federalism and peaceful co-operation. Internationalists such as J.A. Hobson redefined 'internationalism as a relation between peoples rather than states' (Kaufman 2003: 27). In the aftermath of World War II some of the pan-European movements, such as the 'United European Movement' and the 'Socialist Movement for the United States of Europe', re-emerged. As Eric Kaufman (2003: 32) argues, '[t]hese pedigrees reached into the formative institutions of the European Union, highlighting the connections between the inter-war social movements and the institutions of an incipient European Community.'

It is important to reflect on these ideological continuities as they articulate a cultural-racial pro-European orientation despite the fact that Britain joined the European Economic Community as late as the 1970s. It was in 1973 that Denmark, the Republic of Ireland and Britain joined what had started as the 'European Coal and Steel Community', founded by France, Italy, the Netherlands, Germany and Luxembourg in 1951. The steady legal process of establishing close administrative and governance links with the European Union, therefore, has had an enormous impact on contemporary discourses of multiculturalism, national identity and community cohesion that are interrelated with discourses on Europeanisation and cosmopolitanism.

Back in 1990, Sam Allen and Marie Macey (1990) discussed issues of race and ethnic relations in Europe with reference to the situation in Britain. What became clear was that the emergence of nationalism, religious fundamentalism and notions of race conflicts, as 'merely' defined by skin colour (white-black), would miss the point of complex racialising boundaries in Europe. Tariq Modood and Pnina Werbner (1997) argue that the dominant notion of British multiculturalism has shifted in the last ten years in accordance with social processes and changed politics all over Europe (similarly, Gilroy 2004; also Vertovec 2007). Therefore, it is important to take into account the impact of differently organised racialised boundaries in continental Europe that, as argued here, are an outcome of *historically distinctive contexts,* and are after all related to the Holocaust in continental

Europe (Vieten 2009). It is proposed that a broader process of *Europeanisation* is changing the vernacular face of Britain, a process that is influencing contemporary discourses of cosmopolitanism and gender, too.

Despite Britain's delay in joining the EU, its membership since the early 1970s has imposed an increasing pressure to open its borders for 'some 200 million EEC nationals' (Gibney 2004: 115), who possess the principal right to look for work and remain in the UK. In line with these changes of migration patterns Blair proclaimed the re-invention of Britain. Slogans such as 'Britain's history as a hybrid nation', 'its readiness to do business', but also the ambitious vision of being 'a global island' (Leonard 1997: 10), laid claim to a continuity of national traditions aspiring to global cosmopolitanism. In Britain a complementary system of civil inclusion is advancing rapidly in line with European agendas that have taken the place of essential national jurisdictions. It means that the goal of European *social cohesion* implies a strong push for Europeanisation that contradicts some legacies of a more globally oriented commercial cosmopolitanism.

To summarise: throughout history Britain accommodated a particular context of 'subalternity' and difference. Until recently the fairly unique cultural mixture and presence of global communities was characteristic to Britain. However, the notion of a *multicultural* British nation is predominantly confined to London and visible across some more conflict ridden cities such as Leicester, Birmingham, Manchester or Bradford, as far as the racial-ethnic and religious mixture of its populations is concerned. But this does not represent the dominant white and more classed British social fabric across the country (Vieten 2011, 2013 forthcoming). Contradictory and porous social spaces of vernacular cosmopolitanism exist, nonetheless. When looking at the notion of the Other historically we can recognise an ideological fusion of shifting racialised boundaries in the hegemonic narratives of the British national community. The predominant focus on the *black Other* as the *significant Other* in Britain is connected to its postcolonial Commonwealth legacy. That means that otherness and differences can co-exist and produce a tension along a paradigm of hegemonic power. 'What is at issue is the zone in-between complete difference (otherness, Alterity) and complete similarity in socioeconomic profile, opportunities and cultural capital (assimilation)' (Nederveen Pieterse 2007: 97).

In terms of the meaning of 'multiculturalism' Bauman (1999: 197) refers to Alain Touraine's (1997) distinction of 'multicultural' and 'multicommunitarian' societies. He argues that it is the second term that labels hermetically closed communities where cross-cultural exchange and switching of allegiance is banned. The latter would indicate a rigid system of 'communities of communities', which refers partly to a problematic tension of social and spatial geographies in Britain. The terror attacks of fundamentalist individuals in 2005 have caused a major shift in the perception of a principal British tradition of 'indifference' and tolerance (Wemyss 2006, 2009) to group differences that have to be explored more concretely in the following when looking at the rhetoric and arguments by Held and Bhabha and the feminist contester of liberal cosmopolitanism, Chantal Mouffe.

First, I will briefly introduce the two male writers while biographically embedding their distinguished disciplines and research agendas. This will then be followed by an exploration of Held's and Bhabha's writings on cosmopolitanism in the 1990s while bringing in Mouffe as a critical feminist challenger. For in Britain, not unlike Germany, the period after 1989 stimulated academic discourses engaging with cosmopolitanism. The fall of the Berlin Wall and the collapse of the Eastern European communist system impacted differently on the British outlook, which traditionally focused more on global trade and diverse culture. Finally, the more recent writings on cosmopolitanism in the post 9/11 discursive frame will be analysed. Increasingly a 'security – immigration' nexus shapes the general rights discourse in Britain; a nexus that responds to a globalised discourse of terrorist threats. Hence it is of central importance to explore in what ways discourses on cosmopolitanism resist a broader 'securitisation' discourse (Bigo 2002) and whether and how different authors are able to maintain their distinctive approaches to cosmopolitanism post 9/11.

As we will learn later on, commercial and liberal perspectives are closely connected here, and in this regard might shape, for example, David Held's position towards global cosmopolitan democracy and also Bhabha's focus on postcolonial and multicultural frames in distinctive ways.

David Held's and Homi K. Bhabha's Proposals of New Cosmopolitanism in the 1990s Read against a Post *Marxist* Feminist Critique

David Held

Held was the Graham Wallas Professor of Political Science at the London School of Economics (LSE) until recently. Since January 2012 he is Master of University College, Durham and professor of politics and international relations at Durham University. Held's research activities initially combined introductory work on Jürgen Habermas (1982) and a strong research emphasis on the tension between state and citizenship in Britain (Held 1984) and Europe (co-authored with Bornstein and Krieger 1984). Since the mid-1990s he has published on cosmopolitanism (1995, 1996, 2004, 2008, 2010a, 2010b), and, among others, the politics of the United States of America (Held and Koenig-Archibugi 2004). At the heart of his research interests is the political analysis of democracy and citizenship as well as law and justice on a global scale. In line with this focus he looks at social and economic contradictions within different nation states and in turn he problematises their relevance for international politics. His insights into German philosophical and sociological thinking also add to a very pronounced British articulation of global citizenship dimensions and cosmopolitanism, taking on board continental European traditions of social welfare, social democracy and cohesion as we will see more concretely later.

Back in the 1980s, Held had started to look at the correlation between advanced industrialised societies and the situation of Third World countries. He urged Western scholars to analyse more thoroughly the links between different types of state activity and the organisational rationality of the administrative apparatus in relationship to socio-economic structures (Held 1982: 193 and 194). Held kept this global outlook on the international political dynamics of globalisation into the 1990s. He regards globalisation processes as disrupting the familiar notion of territorially bounded political legitimacy and affecting the traditional Western outlook on democracy. In making these assertions Held discusses 'the people' in abstract terms, grounding his democratic ideal of 'the people' on a liberal notion of an individual self and an individualised Other.

By the middle of the 1990s Held's outlook on the function of law, economic frames, and the regulatory effectiveness of the nation state and the role of political resistance shifted fundamentally from a critical Marxist to a liberal position. In contrast to his writings in the 1980s the notion of unbiased law and (equal) rights has become the rationale for mediating interests as a matter of an apparently 'value-neutral' framework. Since the 1990s Held was based at the LSE in institutional proximity to Anthony Giddens.[20] This underlines a nearby intellectual relationship crossing the disciplinary boundaries of sociology and political theory. In addition, there also exists a lively intellectual exchange between David Held and Ulrich Beck[21] – the latter also is institutionally linked to the LSE.

To summarise: since the mid-1990s, Held has no longer challenged the ideological formation of liberal capitalism. In this regard he rides with the mainstream tide on the neo-liberal wave and post 1989 ideological perspectives. Though Held keeps his awareness of the structural dimensions that affect individual 'autonomy' and undermine equal democratic participation of disadvantaged individuals, his previous Marxist analysis is replaced by neo-liberal ideology. This liberal analysis of the social sphere endorses Giddens's and New Labour's agenda that spread in the 1990s all over Europe. Fraser (2009: 107) summarises,

> In Western Europe, the social-democratic focus on redistribution largely gave way to in the 1990s to various versions of the Third Way. This approach adopted a neo-liberal orientation to labor market 'flexibility', while seeking to maintain a progressive political profile. To the extent that it succeeded in the latter effort, it was by seeking not to mitigate economic inequalities but rather to overcome status hierarchies – through anti-discrimination and/ or multicultural policies.

---

20   Giddens became associated with New Labour when the then Prime Minister Tony Blair adopted aspects of Giddens's programmatic outline for his government project of 'Third Way politics'. Further, Held and Giddens had co-founded Polity Press in 1985, among others publishing Habermas's books and thus, also contributed to his international recognition.

21   Beck has been *British Journal of Sociology LSE Centennial Professor* in the Department of Sociology since 1997.

When looking more closely at Held's advocacy of *cosmopolitan democracy* in the 1990s next, I focus on the tension between Held's reading of individual citizenship and his recognition of the Other as the non-citizen, who is not able to participate (fully) in local and national democracies. This therefore adds urgency to the question of the degree to which minoritised groups and illegal(ised) Others might be structurally included in Held's model of cosmopolitan democracy. Given that there is an ideological proximity between mainstream political developments and academic research I look at the ways Held draws symbolic boundaries as far as the formation of contemporary political communities is concerned. Here it is important to extract how Held addresses gendered, ethnic, racialised and classed status crosscutting British, European or Western based assumptions of individualism, universalism and particularity.

John Lysaker (2002: 8) emphasises that representative 'self-government' implies a tyrannical tendency, in which the majority is politically allowed to define the quality of the good and the rule of its distribution. This is important to acknowledge, as political representation does not necessarily include the material right for any minority individuals from less visible groups to be equipped to *represent themselves*, whether they be working class, female, black, Muslim or gay. Thus, the reasonable rule of the law of the majority could structurally exclude the needs of people who are not able or not allowed, to articulate their own needs as already discussed in the previous chapters.

As some liberal ideas are central to Held's work on cosmopolitan democracy I am going to refer briefly to his core beliefs. Regarding the notion of democracy Held (1996) takes for granted that 'the idea of self-determination' appeals to *citizens as members of a political community*. Characteristically the 'conditions of their own association' (1996: 145) have to be chosen freely. In addition, the formal structure of democracy has to be set up in a 'fair framework' (ibid.). In Held's perspective the legacy of democratic ideals appeals genuinely to citizens who define the boundaries of 'the people' who subscribe to and enact a particular model of democratic rule. As the notion of boundary is central to both the notion of national community and the threshold to cosmopolitan belonging, Held's notion of democracy and the role of citizens are discussed more closely. At the centre of Held's approach to democracy is the notion of individual autonomy.[22] According to Held (1996: 147):

> [p]ersons, should enjoy equal rights and, accordingly, equal obligations in the specification of the political framework which generates and limits the opportunities available to them: that is, they should be free and equal in the

---

22   Held refers to Immanuel Kant's idea that each individual has the right to freedom of choice and self-development governed by law abiding behaviour, 'with laws which ensure that the freedom of each can co-exist with the freedom of others' (Kant 1970: 191, cited in Held 1996: 221).

determination of the conditions of their lives, so long as they do not deploy this framework to negate the rights of others.[23]

Firstly, he assumes an intrinsic bond between equality and freedom of choice. In principle all persons are considered as being equal and are thus able to make decisions regarding their living conditions. Here, the rights of Others appear as a point of reference to the gaze of 'equal persons', who should 'not deploy' the framework of rights. Secondly, he brings in 'regulatory structure' as the most important angle to advance democracy. Held's advocacy for (representative) *formal democracy* does not challenge the hegemony of materially privileged groups, who dominate the public sphere and therefore define the content of the 'public good', structurally excluding those who lack the relevant sources or skills. In Marxist phrasings this structural asymmetry could be explained by class antagonism; from a feminist perspective we might argue that gender/sex antagonism is inscribed in all societal asymmetries.

Held proposes a triad of (1) democracy as superior form of governance; (2) plural networks; and (3) formalised decision processes. He (1996: 223) regards 'empowering rights' or 'entitlement capacities' as being central to cosmopolitan democracy. These rights are based on 'free agreements' and echo liberal ideas of equivalent (market) power, as he claims, '[t]here may be no religious, metaphysical or foundational grounds for becoming a democrat, but if one chooses to be a democrat, one must choose to enact these rights' (ibid.). This statement is characteristic to his view in the way he stresses that only individuals who freely accept the rule of democracy can enact participatory rights. In line with this view, 'belief' systems are only relevant as a kind of second order to the values of democracy. According to Held (1996: 224) democratic principles are the 'most superior form of governance' whose formal standards must be approved while neglecting specificities such as 'citizenship or universality'. As he writes in 1995:

> [d]emocracy is the only grand or 'meta-narrative' which can legitimately frame and delimit the competing 'narratives' of the good. It is particularly important because it suggests a way of relating values to one another and of leaving resolution of value conflicts open to participants in a political dialogue, subject only to certain provisions protecting the shape and form of the dialogue itself. (1995: 116)

Therefore, his construction of a cosmopolitan order relies on formalised negotiations between group agents and individuals based on an understanding that 'democracy' is a self-sufficient concept.

Further, Held identifies 'five disjunctures' (law, polity, security, identity and economy) as the shifting patterns of power that influence the constraints of the

---

23 Held explicitly mentions that this conception is modified and thus somehow different to the concept he used in his earlier writings.

nation-state system. In his view of cosmopolitan law the terms 'subordination' (1996: 234), 'subsidiarity' (1996: 235) and 'test of extensiveness, intensity and comparative efficiency' (1996: 236)[24] are significant. Held's proposal of a multi-layered system of global governance refers to constitutional channels that exist in some Western federal states, such as the United States of America, Switzerland or Germany. Likewise, the expanding supra-state system of the European Union (EU) operates through a similarly organised federal administration. In the EU sophisticated policy regulations either bind Member States (i.e. directives; EU parliament) or offer legal protection directly to EU citizens (subjective legal rights; *individueller Rechtsschutz*). However, the European Supreme Court can only take legal action after a formally established process of legal 'subsidiarity' enacted in the different nation states. All in all, this multi-layered delegation of formal responsibility and sovereignty matches considerations about the role of federal representative democracy.

In line with this systematic understanding of federal governance, Held's suggests that local, regional and global issues of governance should be measured according to their different impact on 'the people'. For example, topics such as policing and matters of education should be treated as a local affair; similarly, politics that affect people within a particular national territory should be solved within the national frontier (1995, 1996). By contrast, environmental problems should be mediated, locally, nationally and on regional and global levels. At the end of the day, the collective reach of the problems should define the limits of sovereignty by concrete decision makers (ibid).

Nonetheless, Held (1996: 123–125) regards transnational grass roots movements such as Amnesty International – apart from the UN – as relevant to the furthering of global democracy. Besides, he recognises the discursive place of alterity that could undermine cosmopolitan bonds:

> [a]wareness of 'the other' by no means guarantees inter-subjective agreement, as the Salman Rushdie affair has only too clearly illustrated … there is no common global pool of memories; no common global way of thinking; and no 'universal history' in and through which people can unite. (1996: 125)

Held makes reference to the controversial book *The Satanic Verses* and the public debate associated with the life threatening ban (fatwa) issued against Rushdie at the end of the 1980s, which was mentioned in the first part of this chapter. The life threatening ban uttered by Muslim orthodox fundamentalists became a prominent signifier of transnational ideological encounters between hybrid secular difference and fundamentalist faith orthodoxy. While suggesting that there is no 'common memory' Held makes clear that the way we engage with

---

24   In Germany the high court system operates according to the scheme Held suggests; it is called *Verhältnismäßigkeitsprüfung* ('applying the principle of proportionality').

these different memories and conflicts matter for the way in which contemporary cosmopolitanism is shaped.

Though Held clearly admits that there are limits to any legitimacy regarding responsible decisions of national governments, he nevertheless retains a pragmatic perspective. He argues that widely established institutional bodies should intervene in conflicts. In his plea for liberal cosmopolitan democracy Held uses a rationale that 'naturalises' the superiority of market democracy, accepting its hierarchies and widely neglecting the political dynamics of an increasing lack of functioning political institutions. Problematically, the tension between legal citizenship and broader considerations regarding Others is neglected. Thus, his wish to keep established nation states and maintain international state institutions precludes an effort to have a more in-depth approach of addressing all people and inhabitants of the world as civic agents of cosmopolitan democracy. That means Held is primarily concerned with multilateral conditions which shape the *formal* position of *a citizen* to national sovereignty and vice versa.

As made clear in Chapter 2 this notion of *a citizen* is presented as an idealistic status and as a neutral/abstract value container though largely it is *framed* by hegemonic life circle normativity (add: male, middle class, white, heterosexual). With respect to gender/sex dynamics the whole range of discriminatory practices women face globally are left out of this theorisation.

Held further suggests that new layers of sovereign orders, such as the Human Rights Convention and EC Treaty, have reshaped the overall legal construction of citizen rights. But agreeing that the notion of citizenship has changed should also imply a critical understanding of contemporary notions of *social citizenship* that takes into account broader transformations between national, transnational and finally, international public spheres. In contrast to a merely legal perception of citizenship, T.H. Marshall (1950, 1981) identified civil, political and social rights as being the essential characteristics of citizenship. These different layers of rights are encompassed traditionally by national welfare systems. Thus, access and distribution of rights are regulated and delivered by national states. Yuval-Davis and Werbner (1999: 4) propose that citizenship has to be understood as a relationship 'inflected by identity, social positioning, cultural assumptions, institutional practices and a sense of belonging'. These differentiations matter as they influence the way we theorise citizenship, democratic participation and wider concerns of borders and boundaries. Furthermore, by insisting that we see citizenship as a matrix of intersected complexity we achieve a broader consideration of an ethically loaded discourse on human rights. However, Held's discussion of human and citizen rights refers to the institutionalisation of rights as the pragmatic agenda of states at that stage of his 1990s writing.

Further, we learn that Held holds an idealistic perspective on the 1989–90 collapse of the Communist system. According to Held (1996: 139) the 'revolutions of 1989–90' in Central Europe demonstrate 'the importance and closeness of questions surrounding legitimacy and democratic principles and procedures in Western democracies' and are led by 'the rationale and basis of order and toleration, of democracy and accountability, and of legitimate rule' (ibid.). And rightly, the 1989–90 turning point concerning societies in Central and East Europe directs us to the critical potential of *vernacular cosmopolitanism* as national independent movements challenging the hegemonic notions of autocratically bordered states. The peaceful demonstrations in Leipzig and East Berlin, for example, engendered a liberty movement which spread to the other countries of the communist bloc, initiating its collapse. Crucial to these processes, however, was the previously started *Glasnost* ('opening') politics of Mikhail Sergeyewitch Gorbachev, General Secretary of the Communist Party of the Soviet Union between 1985 and 1991. In addition, the post-1989 development of Germany, for example, also underscores the marginalisation of critical socialist intellectuals and dissident-advocates of the previous civil democratic movement of the GDR. At the end of the day, the initiative to combine socialist and liberal rights agendas was ignored or banned and particular rights of women restricted (Behrend 1995). That means that the actual cosmopolitan spirit of the people who took the protest against closed borders to the streets (Stevenson 2003) was undermined autocratically by established political elites and their normative standards in the West, post-1989.

In this respect we can recognise Held's perspective as looking from a very British and liberal market angle keen to idealise the notion of individual liberty while at the same time underestimating the collapse of social participatory rights in East and central Europe.

It is interesting to bring in Chantal Mouffe, a prominent British post-Marxist and feminist voice and contender of liberal cosmopolitanism at this point.[25] As Jacob Torfing (1999: 3) states, Mouffe's intellectual project intends to combine 'post-structuralism and post-Marxism with a blend of Lacanian subject theory.'

In line with her co-authored publication (Laclau and Mouffe 1985) of the mid-1980s, in 1990 Mouffe (1990a: 57–58) similarly explained her understanding of radical plural democracy.

> [t]he aim is not to create a completely different kind of society, but to use the symbolic resources of the liberal democratic tradition to struggle against relations of subordination not only in the economy but also those linked to gender, race, or sexual orientation, for example.

---

25 Mouffe was born in Charleroi (Belgium) in 1943. She studied in Belgium and later in France at the height of student protests and the rise of second wave feminism. In her early student years she was a member of the Socialist Party and particularly engaged with Latin American politics (Torfing 1999: 15). She is now Professor of Political Theory at the University of Westminster; this is after acquiring research experience from, and holding positions in, different parts of the world. Since the late 1970s the impact of social antagonisms has been at the heart of her research interests. Inspired by Gramsci's thinking about ideology and hegemony, a critical post-Marxist notion of social antagonism is very important to Mouffe's (1979) approach to politics and political community.

Mouffe's approach crosses the meaning of class as the most relevant agent of collective conflicts. In 1990, Mouffe (1990b) criticised John Rawls' approach to social justice. She argued that the 'creation of a collective identity', a 'we', (Mouffe 1990b: 226) would be essential for any kind of (political) public action. According to Mouffe, liberalism, in particular deliberative democracy and its ideal of rationality (see also Mouffe 1996), are not valid theoretical concepts to bridge social antagonisms in society. While Mouffe (1992b: 233) strongly criticises a merely 'instrumental community', she calls for the establishment of new common bonds between citizens that are based on an 'identification with rules'. Also since the 1990s Mouffe has recommended a critical reading of the German political theorist Carl Schmitt. Schmitt fundamentally rejected liberal democracy and advocated a polarised view of 'the political' as the battle of friends against enemies.[26] In 1999 Chantal Mouffe responded critically to the emerging debate surrounding cosmopolitan citizenship and cosmopolitan democracy. In her perspective:[27]

> [w]ithout a demos to which they belong, those cosmopolitan citizen pilgrims would in fact have lost the possibility of exercising their democratic rights of law-making. They would be left, at best, with their liberal rights of appealing to transnational courts to defend their individual rights when these have been violated. (1999a: 42)

On closer examination of her rhetorical strategy in which she intends to set herself apart from the liberal advocates of cosmopolitanism, we come across certain phrases. The expression 'cosmopolitan citizen pilgrims', for example, reflects on Richard Falk's (1995) proposal that global citizens exercise loyalty by belonging to different transnational communities.

However, she rightly emphasises that the existing state orders only guarantee democratic rights to bounded citizens: Mouffe criticises Held's position concerning the global purpose of international law and supranational court systems as being asked to regulate conflicts and claims. Her critical distance to his proposal is indicated rhetorically in the short phrase 'at best' (1999a: 43). To say 'at best' connotes a negative message; there might be good reason to believe that in reality the situation would be worse. Obviously, Mouffe neither shares Falk's idea of a virtual community nor Held's idea of multi-layered governance that could coexist with different local affiliations substituting or accompanying the mono-linear order of nation-state governance. Mouffe argues that democracy is inevitably determined by 'the demos' and 'the people', and that 'humanity', does not offer acceptable allegiance able to compete with state democracy.

---

26   As I have discussed this weakness in Mouffe's critique of liberal cosmopolitanism elsewhere in-depth (Vieten 2010) I will only touch briefly on some of the problematic issues later on when discussing Mouffe's proposal of a 'multiversum' in the post-9/11 context.

27   A very similar argument can be found in 2000: 42.

To summarise: Held (1996: 224–233) regards democratic principles as the 'most superior form of governance'. He argues that even if the current shape of the democratic nation-state vanished, the idea of national politics and states would remain with us. As a consequence of his considerations he proposes an institutionally unfolding multi-layered system of cosmopolitan democracy. By the mid-1990s, Held's outlook on cosmopolitanism is shaped by an individualising discourse that overemphasises the formal freedom of individuals while widely neglecting those conditions based on class, gender and/or ethnicity that hinder freedom rights from being enacted substantially. All in all, the question of how to alter and organise distributive justice and the social inclusion of the global Other are marginalised topics in Held's thinking about cosmopolitan political community in the mid-1990s. His model of 'the citizen', and his notion of cosmopolitan democracy rest on classic and idealistic connotations of a *gender neutral citizenship* that have all but nothing to do with the material imbalance of actual democracies. Significantly, Held's proposal of universal and global citizenship rights does not take into consideration transnationalising social forms of cosmopolitanism within and across various nation-states. He neither acknowledges 'vernacular cosmopolitanism' in connection with local emanations of a multicultural British society nor does he approach the missed possibilities of 'critical socialist cosmopolitanism' that came about in the political transition period in Central Europe. Accordingly, Held addresses cultural diversity and conflict as a matter of international state order rather than as an outcome of new intermingling layers of belonging and the more complex social divisions within and beyond national borders and political communities. It is debatable what it then means for the purpose of an alternative cosmopolitan project when he advocates cosmopolitan democracy from an international politics angle and principle of *formal democracy*.

In Mouffe's critical writings on cosmopolitan democracy and the notion of politics in the 1990s, she demands common consensual values and a clear allegiance that should transcend the particular morality of a private sphere.[28] Mouffe uses the term citizenship exclusively for membership in a concrete political community and in doing so, prefers its formal and legal notion. Not unlike Held she widely ignores critical feminist approaches (Pateman 1989, Lister 1997a, Yuval-Davis 1997a, 1999b) that consider citizenship to be shaped by multi-layered systems of various and varying loyalties to different communities crossing the classic notion of the national political community. However, this social complexity of allegiances is central to an understanding of antagonisms and the ways we theorise 'the political' as social space today.

In the following section I turn to Bhabha, one of the most recognised postcolonial writers addressing conceptual matters of hybridity, culture, colonialism and British history, which are central to his perception of new cosmopolitanism.

---

28   Mouffe touches on the themes of social cohesion and political community in *Pluralism and Modern Democracy: Around Carl Schmitt* (1993: 131 and 132).

Homi K. Bhabha

As discussed in the beginning of this book and the chapters before, 'culture' echoes particular perceptions of political community and national culture depending on the capacity to participate and to *become visible in it*. In this political reading the cultural articulation of ethnic minorities and minoritised social groups (i.e. female; working class; gay and lesbian popular culture) has to be regarded as embedded in particular historical and national frameworks. Hence, British Cultural Studies reflects to a certain degree the plural cultural character of *the social fabric* as *political space* in Britain that can be re-addressed in a critical sociological reading of the perception of 'the political'. Bhabha is a theorist who contributes to the 'problematizing' of cultural phenomena in a political space while creating an 'interface between the hegemonic social and the territorial political' (Dean 2000: 3).

Homi K. Bhabha is the Anne F. Rothenberg Professor of English and American Literature at Harvard University and Distinguished Visiting Professor at University College London. Previously, he held positions in Chicago and at the Universities of Oxford and Sussex. His academic move to the United States places him geographically as an Anglo-American researcher who transcends the European context. Bhabha's personal account of his upbringing and heritage[29] matches the historical record about flourishing cosmopolitan spaces in India in response to the British Empire and its commercial cosmopolitanism as mentioned in the beginning of this chapter. In this regard he could be considered as the offspring of a 'Mercurian' (Zlaskine 2003) community, whose hybrid identity at the margins of Apollonian communities is linked to images of a specific vernacular cosmopolitanism of post-colonial minority groups.

According to Arif Dirlik (1994: 333), Bhabha is 'responsible for the prominence in discussions of post-coloniality of the vocabulary of hybridity.' The prominence of his concept of hybridity has to be related to other central terms he uses, such as 'cultural difference', 'Third Space', 'liminality', 'in between' and 'translation'. Bhabha's academic contributions have to be analysed as part of a larger postcolonial counter debate[30] to hegemonic narratives on nation, society and culture in Britain. Though Bhabha does not focus directly on democracy and citizenship he does talk about cultural difference and its ambivalent inclusion into the narrative of the nation. Furthermore, the way in which he deconstructs the location of the Other is clearly linked to the discursive construction of symbolic boundaries of the British nation. Hence, it is useful to go back to Bhabha's

---

29   Bhabha was born in Mumbai, India, to the 'small Zoroastrian Parsi community in India' in 1949. He moved as a young adult to England to continue his higher education. According to Bhabha the Parsi became a 'translational community in the 19th century and, as they bridged Hindu and Muslim communities, their habit and especially their multilingualism can be called cosmopolitan.'

30   Other key theorists in this discourse are Stuart Hall, Paul Gilroy and Gayatri Spivak.

definition of cultural difference as he suggests a transitive process of otherness inscribed in different cultural realities.

To summarise: in Bhabha's postcolonial criticism of British culture we can recognise a moment of *problematisation* that is inherent in the ambivalent potential of 'hybridity' as a social phenomenon of cultural difference. Bhabha denounces the supposedly 'national culture' as a majority discourse that is contingent and therefore can be transformed. While challenging the rigid construction of binary positions he undermines the dominant narrative of a linear political space. Most importantly, Bhabha tackles the ambivalence of colonialism as an entangled cultural project. As David Huddart (2006: 3) argues, the 'colonizer's cultural meanings are open to transformation by the colonized population: like any text, the meaning of colonial text cannot be controlled by its authors.' Bhabha's insistence on complexity, ambivalence and hybridity brings a transversal notion of the interconnectivity of cultures to the discourses of cosmopolitanism. Nonetheless, there is a danger in the terminology of 'hybridity' if used without a political context. 'Hybridity' as another category of fixing 'belonging' would lose its critical potential. Before I turn to Bhabha's contribution to debates of new cosmopolitanism I briefly look at some of his core understandings of culture.

Bhabha differentiates the notion of cultural difference from the term cultural diversity. As Bhabha (1994a: 134) puts it, '[c]ultural diversity is an epistemological object – culture is an object of empirical knowledge – whereas cultural difference is the process of the enunciation of culture as 'knowledgeable'. The term *enunciation* refers to a split between the performing side of culture as both an emanation *and* as a place of its negotiation. In an interview given to W.J.T. Mitchell in 1995, Bhabha explained this subversive space as 'a kind of enunciative disturbance that throws the process of interpretation or identification into flux'.[31] Accordingly, the notion of cultural difference contains a subversive moment that holds the potential of going beyond 'translation', as going beyond the comprehensive way of seeing the Other. As Bhabha (1994b: 312) describes it:

> [t]he aim of cultural difference is to re-articulate the sum of knowledge from the perspective of the signifying singularity of the 'other' that resists totalization – the repetition that will not return as the same ... that results in political and discursive strategies where adding – to does not add-up but serves to disturb the calculation of power and knowledge.

Bhabha's notion of cultural difference contains the notion of the Other that is not at the disposal of the 'self', echoing Levinas's concern as explored in Chapter 1. The creative counter spaces of cultural differences are in particular connected to hybridity that connotes a moment of displacement. As Robert J.C. Young (1995: 23) argues, 'Bhabha has extended his notion of hybridity to include forms of counter-authority, a "Third Space" which intervenes to effect.' The

---

31   http://prelectur.stanford.edu/lecturers/bhabha/interview.html.

space 'In-between' and the obstacles created in the act of translation can create an uncanny quality in a process where certainty in cultural codes is lost (Bhabha 1994d). Problematically, hybridity, understood as a concept of identity, runs the risk of doing exactly what it intends to avoid, namely to fix boundaries.[32] As Sarat Maharajin (2001: 27) explains:

> [h]ybridity – a vehicle for demarcating and disseminating difference – seems paradoxically to flip over to its opposite, to function as the label of flattening sameness, as 'new international gothic'. At stake is staving off the tendency for hybridity to settle down in a one-dimensional concept.

I will now move to a further inspection of Bhabha's texts on cosmopolitanism in the decade following 1989. In Bhabha's writings on cosmopolitanism in the 1990s, culture, ethnic minorities and the subject of 'hybridity' were given a prominent place. In 1997, *Counterpoint*, the cultural relations think–tank of the British Council, organised the conference 'Re-inventing Britain'. Bhabha wrote the proposal of the conference and gave a keynote speech addressing the hybrid cosmopolitanism of contemporary metropolitan life. The conference reached out for new definitions of art and culture in a global and national community context.

Systematically three aspects are relevant to a discussion of the notion of the Other and difference within this cultural debate on a new cosmopolitanism and gender. These issues include: (1) the meaning of social divisions in relation to culture; (2) the tension of hybrid culture and cosmopolitan location; and (3) the importance of secularism to the project of cosmopolitanism itself.

To begin with the latter, Bhabha explicitly urges us to 're-think secularism' as he regards secularism as essential to the 'new language of transnational social life' (1997: 2). The question is a timely one as Bhabha is addressing the instability and deficits of the secular milieu that were challenged fundamentally in the Salman Rushdie affair of the 1980s. Like Held, Bhabha refers to the fatwa against Salman Rushdie, but he also mentions religiously motivated conflicts in the USA, North Africa and India (ibid.). In Bhabha's view the dense modern metropolis, in particular London represents cosmopolitan habits and secular perplexity. As introduced above, hybridity receives a prominent place in Bhabha's conceptualisation of modern culture and therefore connects his thinking of cosmopolitan spaces directly to his original research themes. According to Bhabha (1997a),[33] it is hybridity, mixed marriages and 'new imagined communities' that generate the cosmopolitan map of the metropolitan global world. This is echoed in the cultural and ethnic

---

32 I will come back to further political implications when discussing Bhabha's contributions to the discourse on cosmopolitanism. Hybridity as a container of identity politics project has been criticised by socialist (feminist) academics, see for example Anthias 2001; Friedman 1999.

33 http://www.britishcouncil.org/studies/reinventing_britain/bhabha_1.htm, not available any longer, but accessible in: *The Manifesto* vol. 14 (29), 1999, 38–39.

mixture of London in particular, as he argues. Bhabha (1997b: part 2, 1) asks for the development of a social 'ethics of "proximity" between self/other and the "otherness of the self"'. In his view the cultural and communal dialogue, as a sphere of ethical, aesthetical and value laden negotiation, has to be reinvented by a 'double relation' or 'hybrid translation' (1997b: part 2, 2). In Bhabha's reading, hybridity delivers the potential for cosmopolitan cultural competence and is less fixed to a specific identity. However, there is a twist in this argument as it argues for *hybrid cultures* as a prerequisite for cosmopolitan competence. Hence, the identification of some coherent elements, even if it refers to hybrid cultural expressions, follows a logic that attempts to fix the meaning of cosmopolitanism to *visible difference* and an, *in-betweenness*. But does this imply that non-hybrid individuals or cultures offer less space for cosmopolitan encounters?

To a certain degree Bhabha's biographical background speaking out from a minority group perspective (the perspective of a non-English academic in Britain, for example) sustains his affinity to the theme of an 'in-between' and the mixing of cultural identities. Nonetheless, we have to be careful not to equate the multicultural presence of group difference with individual cosmopolitan habits. Besides, an elite connotation of cultural hybrid competence might easily adjust to late modern 'mobility cosmopolitanism', condemning the more settled living conditions of a majority ethnic, but lower classed social group.

As discussed above there is a particular tension between the emerging label of a cosmopolitan Britain that favours plural individual identities, and its previous group centred politics of multiculturalism that dominated the public discourse until recently. In 1999, the theme of multiculturalism also was a matter of dispute to Bhabha when he engaged with Susan Moller Okin's (1999) statement that 'multiculturalism is bad for women' (ibid.). Bhabha referred to the dilemma and multiple dimensions of intersecting hierarchies when challenging Moller Okin's feminist claim of less patriarchal Western society. Bhabha (1999) argues:

> [a]n agonistic liberalism questions the 'foundationalist' claims of the metropolitan, 'Western' liberal tradition with as much persistence as it interrogates and resists the fundamentalisms and ascriptions of indigenous orthodoxy. An awareness of the ambivalent and 'unsatisfied' histories of the liberal persuasion allows 'us' as postcolonial critics, multiculturalists, or feminists to join in the unfinished work of creating a more viable, intra-cultural community of rights.

Bhabha detects complex hierarchies within all social groupings crossing hegemonic and minoritised cultures. These hierarchies are apparent in Western claims to 'represent' freedom and liberalism, but also in oppressive authoritative structures of certain orthodox rule. He includes the struggle of feminists in his postcolonial critiques of suppression, suggesting a broader anti-hierarchical struggle for liberation.

In an academic reflection of the public discourse on the perspectives of multiculturalism and individual agency, the conference Minority Culture and

Creative Anxiety aimed to propose ways in which the special competence of minority cultures could reframe the national locus of Britain. In his contribution to this conference, Bhabha identifies explicitly with refugees as Others who are marginalised nationally and internationally. According to Bhabha, '[i]nternal exclusions' replacing 'external separations' in the North and South signal the fundamental erosion of the familiar modern location of nation, region, political community and citizenship. Taking into account the 'minoritisation' of the majority of people on the globe, the term 'minority' used here fuses contingent social status and national belonging. Bhabha (1997b: part 1, 3) suggests *minoritarian cosmopolitanism* as the new mode of cultural identification. He explains:

> [t]o 'minoritise' might be a verb: a positive identification, where the affiliative decision to act in the cause of exclusion, or to participate in the emergence of new social movements, engenders a mode of public discourse articulated with a strong affective and imaginative charge.[34]

In this sense 'minoritarian cosmopolitanism' coincides with an 'other vernacular cosmopolitan alliance' (1997b: part 1, 3). In a lecture in 1995, Bhabha argues that:

> [w]e need a sort of regional, or vernacular, cosmopolitanism, to question the division between central, canonical cultures and everyday cultures. And we can do this by understanding the unique way colonial cultures were themselves cosmopolitan ... [p]eople living under colonial oppression had to deal with a number of values, mores and symbols as an act of survival in a culture over which they did not have power – this was the same for migrants in England and slaves in the South ... [t]hey had to learn the new social languages of their oppressors, and then had to live their lives through those social languages.[35]

What is striking in this passage is the use of the term 'regional' for 'vernacular'. It suggests that Bhabha is in favour of locally coloured expressions of cosmopolitanism embedded in spatial proximity of differences. Remarkably, the term 'regional' is increasingly used to address distinctive global continents rather than various local places within different countries. Further, it is important to understand that Bhabha declares a cultural proximity between the situation of migrants and cosmopolitanism. In his view immigrants' experiences provide a resource of 'social language' that might be able to mediate across social hierarchies. While challenging the rigid construction of the binary and non-contradictory antagonism he undermines the dominant narrative of nationhood (Bhabha 1994b: 148–149). To see the 'liminality of the people' means to accept national culture

---

34   1997: part 1, 4.

35   This is a quote taken from a report written by Jeff Makos for the University of Chicago *Chronicle* 1999.

as a *narrative in progress*. This perspective also gives space to marginal voices constitutive to the national culture as a whole. In Bhabha's (1994b: 148) view:

> [t]he liminal figure of the nation-space would ensure that no political ideologies could claim transcendent or metaphysical authority for themselves. This is because the subject of cultural discourse – the agency of people – is split in the discursive ambivalence that emerges in the contest of narrative authority between the pedagogical and the performative.

This quotation refers to Bhabha's paradigmatic construction of hybrid culture and the in-between as being necessary to expose counter-narratives to the hegemonic claim of British nationhood. Accordingly, the pedagogical project that claims the 'narrative authority in a tradition of people' (Bhabha 1994b: 147) and 'the performative' that is encapsulated in a 'signification' (Bhabha 1994b: 148) of different empirical and contradictory selves can be translated into epistemological means. Hence, alternative means of generating knowledge could challenge the hegemonic national narrative. Bhabha admits that Julia Kristeva (1993) makes a similar point. Kristeva in a comparable vein challenges fixed assumptions regarding femininity while engendering different feminist strategies to de-centre and displace hegemony. In a critical reflection on Julia Kristeva's notion of cosmopolitanism, Evy Varsamopoulou (2009: 32) argues, 'what Kristeva adds is the Romantic and contemporary European favourites: strangers, especially outcasts of some sort, artists and women. In a nutshell, anyone claiming alienation and estrangement from the society in which they live at that moment, perhaps even from most societies.'

Kristeva and Bhabha share a cultural reading of 'exile'. Both Kristeva as a feminist and Bhabha as a postcolonial writer imagine alternative spaces from the symbolic margins of society transcending the boundaries of hegemonic narratives. In this regard the Other, while positioned at the margins of society, is an allegoric wanderer at the border: he or she is both imagined as principally outside, but potentially constructed in an inside. In order to illustrate the link between marginal space and potential cultural criticism Bhabha (1994b: 170) maintains that the gathering of immigrants in London offers 'the space in which new social movements of the people are played out'. Thus, Bhabha's de-centring of hegemonic national narratives that surround the notions of culture as well as the nation contain a *distinctive political perspective* regarding a more inclusive notion of the British nation. In this sense, Bhabha as a cultural theorist enters the political space. He demands a 'discourse of minority', which emphasises the empowering instrument of minority knowledge (1994b: 157).[36] In what ways does Bhabha's political reading of the cosmopolitan potentialities of migrants cross

---

36   Bhabha (1994: 168) writes, 'the colonial space played out in the imaginative geography of the metropolitan space, the repetition or return of the postcolonial migrant to alienate the holism of history.'

the classic modern nation state divide of 'public and private' affairs and how is his view close to feminist provocations challenging established perceptions of the political domain?

Bringing in again Mouffe's view, it is interesting to see what she has to say if we consider a feminist perspective on the 'political and cultural' separation of a public and a private sphere. As made clear above, Mouffe argues that the essence of the political community or *res publica* (1990b: 233) should reflect particular rules of law. In her reading a liberal democratic state which aims to respect individual liberty and pluralism has to 'be agnostic on questions of religion and morality, but it cannot be agnostic on political values since, by definition, it postulates a certain set of those values, which constitute its ethico-political principles' (1992a: 12). However, there is a paradox concerning the boundaries of 'ethical' and 'moral' considerations: on the one hand, she argues that morality and religion belong to a different, *agnostic space*, whereas on the other, she wishes for principles relevant to the public sphere that are linked to ethical considerations. In this interpretation, religious or ethnic group particularity appears as a matter of privacy whereas the content of ethics is privileged as a matter of the public realm; thus it appears as normatively neutral. Hence, we could argue that Mouffe's proposal does not interrogate hegemonic assumptions of political morality/ethics that direct a democratic consensus in the public realm. As we can see here, her proposition of a non-religious and secular but *ethically laden* public sphere in a way corresponds to problematic tensions around the controversy of 'secular democracy' versus minority religion versus 'post-secularism' as discussed in Chapter 2.

To summarise: Bhabha's work, which is embedded in British Literature while advancing Postcolonial Theory, deliberately crosses disciplinary boundaries. In doing so he creates a contrasting field of political inquiry of British national culture. Most importantly, Bhabha insists on *minoritarian cosmopolitanism* as marginalised cosmopolitan practices of disregarded (vernacular) cultures. Bhabha's plea for hybridity and the third space seems to fragment political group coherence and therefore undermine political agency. However, as argued above, his proposal links together different structural social parameters. While doing so, he does not deny that the nation, law and hierarchies influence dynamics between those parameters.

Mouffe attempts to make connections between morality, ethics and 'the political', but fails to consider that they are likewise grounded in culturally dominant systems of knowledge.

A national image of a cosmopolitan and hybrid Britain that adopts 'differentiated universalism' could imply a 'transmutation of British culture into a compounded, composite mode' (Young 1995: 23). A paradigmatic adoption of the 'hybrid' individual, however, ignores the problematic character of social fragmentation of the dominant culture: the amalgamation of ethnic and religious otherness into adjusted cosmopolitan difference appears as a transformation of the 'uncanny' Other into familiar notions of sameness. Consequently, there is an ideological tension between Bhabha's proposal of hybrid cultural difference as *enunciation* that should *alter* the hegemonic perception of national culture, and cultural difference as a primarily exotic commodity of easy consumption.

Nava (2007) calls the current paradigm shift in the make-up of British culture a 'normalisation of difference'. But what does this mean with respect to a contemporary utopian and political outlook on new cosmopolitanism given that Bhabha, for example, claims the marginal space as creating the counter gaze through *identification with otherness*? To answer this, in the remaining part of the chapter I explore more closely how the 'normalisation of difference' as an articulation of hybrid plurality actually faces up to the dialectics of altering 'strange' subjects into Alterity.

Here we have to follow more explicitly the analytical differentiation of difference and otherness that helps us to understand how racialising boundaries are subtly drawn in an apparently open minded cosmopolitan discourse. In spite of the developing agenda of cosmopolitan border- (cosmopolitan democracy) and boundary-crossings (hybrid cultural spaces), contradictory images remain in urban spaces: we come across orthodox ethnic particularity as well as images of hybrid and secular cosmopolitanism in various parts of metropolitan cities. The image of multicultural Britain, in particular, is associated with London and provides the idea of the cosmopolitan late modern British nation. But this image has been damaged by its marginalised underdogs: the meaning of social antagonism, of community cohesion and of political violence shifted dramatically in the new millennium.

Let us think back to the explanation in Chapter 1 – and throughout this book – of the change at the symbolic threshold of 9/11. As far as the British context is concerned, 7/7 2005 symbolises another urgency to come to terms with the disillusion of a locality wished to be detached from global processes of insecurity. Further, it is likely that a broader discourse of militarisation (inside and outside society) corresponds to the end of spatial order as we knew it. As argued elsewhere (Yuval-Davis Et. al. 2006) the political and territorial categories of peace and war and the clear-cut differentiations between domestic and international politics are in turmoil. This has resulted in tightened border control and the ideological mapping inside national political communities. As the meaning of 'security' and 'rights' become blurred in a post-democracy context it is essential to examine further how discourses on cosmopolitanism and the notion of *the Other* have developed in a post-9/11 framework.

The Aftermath of Extremist Network Terror in and Beyond Europe: Civic Cosmopolitanism, The 'Cosmofeminine' and Global (In-)Justice

Repeating the structure of Chapter 3, I will look first at Held's writing on cosmopolitanism in a post-9/11 context, and discuss his considerations, accordingly and will then bring back in Bhabha and Mouffe as those eminent voices that challenge a Kantian-Habermasian centred debate on normative cosmopolitanism.

Since the mid-1990s Held (1995: 221, 227–233, 2002a: 309–310, 314; 2003: 185, 197, 2004: X, XIV) has emphasised how essential Kant's philosophy is to his own concept of democracy and thinking on cosmopolitan concepts. In contrast to his earlier writings on cosmopolitan democracy, however, the cause of the marginalised and illegal Other has explicitly become part of Held's cosmopolitan research agenda during the last decade. While referring to Seyla Benhabib (2002), he admits that 'free movement of people and ideas' is not sufficiently covered by a Kantian principle of hospitality (2002a: 315).[37] Therefore, we can expect a revision of some Eurocentric positions prioritising Kantian philosophy and instead exposing its deficits.

Looking more closely at a text published in 2002, Held repeats the core arguments of his 1996 book. Further to the coverage of the 'five disjunctures' (2002a: 307–308) he introduces three key elements of cosmopolitan values based on his prior work on cosmopolitan democracy. These values include: (1) the 'individualist moral egalitarianism or, simply, egalitarian individualism'; (2) 'the principal of reciprocal recognition'; and (3) the value of impartiality, as 'contemporary cosmopolitanism stresses that equality of status and reciprocal recognition require that each person should enjoy the impartial treatment of their claims – that is treatment based on principles upon which all could act' (2002a: 311).[38] Interestingly, in his most recent publication on cosmopolitanism (2010), Held names another set of 'five disjunctures' (2010: 35 ff.) regarding democracy and globalisation. He accepts the lack of clear-cut political sovereignty as far as nation states are concerned and the push to alter global regulatory regimes from the bottom up. Further, he agrees to strengthen alternative regulatory regimes as unbounded and de-territorialised political issues such as ecology, economy, drug criminality or terrorism, for example, jeopardise all inhabitants of the world.

I return to Held's (2002a: 312) term 'impartiality', or 'impartialist reasoning' to discuss his pronounced perspective on the Other in the early 21st century. Whereas Held stresses that the content of this principle is guided by formal processes, and a general inter-subjective perspective has to be taken into consideration, he declared that his proposal is purposefully highly abstract and open to negotiation. He admits that International Labour Organisation (ILO) standards, such as the 'freedom to join trade unions and equal payment for women and men' (2002a: 319), are Western standards. While Held situates the Western rooting of legal protections, he accepts indirectly the geographical and thus, geopolitical, argument of those opponents of particular individual freedom rights. Thus, the rhetorical structure of his argument constructs a binary between Western progressive equality and protective

---

37   Held (1996: 227, quoting Kant 1970; 105) explains in his 1996 writing on the cosmopolitan order that his reading of Kant's cosmopolitan programmatic implies that hospitality is an absence of hostility: '[t]he right of a stranger or foreigner "not to be treated with hostility" when arriving in someone else's country'.

38   This text passage is entirely repeated in Held's chapter 'From Executive to Cosmopolitan Multilateralism' (Held and Koenig-Archibugi 2003; 9).

legislation on the one hand, and a lack of individual right schemes in the non-West on the other. Further, Held (2002a: 319) reflects on the post-colonial challenge to Eurocentric and Western moral and legal frames, when he declares that '[d]issent about the value of ideas such as equal consideration equal liberty and human rights is often related to that experience of Western imperialism and colonialism.' Though rhetorically taking non-Western criticism of liberal individualism into account, the core assumption of individual liberal rights pertains. In 2010, Held revised his position slightly; nonetheless, at the core of his 'cosmopolitan principles' is 'egalitarian individualism' (2010: 70). He differentiates important layers such as '(i) equal worth and dignity; (ii) active agency; (iii) personal responsibility and accountability; (iv) consent; (v) collective decision-making about public matters through voting procedures; (vi) inclusiveness and subsidiarity; (vii) avoidance of serious harm; and (viii) sustainability' (2010: 69).

Apparently, Held shifted his rather classic international politics based perception of the early 21st century to a Fraserian (Fraser 2005; 2007) inspired post-Westphalian outlook on blurred political community boundaries and a transformed spatial political order. As already observed in 2007 (Vieten 2007), Held's proposal of a *social democratic cosmopolitan democracy* in 2004 contradicted some of his core views published in the 1990s that back then were clearly defined by neo-liberal ideology. From 2007[39] on he has moved towards a new stage of reflection on the impact of globalisation on democracy and cosmopolitan perspectives. In 2010 he argues, 'the shift in the agenda of globalization I am arguing for – in short, a move from liberal to social democratic globalization – would have pay-offs for today's most pressing security concerns' (2010: 169). Interestingly, Held is bringing in the Tobin tax here (ibid.), a global financial transaction tax, which was first called for by the left wing grassroots movement *ATTAC* and became a theme off and on at different *Global Social Forums*. I will come back to the theme of counter globalisation later in Chapter 6.

To return to Held's (2004: 13) view of what a *social democratic concept* of global governance and of cosmopolitan democracy should look like: Held proposes an alternative version to the liberal market consensus. In doing so he calls for a global social democratic contract,[40] a

> [c]ompromise between the powers of capital, labour and the state, which seeks
> to encourage the development of market institutions, private property and the

---

39   I would regard *Global Inequality* (Held and Kaya 2007) as the turning point to Held's recent standpoint. It was Nancy Fraser's proposal of a 'post-Westphalian democratic justice' (2007: 252) that got central attention in Held's introduction (2007: 22, 23). Fraser (2007) made the criticism that advocates of deliberative democracy (Jürgen Habermas, for example) or those asking for an agonistic political frame (Chantal Mouffe, for example) are equally arguing from a 'Keynesian-Westphalian territorial frame' (2007: 256, footnote 7).

40   Significantly, Held's book title *Global Covenant* echoes Hobbes's Leviathan-covenant (see Williams 2003 for details to the controversy between Kant and Hobbes).

pursuit of profit within a regulatory framework that guarantees not just the civil and political liberties of citizens, but also the social conditions necessary for people to enjoy their formal rights. (ibid.)

The *social-democratic compromise* delivers an alternative political framing of an otherwise unjust global economy.

It is interesting to bring back here Mouffe's proposal of a 'multiversum' and to look in greater depth at her arguments. Mouffe continued with her polemical attacks against Held, Richard Falke, Beck and Giddens in her 2004 and 2005 publications.[41] In her view, Held and other liberal voices were 'not properly political' and this would imply that they do not challenge 'the prevailing hegemony' (2004: 67). As an alternative model she proposed a 'multipolar world order' which acknowledges the 'pluralist character of the world' (Mouffe 2004: 62). In reference to David Chandler's arguments[42] Mouffe made the point that any claim to extend individual rights beyond nation-states ignores the essential problem that there has to be an efficient powerful subject to guarantee rights and protection. She argued that the de-legitimisation of national sovereignty undermines existing democratic institutions (2004: 64 and 65). To Mouffe (2004: 66), the focus on global concerns can be regarded 'as an attempt to privilege morality over politics' she argues:

> [t]he cosmopolitical approach puts more emphasis on the legitimating function of human rights than their democratic exercise, and Chandler rightly sees the cosmopolitan construction of the global citizen as an attempt to privilege morality over politics. ... the new rights of cosmopolitan citizens are a chimera because they are moral claims, not democratic rights that could be exercised.

Her take on 'morality' here is particularly interesting as she differentiates between a universal claim of specific values (morality) and the concrete realm of politics. Also, Mouffe (2006: 272) attacks advocates of western universalism such as Martha Nussbaum, Habermas and John Rawls, who pursue universalism of 'Stoic/Kantian traditions'. In doing so she confronts the idea of cosmopolitan democracy with its lack of democratic sovereignty and proposes that a de-politicised notion of global governance aims to manage moral purpose rather than reassure democratic legitimacy.

As far as pragmatic aspects of *Realpolitik* are concerned, millions of illegalised victims of genocide past and present, the 'sublime silence of eternity' (Luxemburg cited in Geras 1998: 168), make very clear that a valid passport and a legal citizenship status overrule any global aspirations of human rights and cosmopolitan existence. As some of Mouffe's objections are crucial to a critical discourse of

---

41　'The noble intention of the diverse advocates of democratic cosmopolitanism' (2004: 65).

42　David Chandler has been Professor of International Relations at the University of Westminster since 2004.

cosmopolitanism and gender, particularly concerning the dialectic change in the notion of difference as explained in Chapter 1, her objections to liberal cosmopolitanism have to be discussed further. Carl Schmitt's slogan 'the world is no political unit but a political pluriversum'[43] is mentioned by Mouffe (2004; 2005) in various essay titles with slight modifications.[44] Further, Mouffe refers to Schmitt's book *Nomos der Erde...* published in 1952 (for a critical discussion see Dean 2006; also Buck-Morrs 2008). Schmitt's vision of a 'new equilibrium, this time under the hegemony of the United States' (Mouffe, 2004: 71) and 'the opening of a dynamics of pluralisation' (ibid.) matches the late 20th-century experience of the post 1989 collapse of the Cold War bilateral world system.

As Mouffe uses the concept of 'multiversum' to challenge the liberal notion of universalism it is helpful to trace back the notion of 'multiversum' as it was introduced in the German discourse in the 1920s and linked by Scheler to *Europäität*[45] as outlined in the previous chapter though it originated in an Anglo-American context: Schmitt mentions that the term 'pluriverse' was used by English (Anglo Saxon) theorists of pragmatism in 1925.

The philosopher William James used the term in his 1909 lecture on 'A Pluralistic Universe'. James developed two analytical angles that differentiated between a monistic perspective, the 'all-form', and the pluralistic outlook, 'each-form' (1909: 34). In relation to 'the political', James argued that 'the pluralistic world is thus more a federal republic than like an empire or kingdom' (1909: 321, 322) and stated that 'our "multiverse" makes still a "universe"' (1909: 325).[46] Thus, in James's original phrasing, plurality is characteristic of the universe and presumes that there is no fundamental contradiction between universal order and plural existence. Further, and this conveys sounding with Kantian ideas of multilateral arrangements, the talk is of a 'federal republic'.

Hence, we could argue that multiple and plural positions are intrinsically connected to universalism that might have repercussions in a federal order. However, this notion of the *multiversum* would be in line with ideals of cosmopolitan democracy that aims at the political integration of plural states in line with a territorial order.

The malaise here, and as argued elsewhere (Vieten 2010), is that Mouffe's multipolar world re-territorialises *plurality* as a matter of multiple political sovereigns. But what does this tell us about her notion of the cosmopolitan and

---

43   'Die Welt ist keine politische Einheit sondern ein politisches Pluriversum', cited in Hofmann (2003: 7).

44   *Cosmopolitan Democracy or Multipolar World Order?* (2004); *Eine kosmopolitische oder eine multipolare Weltordnung?* (2005).

45   See above beginning of Chapter 3.

46   'Our 'multiverse' makes still a 'universe': for every part, though it may not be in actual or immediate connexion, is nevertheless in some possible or mediated connexion, with every other part however remote (it is "continuity, contiguity, or concatenation")' (James 1909: 325).

the Other in terms of an alternative spatial societal order across the globe? Mouffe regards cosmopolitans as having an interest in global civil society and as being powerful 'business and financial elites' (ibid.). Also, she attacks cosmopolitanism as the 'globalisation of the Western model' (2004: 74). Mouffe (2004: 72) identifies cosmopolitans automatically with liberalism and her post-Marxist view here has resonances with Behrend's critical perspective on a *Weltbürgertum* as made clear in Chapter 3. But the English language does not have this positional difference of cosmopolitan agents as it is charged in German with classed and racialised connotations. Further, echoing the classic Westphalian, territorial paradigm Mouffe neglects the patchwork of multi-layered social divisions engendering transnational links and also cosmopolitan habits that do not match the glamorous image of cosmopolitans as global travellers and citizens of the world. Working class migrants, for example, cannot 'treat the world as their oyster' (Kofman 2005: 85), but develop sophisticated networks and cosmopolitan routes of their own (Werbner 1999, 2011). As May Joseph (1999: 8) points out, 'new cosmopolitanism fractures the idea of easy movements'; complex border crossings challenge the privileged notions of legal as (nation) state citizenship.

What needs further attention is that Mouffe takes sides with a revolutionary view that ignores those Social Democrats, for example contemporaries of Schmitt such as Hans Kelsen and Herman Heller, who struggled with class antagonism while negotiating conflicting interests and hoping to settle for compromises. 'Heller as early as 1928 discussed the "contradictory inner dynamics of creating and maintaining political units."' (Vieten 2010: 106) If we follow Mouffe's line of thought we might say that social democratic compromise failed Europe and, in particular Germans, eventually and thus is part of the negative lessons we have to learn from history. But do we then leave cosmopolitan utopia aside as radical change cannot be based on negotiation and compromise? What about those totalitarian subjects that threaten individual life randomly and target our democratic freedom? Who is using a totalitarian framing?

These questions prepare the next step of inquiry, which looks more closely at post 9/11 writings of Held and Bhabha, and talks about war and terrorism more explicitly.

In the following I turn to some paragraphs of Held's work in 2004, and in recent publications of 2010. Certain passages of *Violence, Law and Justice in a Global Age* (2002b) re-appear in the preface and introduction to Held's book *Global Covenant – The Social Democratic Alternative to the Washington Consensus* (2004). He addresses an 'uncanny' Other in a notion of *alterity* confined to individual fanatical Muslims. The terrorists of 9/11 are described at length as 'terrorist aggressors', 'triggered by religious identity, zeal and fanaticism', who 'must be treated as criminals' (2004: 193, 195). In his more polemical take the terrorists are singled out as deviants and any linkage to complex global economic and power imbalances that might have an impact on the cause of extremism is missing. In 2004, Held (2004b: xi) views the New York mass murder as 'an atrocity of extraordinary proportions' and as 'a crime against the United States and against humanity'. The formulations he is using draw a clear line between a civic human consensus and an outside; thus the new global terrorists are regarded as acting outside civilisation. Rhetorically, Held addresses the US and their allies by stressing a moral difference to those who did not join the war alliance:

> [a]fter 9/11, the US and its allies could have decided that the most important things to do were to strengthen international law in the face of global terrorist threats ... they could have decided ... But they have systematically failed to decide any of these things. (Held 2004: xii)

Despite this rift between an US led war and its rejection by some European and other states, clearly the declaration of a 'civic we' dominates Held's rhetoric:

> [t]he founding principles of our society dictate that *we*[47]do not over-generalize our response from one moment and one set of events; that *we* do not jump to conclusions ... that *we* do not re-write and re-work international law and governance ... *we* do not think and act over-hastily ... Terrorism does negate our most elementary and cherished principles and values. But any ... response ... must be consistent with our founding principles. (ibid.)

The 'we' noticeably suggests a principal inclusion of those who took the Hobbesian pathway of war. In this regard Held differentiates notions of the Other in terms of plural difference and 'uncanny' otherness. He keeps this tone when arguing, '[w]e have to come to terms not only with the reality that a single country enjoys military supremacy ... the new American security project displaces a much urgent focus on a broad conception of human security' (Held 2004: xii–xiii). And in a rhetorical response to a criticism of 'old Europe', provoked by the Franco-German non-participation in the military action in Iraq, Held (2004: xiv) stresses that 'Kagan ... interprets the EU as a Kantian haven of peace and economic change, albeit parasitic upon the Hobbesian protector'.

It is interesting to see that the two alternative ethical models of a *Kantian 'cosmopolitan eternal peace' vs. Hobbes's 'Leviathan'* as accentuated in Chapter 2 above, do have repercussions in this debate. Identifying positively with the British civil discontent of the million people that marched in London in 2003 while articulating civic public protest against Blair's war alliance with the US, Held also expresses normative identification with the Kantian perspective. A normative rift between different ethics of politics does not really work against the notion of the Other as an alterity. Intrinsically, otherness refers to a context where 'a culture or an identity is incompatible with ours' (Cohen 1994: 199). In this reading, the Islamic terrorists are located in an outside, as the alterity to 'us'; the US American war is part of the global/European civil society of 'us.' In what ways is this view still prevalent in 2010?

---

47   I stressed the 'we' in this quote with italics.

When turning to Held's recent publications (2010a, 2010b) explicitly addressing a post-9/11 frame of war, cosmopolitanism and justice, it becomes clear that further reflection altered his rather rigid boundary drawing, though his judgement that 9/11 was an 'atrocity of extraordinary proportions' (2010a: 128) and 'a crime against America and against humanity' (ibid.) remains the same. What is more striking, the moral distinctions previously upheld with regard to the role of Europe and the US are absent in these texts. Nonetheless, he demands that the (Western) universal notion of justice and a global law has to be adopted effectively in different regions and cultural contexts. As Held argues (2010a: 138)

> The attacks of 9/11 appear to have been perpetrated in the name of Islam, albeit a particular version of Islam. It is this version of Islam which must be repudiated by the wider Islamic community, which needs to reaffirm the compatibility of Islam with the universal, cosmopolitan principles that put life, and the free development of all human beings, at their centre.

The Islam as addressed here refers to Muslim countries as well to Muslim citizens in Western countries who blame the West for all failures (2010a: 138–139).

Still Held's statement poses a strong affiliation between 'impartial' law and moral judgement derived from Kantian (2010a: 136, 137) and Habermasian consecutive dialogical aspirations of democratically electing global citizens.[48]

At the end of the day, two angles are prominent in Held's writings throughout: firstly, there is a more fundamental interrogation of global spatial order, which politically affects local and national organisation, and secondly, there is advocacy for *particular European values*. In line with his second angle Held turns to the most advanced instrument of regional governance in Europe: the European Union. Held's (2004: 163) reform project of Social Democracy is framed by his reading of the 'achievements of the post-Holocaust multilateral order'. His proposal is for the European Union to have a leading role as far as multilateral international politics is concerned.[49] Since 2003, Held's publications have embraced the narrative of a particular tradition of enlightened European humanity that is linked rhetorically to the European Union. All in all, Held takes into account the 'existence of progressive social, political and economic forces seeking to advance a rather different kind of world order' (2004: 167). In contrast to his 1990s preference for market liberalism, Held (2004: 162) condemns 'neoliberalism', 'anti-globalization movements' and 'neoconservatism' (2004: 17), as they are 'key political opponents' (ibid.) of cosmopolitanism.

---

48   Held refers explicitly to Habermas; 2010a: 60.

49   'Europe could have a distinctive role in pursuing the cause of global social democracy' (Held 2004: 167). 'As things stand, the EU has no coherent position on these matters [a strong opposition to the White House politics, UMV], and no credible defence and strategic capacity to offer at this time' (2004: xiv).

Held's proposal of *social democratic cosmopolitanism* incorporates to a certain degree reformist perspectives. He strongly advocates this outlook as a structural response to unfair global liberal market democracy. Held's move towards social democratic aspirations since 2004 contradicts his 1990s writing as he was singing the British liberal tune of free market democracy – a liberalism that failed its poorer citizens when causing more social injustice and rifts in British society. These are structural legacies which not only the current government but civic society as a whole has to deal with.

The emerging 'imagined community' of a European region (European Union), however, is evolving by marking discursively new civil outsiders. In particular, the problematic tension between an autocratic post-democracy and the structural exclusion of 'uncanny' Others, such as illegalised migrants, orthodox Muslim communities and otherwise constructed outsiders is not being taken up as a serious conceptual problem of any form of democracy and statehood. As argued in Chapter 1 the notion of the Other as the stranger is ideologically contingent and in flux. As Ladwig (2003: 56) puts it '[i]n fact, the stranger does not have to be unfamiliar, he does not have to be regarded as belonging legally or ethnically. You also can keep your distance from the "Other" by declaring him to be a stranger.'[50] Thus, the position of the global stranger is contingent to ideological purposes and efforts of cohesive community building.

Finally, I turn to Bhabha's writings on cosmopolitanism in the 21st century. In what ways does Bhabha understand the complexity and diffusion of political borders and boundaries of the nation, the place of Europe and its relation to cosmopolitan belonging differently? Bhabha regards individual border crossings as 'ways of living at home abroad or abroad at home' (cited in Huddart 2006: 79).

In 2002 Bhabha co-edited (Breckenridge et al. 2002) an anthology devoted to cosmopolitanism, which echoed some of Bhabha's earlier considerations of the 1990s. All the editors of this book agree that cosmopolitanism should be debated broadly as an alternative theoretical and political framework to tackle dilemmas of nationalism, globalisation and multiculturalism (Pollock et al. 2002: 2). In line with Bhabha's 1990s plea they argue that cosmopolitanism 'should be considered entirely open, and not pre-given or foreclosed by the definition of any particular society or discourse' (Pollock et al. 2002: 1). We can thus see how Bhabha's earlier approach to cosmopolitanism defines the central tone of the anthology. Although the phrase 'producing evil in the world' (2002: 2) echoes the mainstream discourse of 'terrorism as evil', they are not engaging directly with the theme of terrorist individuals or groups. In opposition to concepts that address cosmopolitans as elite and privileged individuals, Bhabha et al. (2002: 6) regard cosmopolitans as 'victims of modernity'.[51] However, this position does not presuppose a lack

---

50   'Der Fremde muß nicht tatsächlich *unvertraut*, er muß auch nicht von vornherein – etwa rechtlich oder ethnisch – *nichtzugehörig* sein. Man kann vom anderen auch Abstand nehmen, indem man ihn zum Fremden erklärt'.

51   This perspective is also shared by Beck; I will come back to this later in Chapter 6.

of subjective agency. It rather clarifies that 'cosmopolitans' remain somewhat invisible at the social and cultural margins of the modern nation state system:

> Cosmopolitans today are often victims of modernity, failed by capitalism's upward mobility, and bereft of those comforts of national belonging. Refugees, peoples of the diaspora, and migrants and exiles represent the spirit of the cosmopolitical community. Too often, in the West, these peoples are grouped together in a vocabulary of victimage and come to be recognized as constituting the 'problem' of multiculturalism to which late liberalism extends its generous promise of pluralist existence. (Bhabha et al. 2002: 6)

This passage is particularly interesting as it conveys an alternative reading of the figure of the cosmopolitan. The description hints at vernacular and less glamorous representations of cosmopolitanism and in that sense captures what Werbner (2011) describes as 'postcolonial vernacular cosmopolitanism', Stuart Hall (2004) calls 'practical cosmopolitanism'[52] and Nava (2007) approaches as 'visceral cosmopolitanism'. As framed theoretically in Chapter 1 though, the relevant symbolic representations of the contemporary Other have to be read more carefully: whereas 'the exile' suggests the image of a political persecution by another nation state, the 'migrant', but *only* as the *illegal* immigrant of the 21st century, can become the signifier of an 'uncanny' Other. It means that immigrants do not per se and any longer qualify as 'victims' and signifiers of subordinated status in a contemporary context. Class and gender divisions, in particular, but to an even greater extent legal status, define living conditions at the margins, classifying the 'outside' across society.

In another publication, Bhabha (2003) takes a more explicit political perspective on the problematic situation of contemporary Others. He writes 'migrants, refugees and nomads don't merely circulate. They need to settle, claim asylum or nationality, demand housing and education' (2003, n.p.). In response to the politically framed construction of social outsiders Bhabha asks us to identify with the most vulnerable Other. As Bhabha (2003, n.p.) demands:

> [I]n such circumstances, the minority, always a partially denationalised political subject emerges as 'political and incipient' social form that seeks to recognize itself and represent its freedom through an identification with the other's difference – its claims, interests, and conditions of life.

As we can see, the *minoritarian cosmopolitanism* advocated by Bhabha in 1997 was further conceptualised in 2002, and has become explicitly political in his 2003 text. The latter is the place where Bhabha engages directly with the theme of terrorist attacks and violent threats. While looking back at the cultural discourses of the 1980s he recognises a shift from 'presidential parlance' on 'evil empire' in

---

52　http://www.opendemocracy.net/arts-multiculturalism/article_2191.jsp.

1983 to 'axis of evil' in 2002 (2003 n.p.). Bhabha criticises the ruling binary of 'world of Order' (ibid.) in contrast to the 'world of Disorder' (ibid.), making very clear that the critical potential of the 1980s meant 'a complex aspiration to equality without equalization' (ibid.). This phrase highlights the problem of an ideological 'neutralization' of difference as becoming 'sameness'. The idea of sameness, however, is part of a hegemonic attempt to secure the dominant social order.

As Judith Butler (2007, 2010) argues while thinking about the stateless, 'The jettisoned life is thus saturated in power; though not with modes of entitlement of obligation … it is enough to remark that to produce the nation that serves as the basis for the nation-state, that nation must be purified of its heterogeneity except in those cases where a certain pluralism allows for the reproduction of homogeneity on another basis' (2010: 32).

To gain a deeper understanding of Bhabha's different approach to cosmopolitanism I turn to a lecture he gave in 2004 at the UC Santa Barbara (US) on '*A Global Measure – Writing, Rights and Responsibilities*'. Talking about global transitions he points out that 'security has become a cultural lens.'[53]

This remark is important as Bhabha asserts very clearly how national, regional and global security has become a token of cultural[54] racism. Further, in this lecture he criticises Hardt's and Negri's vision of a nomadic flow and the post-national mode. Outlining his explicit political perspective he discusses the Tobin tax, and proposes 'aspirational tax schemes' that matter to global redistribution of goods and justice (ibid.). The idea of the Tobin Tax, as already mentioned above, was called for by anti-globalisation groups such as ATTAC. Coming back to Bhabha's co-edited book (Pollock et al. 2002), we can note that they connect their intellectual project to critical feminist debates (Pollock et al. 2002: 7–8), opening a space of contestation to universalism in different ways to Mouffe's post-Marxist view as they are directly reflecting the articulation of diverse subaltern voices.

> We would have the cosmofeminine as the sign of an argument for a situated universalism that invites other universalisms into a broader debate based on recognition of their own situatedness. A focus on this extensional understanding of domesticity and intimacy could generate a different picture of more public universalisms, making the domestic sphere subversive of thin claims to universalism. (Pollock et al. 2002: 9)

In line with Bhabha's considerations in the 1990s about *minoritarian cosmopolitanism* and the acknowledgement of feminist approaches, it is 'the cosmofeminine' (Pollock et al. 2002: 9) that pronounces an advanced critique of liberal cosmopolitanism. However, from a radical feminist perspective this term might be problematic as the 'feminine' is identified with domestic work and personal intimate relationships. Accordingly, it mirrors the vernacular experiences

---

53   http://video.google.com/videoplay?docid=8103256612901010466.
54   This cultural racism (Balibar 1991) conveys culturalist views.

of gendered notions of the private domain. For critical purposes though it is acceptable to use it as a provocation to de-centre the European legacy of male cosmopolitan ideals. The 'cosmofeminine' argues for a broader perspective in studying emanations and experiments of cosmopolitanism as a re-location of particular and diverse human experiences. In contrast to a hegemonic discourse, Bhabha et al. (2002: 4) set themselves apart from political binaries while claiming:

> [w]e are properly resistant to a radical revanchism that seeks a return to the certainties of a world of the either/or: either First or Third world; either communism or capitalism; either planned economies or free markets; either the secular or the sacred; either class politics above all other differences or a betrayal of the spirit of History itself.

The rejection of 'either/or' allegiances and another formulation of 'the twilight of transition' (Pollock et al. 2002: 4–5) is in line with a reading of cosmopolitanism as individual, transcending cultural capital. The idea to 'provincialize Europe' (Pollock et al. 2002: 6) again echoes Chakrabarty's proposal and links here to a critical choice to de-centre the dominance of cosmopolitan thinking rooted in narratives of the unique European Enlightenment.

Concluding Remarks

The United Kingdom's Empire led to rather fragmented patterns of differences: the apparent multiculturalism has to be regarded as the central theme surrounding critical debates about difference and liberal individualism, as well as political community belonging. Accordingly, multiculturalism and liberal notions of democracy underlie contradictory and porous social spaces of commercial and colonial cosmopolitanism. As outlined above London epitomises 'multicultural Britain' and as the trade centre directs both global economic interests and various stages of classifying and dividing Others into citizens, subjects and Aliens. The predominant focus on the *black Other* as the *significant Other* in Britain is connected to the Commonwealth and post-colonial legacy.

It is this topical background that is echoed in Held's and Bhabha's writings on new cosmopolitanism as discussed. Bhabha, for example, argues that 'cultural pluralism' (Pollock et al. 2002: 6), in the notion of multiculturalism, is constructed as the marginal space of 'refugees, peoples of the Diaspora, and migrants and exiles' (ibid.). To foster cosmopolitanism would mean to identify with these subjects at the margins of national societies. But as argued in Chapter 1 it is important that we differentiate between plurality/diversity that resides inside nation states, and the discriminatory practices against significant otherness that is constructed as being inside/outside the national realm. The most obvious allusion to the conflicts surrounding multicultural Britain in the 1990s is the secular vs. religious fundamentalism controversy over Salman Rushdie at the end of the 1980s. Held refers to the 'fatwa' while stressing the priority of Western secularism and freedom of speech; it is Bhabha who analyses the content of Rushdie's contested novel in his 1990s essays. In the latter's reading, Rushdie articulates hybrid cosmopolitanism as a postcolonial encounter with otherness. Whereas the reference to Rushdie is prevalent in all authors' writings in the 1990s, their understanding of 'the political' and the impact of globalisation processes on the make-up of the British nation diverge in a post-9/11 context. Held s' and Bhabha's perspectives appear as moving closer to each other. Looking at Held's intellectual development following 9/11, we see that he revised his 'liberal market position' and turned to a reformist and social democratic perspective, i.e. the idea of global social democracy or *social democratic cosmopolitanism*. To make a pragmatic start, Held advocates the European Union as one of the regional power institutions equipped to advance equality, social justice and law globally. Whereas Held explicitly advocates a strong European Union, Mouffe as his critical contender talks indirectly about Europe, and the EU, as one of many regions that could balance the hegemony of the unilateral US. At the end of the day, her version of a *multiversum* similarly presupposes a strong Europe as a regional bloc[55] that might qualify as a serious military and economic power. Thus, Mouffe's vision of transforming radical democracy still operates in a Westphalian paradigm of territorially bounded (nation) states. Mouffe's classic territorial view resonates here with Held's perspective, though the latter more recently changed his position towards a Fraserian 'post-Keynesian Westphalian framework' (Fraser 2005). Hence, the post-Marxist and feminist critique underestimates how the same Europe is rooted in culturalist[56] aggressions against the spiritual Other. The EU is creating a strong security and surveillance supra-state order, as argued in Chapter 2, with very different consequences concerning desirable migration as social mobility and unwanted migration as 'illegal' movement. Mouffe's critical anti-liberalism argument could be regarded as a counter discourse to capitalist hegemony, but it contains the pitfalls of 'travelling' concepts that are taken out of context or are stuck in an ideological container. In response to a peculiarly British discourse of liberal cosmopolitan democracy and middle class consensus, Mouffe's critical interventions aim to challenge its ideological claim of political impartiality. Her radical and also polemical rejection of liberal cosmopolitanism, nonetheless, has to be situated equally with reference to the historical context of the British discourse. Mouffe broadly ignores the variety of vernacular cosmopolitan actors and the ambivalent, darker dimension of the discourse of cosmopolitanism that refer to the two symbolic and social positions of *Weltbürger/Kosmopoliten*

---

55   Apparently, the former French president Jacques Chirac uttered some of the early 20th-century connotations of *Europäität* and Schmittian idea of a multipolar world order. Chirac argued his proposal of a European constitution 'was part of his vision for a strong Europe in a "multipolar" world' (Lichtfeld; *The Independent*, 12.03.2007).

56   For an explanation see Chapter 3.

that encircle new boundaries and legal borders separating world citizens from illegalised cosmopolitans.

Finally, Mouffe fails to see the reformist contribution of liberal, positivist 'hybrid' and cosmopolitan European lawyers and social thinkers such as Heller, whose legacy set up the German welfare state that helped to comfort class antagonism and capitalist economy in Germany.[57] This silence in Mouffe's writings in the 1999 text hints at a long lasting ideological battle between 'revolutionary' Communist and Radical Socialists on the one side, and reformist Social Democrats, on the other. Also, as Thaler (2010) argued recently, the strong division between 'morality' and 'politics' is somehow flawed as 'pure politics' (Thaler 2010; 797) does not exist, and an attempt to uphold this as rigid truth might only preclude *different n*ormative assumptions; perhaps fed by a different and distinctive *universalising* horizon.

Also, it should have become clear that the conceptual problem with 'the political' arises because of the hegemonic notion of 'the social'. The social is challenged analytically through postcolonial and feminist criticism of the political vs. private realm: 'the social' evolved differently as an outcome of historical struggles and distinguished notions of inclusion and exclusion. It is Bhabha who transcends a primarily Eurocentric focus while reformulating the notion of the *national narrative* through a postcolonial lens and acknowledges contradictions across all communities and cultures, initially. Hence, Bhabha's focus on *minoritarian cosmopolitanism* and the counter image of the 'cosmofeminine' maintain the utopian potential of those British legacies that have historically articulated vernacular cosmopolitanism alongside commercial and colonial cosmopolitanism.

Despite their distinctive approaches Held and Bhabha (and even the feminist challenger) express in their topical reference system the impact of the British historical context and articulate the dynamic acculturations of its different ethnic minorities. It is here where the contestation about adequate responses to liberalism, fundamentalism and recognition of difference, takes place.

---

57   This territorial welfare regime has its own ethnic-*völkisch* ideological baggage as criticised elsewhere (Vieten 2010).

Chapter 5

About Dead-Ends, One-Way Streets and Critical Crossroads

As argued here, mainstream visions of new cosmopolitanism in Europe contain darker sides (Kofman 2005): Beck's 'European Empire', recently 'transforming' into a credo of 'self-provincialization' of that same Europe and its social theory, and Habermas's 'Constitutional Patriotism', are based on a German discourse tradition of linking culture with civilisation. It is this dark side underlying the ideological link between territoriality and moral identifications that accompanies a 'lighter' version of the Europeanised world citizenship as *EU-Weltbürger*. Though Held's and Bhabha's perspectives are inclined to a tradition of liberal individualism as well as global culture and international politics, crucially their understanding is anchored in traditions of British commercial and postcolonial cosmopolitanism. These traditions are intertwined with imperialism and colonialism and bring to the fore further discrete *moral equipment* to contemporary entanglements of cosmopolitanism. To put it in a nutshell, 'if the communitarian critique to abstract liberalism has taught us anything at all, it is that liberalism – and by association, contemporary cosmopolitanism – is not without its own cultural roots' (Sanches-Florez 2010: 2).

As it is argued here there is a problematic proximity between academic knowledge and state policy that keeps a certain form of hegemonic power in place and which I call a *helix of hegemony*.[1] It is here where writing on cosmopolitanism and gender in Europe, for example, sends signals to local and global societies in transition.

While tracing back the historically and nationally specific framing of different voices that engage in the debate of new cosmopolitanism I explored how distinctive approaches are affected by *particular* intersecting social locations, for example secular-religious identity, class, ethnicity, nationality, generation and gender/sex, inside a larger Western and European discourse. Hence, to break down the phenomenon of *new cosmopolitanism* into plural discourses stresses the complex and contradictory social locations (Mahler and Pessar 2010) of academics unfolding in a web of collective imaginations and particular memories, but also in specific contemporaneous inter-textualities. Van der Veer (2002: 178) rightly asks us to 'avoid both centre-periphery models and the identification of originary moments, but try to describe historical entanglements.' However, this is not only

---

1   The *helix* here should represent, as a systemic intertwined structure, the parallel dynamics of state-politics and academic knowledge, see Vieten 2007.

relevant to a critical approach to colonial cosmopolitanism and the role of Europe as a whole (van der Veer 2002); it also matters how intra-European debates are entangled. Exploring these roots and routes is an intellectual effort to move our thinking about cosmopolitan utopia further.

Before moving in the final chapter of this book to a discussion of critical feminist and postcolonial alternatives to Euro- and largely andocentric localities of new cosmopolitanism, I will pinpoint in this chapter the crucial findings of the archaeology of specific cosmopolitan discourse traditions as explored in Chapters 3 and 4. The central aspects of the historical national (nation state) pathways[2] towards cosmopolitanism are summarised systematically and presented in distinctive model typologies.

Scheme 1

Britain	Germany
Commercial and colonial cosmopolitanism (Empire)	Cultural(ist) cosmopolitanism (*Weltbürger* and *Kosmopolit*)
Vernacular cosmopolitanism and political centralism (multiculturalism as 'communities of communities', Commonwealth and the city)	Ethno-nationalism, anti-Semitism and federal integration (the Holocaust and a war-colonial regime in Continental Europe; GDR vs. FRG-federal structure)
The 'colour' of difference (slavery; racism, dual nationality; anti-discrimination law)	The 'faith' of difference (racisms; xenophobia; single nationality / ethno-citizenship)

In Scheme 1 we find the two most characteristic discourse streams of cosmopolitanism that can be identified by digging into the archives of the British and German nation state historiographies: significantly different patterns of cultural inclusion and stages of territorial and social integration become apparent. A commercially anchored notion of cosmopolitanism in concordance with colonialism framed the global outreach of the Queen's and Kings' subjects, contested national identities and citizenship in Britain. In Germany, intertwined ambitions of '*Kultur*' and a *völkisch* goal to 'educate' ('*Bildung*') the nation and 'humanity', supported the rise and growth of a hegemonic ethno-nationalistic discourse of *culturalist* cosmopolitanism that is mirrored in the most extreme form in the Shoa as the systematic mass-murder of Jews as well as Sinti and Roma. The term 'culturalist' aims to catch the underlying structural racisms

---

2   This is not to say that these pathways are the only relevant streams of cosmopolitanism discourses; this model rather stresses the most influential themes that have a consistent impact on contemporary discourses.

(i.e. anti-Semitism) of the discourses of cosmopolitanism that created two social-cultural symbolic positions within an ideological discourse of cosmopolitanism. The 'faith of difference' in Scheme 1 should contrast 'the colour of difference' while indicating that spiritual unity and institutionalised anti-Semitism were core elements of the popular movements for democracy in Germany in contrast to Britain where the colonial non-white Other became also the visible signifier of postcolonial struggles.

As argued here the model of commercial cosmopolitanism rather accomplished a *differentiating system of 'encompassment'* whereas culturalist cosmopolitanism with its focus on cultural-federal integration, single allegiances and social cohesion could be understood as a *differentiating system of 'segmentation'*. Bauman (2004) proposes the taxonomy of *differentiating systems* (encompassment; segmentation; Orientalism; (Bauman 2004)). These systems orientate the ways in which group differences are played out within particular social contexts. With reference to Britain and Germany we can distinguish significant themes that subscribe to a system of encompassment (Britain) and a system of segmentation (Germany) – see Scheme 2. Related to these significantly different approaches to social cohesion, the place of collective (minority) identities and the location of governance and political integration are characteristic aspects of how differences became constructed and perceived.

Scheme 2

Encompassment **(Britain)**	**Segmentation** **(Germany)**
London as the centre (local) and multiple territorial peripheries	Federal integration of territory
Individualism	Communitarian perspectives of social cohesion
Indifference to collective difference	Convergence of difference

As far as the British context is concerned Scheme 2 sketches a specific administrative, economic and cultural structure with the overall focus on *London*: the political centralism, but also the cultural uniqueness of London represents cosmopolitan images comprising indifference against but also tolerance of the Other. Accordingly, London gives resonance to an urban place that accentuates individual encounters of strangers despite multiple divided spaces of collective difference. 'Colour' became the prominent signifier of multiculturalism, minority difference and the collective struggle against racism in Britain in the 20th century. As argued above, it is the mixed legacy of the British Empire, the slave trade and a constitutional monarchy that first allowed unrestricted entry to its Commonwealth subjects until 1962, and shifted to the perception of the Other as defined by skin colour against the post World War II order. This happened at a time when Britain re-connected more intensely with a white continental Europe unfolding alongside post-colonial transformation. Post 9/11 and 7/7 2005 anti-Islam racism and the fear of a fundamentalist violent Other placed attention more exclusively on religion as a politicised angle for othering difference.[3]

In contrast to Britain, federal integration and a long lasting preoccupation with the overlap of territorial borders and political community belonging direct a different system in Germany. The meaning of a French inspired notion of 'republic' and a nationalistic demand to 'unite' the democratic movements of the 19th-century German states accommodated regional-provincial difference as a matter of territoriality and spiritual allegiance. The pre-1989 FRG's constitution had expressed in writing the wish to unite again with the eastern part of Germany, as today in the 21st century it is the constitutional goal to strive for a united Europe. Here, *convergence of difference* is organised and labelled in features of different struggles for 'unification' on the basis of a stronger demand for collective social cohesion.

When looking at the contemporary versions of British and German citizenship we come across different concepts that allow individuals to have dual (or even more) passports in Britain whereas Germany keeps its mono-cultural perception of one single allegiance to a nation. Although in 2010 the German *Staatsangehörigkeitsgesetz* relaxed its strict rules on the possibility of keeping another passport, which means in effect allowing dual passports for other EU citizens,[4] this exemption is not granted to the largest ethno-national minority community in Germany, the Turks. That means that it is a *transformed, but still existing* idea of 'ethno-cultural' bonding that admits 'entrance' and boundary crossing of the concrete national political community. In the 21st century, however, it is the *civic-cultural European bonding* that gives the guidance. With respect to Britain and Germany as two powerful national players in the EU, the meaning of 'national belonging' unfolds in distinctive ways that have an impact on the perception of difference and the Other reaching into contemporary engagements with cosmopolitanism and gender in Europe and beyond.

I return now to the arguments of the different academics and intellectuals, highlighting how they made reference to the systems introduced above in their writings in the 1990s and the following decade post 9/11.

---

3   The recent 'gangster consumer riots' of August 2011 might change this perception.

4   http://bundesrecht.juris.de/bundesrecht/rustag/gesamt.pdf; see Paragraph 12 (2), also exception for Switzerland.

Discourses on Cosmopolitanisms in the 1990s: Departures, Locations and Conflicts

Britain: The City and the Space of Multiculturalism

Despite very distinctive upbringings and research agendas all three British academics either are based academically in London (Held[5]; Mouffe) or the multicultural space of London (Bhabha) is a prominent theme in their writings. As argued above, London does *signify* Britain in terms of its colonial past and multicultural presence. Hence, London is the 'local' angle from where considerations about the state of the nation and contemporary perspectives on cosmopolitanism depart. Bringing in testimonies of political feminist critique, we can note that early signs of fundamentalism were recognised for example by the London based feminist group 'Women against Fundamentalism' (Sahgal and Yuval-Davis 1992).

What is striking is that Mouffe, like Held, regards 'the political' predominantly as a matter of international state affairs that is approached in line with Anglo-Saxon traditions of pragmatism or realism. More specifically, Mouffe's criticism of liberal cosmopolitanism concentrates on images of cosmopolitanism related to the 'commercial' centre that characterises and encircles middle class, urban and liberal attitudes. Further, Held's advocacy of liberal individualism and a cosmopolitan market democracy was very much in line with the dominant neo-liberal economic discourse in Britain of the 1990s. Finally, the cultural space of London is significant for Bhabha's critical thinking about the margins of the nation and the role hybridity, enunciation and non-European immigrant communities play in de-centring the cultural space of the national centre. The latter, in particular, advocates that immigrants and minority cultures would contribute to a cosmopolitan, but multicultural Britain.

As suggested above, an *encompassing system* features the principal configuration of a hegemonic centre and a multicultural periphery; this periphery can evolve as the sometimes impoverished and ethnically mixed spaces of the centre. Stuart Hall (2004: 2) points out that cities and London in particular, have to be understood traditionally as porous spaces where individual encounters happen despite the existence of social divisions. He writes, '[t]he boundaries between these spaces, however, have never been absolute' (Hall 2004: 2). Attractive prosperous cities have led to the development of a cultural mixture or as Hall calls it an 'unplanned cosmopolitanism' (ibid.). It is London that attracted exiled intellectuals poets and politician for centuries from all over the world; it is London where Salman Rushdie lives in exile. Held and Bhabha take up very explicitly the debate about the life threatening fatwa against Rushdie in their 1990s publications. Accordingly, the canon of all British texts resembles ideological conflicts surrounding sub-themes

---

5   Held's very recent move to Durham doesn't change this topical focus. All in all, it can to be left to further speculation how far the scandal at the LSE mentioned above also had an impact on this change in location.

of a system of encompassment with strong features of the principal agenda of liberal individualism and multicultural democracy.

Germany: Provincial Nations and their Ideological Maps

I turn now to the German academics. Habermas is associated with Frankfurt (Hesse) and the *Frankfurt School* respectively, while Beck's research centre is located in Munich (Bavaria). Finally, Behrend held a lectureship[6] in East Berlin (Humboldt University) and lived in the GDR, unlike the two other more prominent scholars. Further, these different urban locations express federal regionalism. Here, East Berlin represents the capital city of the GDR until 1990, and, as far as research at the Humboldt University is concerned, Marxist social analysis was shunned post-1990. The *Frankfurt School* where Habermas established his career[7] represents a particular tradition of German Critical Theory. But the School as a symbol for the outspoken and internationally renowned exiled theorists Adorno, Marcuse or Benjamin, in fact became famous in its US American exile. In this respect *Frankfurt* as the location of German Critical Theory prescribes a kind of fictional space. It refers to the intellectual peak of political and critical *modern* thinking and to Weimar, and also to its demolition by the Nazis.

According to Wendy Brown (2006: 3), 'In contrast with Kant and the Kantians, the Critical Theorists understood the social world to impress itself upon thinking and regarded new forms of thinking as essential to grasping new historical circumstances.' Marcuse was at the centre stage of the 1968 German student revolt that originated in Frankfurt; this underlines, too, the de-centred historical stage of the FRG. Finally, there is Munich and its historical connection as first centre stage of Hitler and the rise of early National Socialism and *völkisch* ambitions to conquer Europe, and then the world. Against this background we can conclude that in a way the different cities, their histories and particular institutional embeddings reach out into the contemporary projects of Habermas, Beck and Behrend.

In Habermas's view 'social cohesion' is linked to cultural integration, but he agrees that in a contemporary world democracy means respecting multicultural identities. But this still has to be achieved along the lines of normative integration. In his plea for a European constitution, he adopts a (West) German post-Holocaust paradigm of the impartiality of law and justice. Hence, Habermas's view reflects the concern that the interests of the other as an individual were dismissed in the totalitarian regimes. However, the post-totalitarian German system tends to dismiss the normative hierarchy that still persists through the value-laden positioning of majority and minority collectivity. This is a weakness in Habermas's considerations

---

6   Behrend, who formally held a PhD and the German Habilitation, was not moved to a professorship as she was a dissident critical intellectual yet in the GDR.

7   Although his Habilitation was rejected first by the famous Frankfurt intellectual Adorno and he received the 'viva legendi' in Marburg under the sponsorship of Wolfgang Abendroth.

as he keeps idealistic and abstract liberal functions of law and republicanism. Similar to Habermas, Beck's 'risk and society' approach focuses on the theme of social stability when engaging with the consequences of disrupted national social consensus and mediating institutions. His perspective likewise follows a hegemonic narrative of national social cohesion before the 'risk and insecurity' demons of the 'Second Modernity' captured the national social fabric. (For an excellent in-depth critique of Beck's argument, see Holton 2009). Also, I write 'narrative' as Götz Aly (2005, 2007) concluded that a part of the *social welfare* history is missing in the hegemonic narrative. The national 'community cohesion' in Germany has some roots in a *völkisch* project of homogenising and 'comforting' the political community. Aly revealed that one purpose and effect of the German National Socialism was its racist socialism by which low (working) classes of the *völkisch* 'Aryan' majority gained direct material advantages from state anti-Semitism and the war colonialisation of Europe.

Behrend, whose interventions came from an intellectual minority position, viewed the social realm of the nation and the political community from an ideologically and biographically contrasting angle. She urged an acceptance of the plural and all-inclusive German nation that eventually might overcome racist, sexist and classist attitudes. Nevertheless, her critical Marxist and feminist projection addressed German national identity as overlapping with its *current* national territory, albeit with an emancipatory outlook on a non-ethnic nation.

Though sharing almost the same generational positionality, Habermas and Behrend look at the contemporary discourses on cosmopolitanism from biographically specific perspectives that are intrinsically linked to the period of German National Socialism, Communist dissent and the Holocaust. Interestingly, Habermas and Behrend use the German phrase *weltbürgerlich* or *Weltbürger* in their publications. When talking about cosmopolitanism as the contemporary condition Habermas uses '*kosmopolitsch*', a term which has equally an explicit connection to a German cultural discourse of cosmopolitanism. Here we have a generational link between both German academics that are situated in different positions via this history and terminology.

Similarities, Disparities and Crossings

In Britain the loss of Empire and its global territories did not generate a hegemonic plea for a one and united 'national territory'. The struggle and goal for the autonomy of various regions (for example Wales; Scotland), the political violent resistance and by now, peace process in Northern Ireland, and England's sceptical attitude towards 'Europe', however, mark its overall *geopolitical* perspective. But these concerns did not become the decisive ideological box for the negotiation of allegiance and integration as far as the contributions of Held and Bhabha are concerned. Rather it is the performance of global diversity in the English heartland of commercial locations, i.e. London, where academics and ordinary folk engage with the legacy of constant group migrations, colonialism and individual acculturations.

As made clear above, the legacy of various forms of territorial changes such as integration, separation and 'unification' map political territory as ideologically laden in Germany. In this regard dynamics of 'social cohesion'[8] correlate to anti-Semitic stereotypes of 'rootlessness', 'detachment' and 'disloyalty'. Behrend's rejection of liberal cosmopolitanism and her Marxist-informed distance from the term '*Weltbürger*' is also echoed in Mouffe's post-Marxist criticism of liberal (commercial) cosmopolitanism.

Further there is an ideological proximity between Behrend and Mouffe as feminist socialists although Behrend's Marxist view is marginalised in a German context. The annexation of the communist society meant a ban from academic professions (*Berufsverbot*) for Marxists that has a precedent in a legal ban of communist parties and *Berufsverbote* in Western Germany in the 1980s. Beck's rather vague political position has to be read against this marginalisation of communist and Marxist positions and can be interpreted as a symptom of the West German *Zeitgeist* of the late 1970s and 1980s when radical left wing politics was largely criminalised and split due to the issue of political 'violence'. In addition, Beck's approach reflects his proximity to the British academic discourse, but also his generational anchoring in a post-Holocaust moral identification.

What is striking is that Bhabha and Behrend, both minority academics, discuss 'culture' in a critical disjuncture and as embedded in the political interpretation of the 'social'. Behrend in her dissident perspective is a 'minoritised' Other, who could qualify for Bhabha's perception of 'minoritised cosmopolitanism'. She holds the historical counter position of *othered Jewish Germans* (or Austrians) who by now are claimed *post-mortem* as part of German heritage and its past, but are still *othered* as communists.

It has been illustrated above how individual academic approaches to new cosmopolitanism relate to both personal and broader cultural themes of Britain and Germany. We can conclude here that 'encompassment' and 'segmentation' shaped discourse angles in both countries specifically; nonetheless, the attacks on the US on 9/11 hint at an abrupt and 'affective' component bringing to the fore the third system of *Orientalism* which re-directed these discursive angles accordingly.

In the next section I summarise relevant transitions and consistent differences regarding the new millennium discourse post-9/11. The most problematic aspects of the ideological crossings between the British and the German discourses are extracted, pointing out its impact on modified notions of the pairs of *mobility/ plurality* and *migration/alterity* as differentiated in Chapter 2.

---

8   The author is aware that a controversial discussion about 'social cohesion' has been taking place in Britain more recently. See for example the discussion of the white paper of 'safe haven' in Yuval-Davis et al. 2005. Though there is no space to discuss this here, it makes clear that the supra-state system of the European Union transforms the perception of 'national' boundaries in Britain and other Members states.

The New Millennium's Rhetoric of Closure: Allegiances, Cohesion and Security

As I have shown above, two dissimilar *differentiating systems* shape nationally situated views and it is important for the contemporary moment to assess cautiously to what degree these systems of 'encompassment' and 'segmentation' are merging into a 21st-century Eurocentric version of civic cosmopolitanism.

European Mobility and the Migrating Other: EU Citizens Unbound

We are currently witnessing the transformation from different models of liberal (Britain) and social (Germany) market democracies to a European liberal market democracy that cherishes global capitalism and commercial perspectives of cosmopolitanism. Eric Kaufman (2003: n.p.) stresses the 'civic-political quality of European cosmopolitanism' in contrast to a rather 'ethno-cultural cosmopolitanism in the US'. He argues further that the 'Schengen agreement preserving the identity of Europe's frontier and citizenship laws highlights the limits of cultural cosmopolitanism' (ibid.). Against the background of these reflections it is vital to consider the different notions of 'mobility' and 'migration' that were decisive to the ordering of social positions within historical discourses of cosmopolitanism in Germany and that were never linguistically differentiated nor symbolically charged in Britain.

In the context of the European Union we come across distinctive notions of 'mobility' and 'migration'. As argued elsewhere (Vieten 2006, 2009), *mobility* of EU citizens is at the centre of the economic 'community' building processes of the European Union. We are confronted with new configurations of 'social mobility' as European citizens' 'cross border migration' is assigned legal and economic privileges. It is important to understand that these new legal layers not only *redefine* entry and exit to nation states, but engender and modify the meaning of cultural bonds in the context of *migration* and *citizenship*. In this new flexibility order, a multi-layered and sophisticated system of citizenship rights is constructed as 'internal market' migration, and 'external' worldwide mobility of professional specialists is welcomed. However, nationals who do not move across national EU borders largely gain no benefits from this system and individuals or specific communities that are not permitted or able to move get stuck, for example among local under-class populations in controlled areas.

Peter van der Veer (2002: 167) stresses 'the argument that Western modernity has depended principally on "the mobile personality" – that is, on a type of person eager to move, to change and invent.' And further in reflection on the gender of the cosmopolitan, he argues, 'In gender terms the cosmopolitan is more usually conceived as a man, an individual who has the ability to live anywhere and the capacity to tolerate and understand the barbarism of the others' (2002: 166). Van der Veer's remark on *gender* is worth noticing as the 'understanding of barbarism of others', though probably mentioned with sarcasm, might provide another departure point for considering the gendered language of European cosmopolitan outlooks.

To make clear the systematic linkages of different categories of *mobility* and *migration,* a third scheme is introduced.

Scheme 3

Mobility	Migration
Weltbürger – cultural(ist) term; addressing (male gendered) middle classes of the world	*Kosmopolit* – cultural(ist) term; describing the racialised Other
EU citizen – legal term; addressing individual rights/*Grundfreiheiten* (fundamental freedoms)	Third Country national – foreigner/alien – legal term addressing the 'national' outsider
Global citizen – conceptual term addressing a citizen of the world; sustaining a privileged condition	Global foreigner/alien – conceptual term addressing a general outsider; creating a discriminating condition

As argued here, there is a striking ideological pathway from a cultural notion of a *Weltbürger* to the contemporary conceptual term of 'global citizens' or 'citizens of the world'. After all, this pathway develops dialectically; the patterns of 'mobility' produce significant shifts in the perception of 'national outsiders' to 'global foreigners' as theorised in Chapter 1 and exemplified in Chapter 2. In addition, this also indicates that the notion of trans-border mobility is changed to a required 'cultural and civic' inclusion for accepted migrants. In opposition to this, the negative connotation of 'migration' even might include the stuck underclass 'migrants' associated with 'non-mobility'.

As Kofman (2005: 92) points out:

> [b]ringing the outsider into the nation meant that the cosmopolitan as bearer of non-national practices and values was depicted as threat to its stability and homogeneity. Today, national outsiders, and especially those whose lives are actually transnationally grounded, must justify their multiple links and contacts.

In the contemporary, 21st-century world we are left with divergent and more complex parameters of differences: the 'Other' as social outsider is still around; especially when considering that 'being local [itself] may become a sign of social deprivation' (Kofman 2005: 86). We are witnessing a process of a *normalisation* of difference (Nava, 2007), while dialectically the notion of *the Other* as the 'irregular' (Broeders 2007: 71) migrating or 'risky' cosmopolitan is being reconstructed as its dialectic twin. Movement of people is still measured, controlled, directed and incorporated into modified economic clusters of productivity. Here, the European Union with its single market economy transforms rapidly symbolic points of references for political allegiances, cultural identifications and therefore socially relevant (trans-)national community space. Coming back to the tension between multiculturalism, gender and cosmopolitanism, London can work as a crystallisation of these conflicts.

In opposition to the image of the cosmopolitan and open minded image of London stands the terrorist violence that randomly targeted any people *travelling* in London on 7/7 in 2005. The terrorist massacres in London were planned and undertaken by young British Muslims from Leeds and Bradford. Though the motives that triggered their fanatical violent actions are multi-dimensional, we can detect a problematic tension between the 'visibility'/'invisibility' and the possible 'empathy for the Other' when taking into account the different spatial realities across England, for example. Social deprivation means, for example, that working class – or by now underclass – white and black populations in North English cities such as Liverpool, Manchester or Birmingham on the one hand, and significant pockets of South Asian working class neighbourhoods on the other, live rather segregated daily lives. However, all struggle hard to position themselves in the 21st-century hegemonic capitalistic liberal market order. It is mainly class division as well as ethno-gendered social spheres that shape the perception of England beyond London (Vieten 2013 forthcoming). This social structure of 'impoverishment' contrasts with the multicultural, economically prosperous and cosmopolitan *image* of London. I write 'image' on purpose as the most recent riots in some of the poorer boroughs of London and some of the North and Middle England cities in August 2011 underline that the symbolic representation of what a cosmopolitan-*Weltbürger* elite wants to see as its place of trade and commerce does not match with the distressing vulnerability and social injustice living right next door. There are arguable limits to the comprehension of what the balance between individual and collective rights would imply and which level of social cohesion could thus be negotiated with people who are not willing to subscribe to a process of negotiation. However, concepts of democracy and cosmopolitanism require material conditions that encourage people to engage positively.

Further, the axes of 'visibility'/'invisibility' come in when thinking of 'contemporary strangers': either young male orthodox Muslims are presented in the media as hostile to the secular cosmopolitan consensus or we see black male refugees entering different EU countries. Whereas female orthodox Muslims are ascribed as being victims of 'their' communities, the female black global outsider is totally removed from visibility: leaving them in the camps and deserts there means leaving them outside our circle of recognition and global social redistribution.

Against the background of this nexus of otherness-exclusion it is important to understand how Held, Habermas, Beck and Bhabha as well as their post-Marxist and feminist contenders contribute in their interventions on new cosmopolitanism to the advocacy of the EU and a 'cosmopolitanization' of Europe as a geopolitical area. In what ways are modified patterns of difference understood that unfold along a global social transformation demanding to go beyond the classic territorial understanding of social solidarity?

Patterns of Plurality and Alterity: European Diversity and The Other

What is striking is that we are confronted rather with minor differences between Held and Mouffe on the one hand, and Beck and Habermas on the other, when it comes down to the strategic role of a more cohesive European region. Four out of six academics advocate *European allegiance*s rather than an alternative utopian vision of cosmopolitan belonging as the timely political response to the global transition of nation-states in Europe. As far as the international academic discourse is concerned there is clearly a crossing of disciplinary and national boundaries adding to a wider phenomenon of transnationalism. Despite Mouffe's efforts to challenge the liberal concept of (British) market democracy she argues equally in favour of multiple regional powers to balance the unilateralist USA and therefore promotes territorial cohesion (Vieten 2010). Her approach corresponds to the model of the *Keynesian-Westphalian* 'national container' though as a trigger for social protest and political organisation. Held's proposal for cosmopolitan democracy turns to the EU as the institutional model for how multi-layered governance might operate; in doing so he effectively concentrates on global IR institutions of governance until 2007. More recently, his perspective turned to a more principal interrogation of the space-social nexus. Habermas and Beck add a specific Germanic layer to this hegemonic discourse of *Europeanisation* while referring to the European Union as the relevant social-cultural mediator of 'their' region. Here, the themes of 'segmentation' – for instance social cohesion and convergence, the meaning of mobility, the regulating function of law and secular cosmopolitanism – dominate their focus on the cultural cohesion project of the European Union.

Apparently, there is this paradigm: British political science and German sociology regard the European Union as the regional mediator of civil and public European interests. However, the pitfalls of the merging of cultural horizons (*Horizontverschmelzung*) derive from strongly gendered and classed cultural assumptions which allow the identification of moral scapegoats to proliferate; moral panic is on the rise, targeting those underdogs that do not subscribe to the sophistication of the knowledge society and its *modus* of hybrid 'transcultural diversities' (Robins 2006).

Habermas not unlike Mouffe though for different ideological reasons (Vieten 2010), concurs with the dominant reading of the 'political' as processes of opening and closure ('*Öffnungs- und Schliessungprozesse*'). In recent years, Mouffe has proposed that 'passion' is central to 'agonistic politics', but even this attempt to bring in the 'darker side' of human dispositions cannot grasp the extreme contestation articulated in current global terrorism: local terrorists act as global warriors, who confront the West with another form of cosmopolitan belonging. This paradox of another dark and untamed potential of cosmopolitanism remains unpacked in all approaches. While advocating regional blocs Mouffe underestimates the hegemonic policy discourse that targets Muslim communities as 'uncanny' Others' (alterity). She neglects the fact that the enlarged regional power of the EU in Europe is establishing itself as a fortress, and as panoptical, in a Foucaultdian sense by introducing a digital net of surveillance.

Beck, not unlike Habermas, addresses Jews as *the Other* to German modernity and implicitly, as *an Other* to the German nation. His similarly positive adaptation of *the* significant *cosmopolitan Other* in a contemporary context of 'reflexive modernity' operates through an identification process which looks for common ground beyond the devastating past. In this regard past otherness is altered to encompassed difference in the present. But to be clear here, the notion of *contemporary otherness* coveys a distinctive meaning: this position goes beyond diversity. The claim of diversity largely echoes debates and socio-legal achievements of collective minority struggles for group *recognition* in the 19th and 20th centuries but it does not capture the meaning of a 21st-century cosmopolitan openness towards the contemporary global Other.

In contrast Bhabha advocates an inclusive transnational cultural cosmopolitanism that traverses the Eurocentric focus on Europe and the EU and Behrend asks for cosmopolitan all-inclusive nations, i.e. Germany. Bhabha is the one who most explicitly talks of 'minoritised cosmopolitanism' and the 'cosmofeminine', which opens up space to feminist and postcolonial voices and experiences.

Concluding Remarks

The *mainstreaming* of *new* cosmopolitanism as a cultural European discourse fits appropriately into a post democratic Europeanisation process that welcomes 'mobile, cosmopolitan European citizens' while disregarding other migrating global cosmopolitans.

Michael Walzer (1980: 195) argues:

> [m]odernization theory … lies behind the widely shared view that the United States and the Soviet Union are evolving toward one another and eventually will develop very similar social systems. This is a view that suits men and women of different political persuasions: it can provide the basis for arguments about Soviet liberalization or incipient *American totalitarianism*.[9]

Given that there is this logic of 'fusion' inherent to modernisation processes, apparently we have reached further stages in establishing the latter alternative of an 'incipient American totalitarianism', which is very much feared by Mouffe and others. More optimistically though this might not be the end of the story: the

---

9　My emphasis.

complexity and ambivalence of modernisation theory holds the power to argue and act against any hegemonic order.

As far as the contemporary mainstream debate on new cosmopolitanism is concerned it seems to be framed by a late modern version of a secular and European 're-conquista';[10] the debate proposes 'European cosmopolitan and democratic civilisation, global human rights and multicultural equality' as an emancipatory narrative to global poverty and injustice. However, modernity and civilisation are and have been everywhere in the hybrid transformations of entangled modernities.[11] Buck-Morss (2003: 99–100) reminds us:

> [i]f we are interested in the genealogy of a global public sphere, we will need to note that the first radically cosmopolitan critique of Western-centric thought did not come to the Islamic world from within. It came from the French-speaking Caribbean, via secular, Marxist transport with a detour to Algeria – and when it appeared it came with a Western wrapping, I am referring to Frantz Fanon's remarkable book, *The Wretched of the Earth*, which (paradoxically was introduced by the European Marxist Jean Paul Sartre) called on the non-Western world to leave Europe 'behind' …

In the process of creating new and different layers of de-territorialised citizenship, virtual participation and global market integration, the meaning of traditionally bounded social concepts is in a transition that opens up new cosmopolitan spaces, accordingly.

As asked in the beginning, what does cosmopolitanism mean if 'citizenship' keeps a nationally based notion of republican citizenship? Does it make any difference to those who do not possess secure citizen rights? We can see that the dominant contemporary discourses of new cosmopolitanism enshrine a concept of European cosmopolitanism via EU citizenship that continues with a vision of a global asymmetric polis. What is lacking is the de-gendering of hegemonic knowledge[12] and a clear political passion to challenge this 'new', but old order.

To make the transition to the final part of this book, I will finish this chapter with a remark by Walter D. Mignolo and Madina V. Thostanova (2006: 214):

---

10   We could also adopt an interpretation of this late modernity project as rooted in secular Protestantism. According to Walzer (1980: 191), '[t]he theory of modernization appears in an earlier form as Weber's "rationalization" – a process culminating in a "rational-legal" society.'

11   This is by now a common statement; see Beck and Grande 2010.

12   Yes, boys and girls, feminists do not only engage with 'women's rights as human rights'; but de-construct normative, moral, cultural, economic and political formations that keep inequality and social injustice in place. In *The Cosmopolitanism Reader* (2010: 453) Garret Wallace Brown and Megan Kime write 'Unfortunately cosmopolitans have so far tended to neglect specifically feminist issues, but some feminists have begun to consider the issue of global justice from the perspective of women, paying specific attention to the question of women's human rights.'

The question commonly asked is: how do you perform border thinking and how do you enact the de-colonial shift? What is the method? Interestingly enough, the question is most often asked by predominantly white and North Atlantic scholars and intellectuals. It is impossible to imagine Dubois asking that question because he prompted it with his own thinking, dwelling in what he called double consciousness. The question is interesting because it acts like a boomerang and returns to the person who asked the question. Why is he or she asking that question? Where is he or she dwelling, in a single consciousness? Why was it an African-American like Dubois and not a German like Habermas who came up with a concept such as double consciousness? Furthermore, double consciousness would not admit the thesis that promotes the 'inclusion of the other' (Habermas, 1998). Double consciousness and the inclusion of the other confront each other across the colonial difference.

Chapter 6

Transversal Conversations on the Scope of New Cosmopolitanism: Beyond the Eurocentric Framework

According to Nwankwo (2005: 10): 'The White fear that arose in the wake of the Haitian Revolution was not only a fear of violence but also a fear of people of African descents' embrace of cosmopolitanism – of their defining themselves through a Black world that included the Haitians.' Hence, a self-empowering notion of cosmopolitanism as 'defining oneself' is at the core of any forceful political change to unjust and unequal living conditions; in that sense feminist politics which fights to alter oppressive societal (civic and intimate), economic and political arrangements is linked to cosmopolitan utopia (Reilly 2007).

Referring to Martha Nussbaum (1997), Costas Douzinas (2007: 175) argues that 'Humanism and cosmopolitanism involve cultivating a critical examination of our way of life; the capacity to identify with others in different groups, cultures or nations, and a "narrative imagination" that helps us to understand and empathise with others.' He talks of 'The cosmopolitanism to come' (2007: 291 ff.) which also means accepting that:

> I can never comprehend fully *her*[1] intentions or actions. I can have no immediate access to the consciousness of the other no perception of otherness. ... In cosmopolitan ontology, each singular being is a cosmos, the point of intertwining and condensation of past events and stories, people and encounters … The other as singular, unique finite being puts me in touch with infinite otherness. (2007: 294)

Here, we find resemblances of Levinas's notion of the 'infinite other'; the acknowledgement of the Other assumes *difference* beyond a (gendered) self-centred mirror, as argued in Chapter 1. Also, there seems to be a gendered allure in Douzinas's imagination while asking for 'empathy' with the unknown (mysterious female?) other. All in all, we can grasp from these remarks that engaging with a particular and unique 'narrative' of the Other suggests an unorthodox capacity of *listening*. This capacity of 'opening' is deemed necessary if we are willing to embrace a more inclusive framework of cosmopolitan global bonding.

Coming back to Nwankwo's (2005) proposal, we can note that she refers to the cosmopolitan consciousness of a black female slave, named Mary Prince.

---

1   My emphasis.

Mrs Prince *narrated* her story on the brink of the Haitian Revolution of the 18th century. Looking at the potential of cosmopolitanism as defining 'oneself through the world beyond one's own origins' (2005: 9), Nwanko argues 'that imperialism and colonialism themselves are forms of cosmopolitanism. Responses and resistance to these forms, then, are often also cosmopolitanism.' As made explicit in the analysis of the contributions to new cosmopolitanism by Held, Beck, Habermas and Bhabha as well feminist contenders Behrend and Mouffe, cosmopolitanism as well as nationalism/national identity is not plain, but filled up with purpose, situational background and gendered subjectivity. Hence, approaching a *Janus-faced* cosmopolitanism, our critical feminist reflection has to consider counter-narratives to the hegemonic stories of global bonding that are told to us. Against a gender-neutral tale of a *cosmopolitan light* 'new globalized world' we have to insist on the revolutionary spirit of some elements of older cosmopolitanism conveyed in socialist utopia as well as through local liberation struggles across the world. And this notion of cosmopolitanism is beyond a 21st-century script that wishes to accommodate *Weltbürger* cultural identity as binding glue to trans-national territorial regimes. Alternatively as Douzinas (2007: 176) puts it, 'institutionalised cosmopolitanism risks becoming the normative gloss of globalised capitalism at its imperial stage.'

This concluding chapter will draw together the main arguments running through the book as far as gendered and dialectic forms of difference are concerned and confront the way new cosmopolitanism is mainstreamed with critical feminist and postcolonial engagements reaching out beyond Europe. In this context, the role of human rights with respect to the controversies encompassing culture, women and human rights and an increasing social regression in late modern societies will be revisited first, before sketching the impact of postcolonial debates and the proposal of *subaltern cosmopolitanism* in the concluding section. Fraser's call for a new form of global redistributive justice leads the final investigation as the present state is the troubling state of globalising injustice.

'Women's Rights are Human Rights': Searching for Cosmopolitan Tools to Deepen Feminist Critique and Action

In Chapter 2 the prominent influence of Kant's writing was discussed, mapping out the two-fold reading of his approach to the possibilities of 'eternal peace and global justice'. In the 20th century, Kant's model of cosmopolitanism inspired post-war (transnational) governance institutions such as the 'League of Nations' (1917) and most importantly for the current situation of the 21st century, the codification of an embryonic form of *cosmopolitan rights* known as the Universal Declaration of Human Rights (1948). Within its global outreach the Human Rights declaration is a programme of *positive* international law and thus has to be mediated through agreement and signature of national governments. Does it come as a surprise that the US did not sign up to it? Nor did consecutive US governments agree to 'the Kyoto

Convention of 1992 all the way to the United Nations (UN) International Convention of Children Rights or the International Criminal Court' (Ugarteche 2007: 65). As David Chandler (2002, 2006) makes clear, the Universal Declaration of Human Rights was established as a moral response to the atrocities that occurred in the 20th century. In the 21st century, this platform is transformed to a master plan of 'political humanism'. Powerful states try to resolve their domestic politics while pushing away old elites and establishing new elites more suitable to their interests. (Chandler 2002: 53 and 221) We can agree with this insight when considering that Iraq's and – more recently – Libya's latest governments, however, are expected to sustain the business-as-usual profits of global capitalist companies as previous leaders did. When searching for challenges to this hegemonic language it appears as if we have to look for guidance in another part of the world: interestingly, we find a place where the hegemonic view of *small* redistribution and liberal market philosophy is contested rather situated in the Spanish and Portuguese speaking world of the *Americas*, the southern neighbours to the US. As Sallie Westwood (2001: 249) claims:

> Latin America is important to our understanding of the regimes of recognition, democracy, citizenship and the nation as sites for the production of recognition ... In Mexico, the Zapatista uprising received world-wide media coverage through the astute use of the Internet and the global press by Comrade Marcos. The Zapatista struggle globalised a local issue in which poverty and land claims were allied with state abuses towards people who are not recognized as citizens or nationals, who are not part of the imaginary of the Mexican nation and who therefore are excluded and denied in relation to citizenship rights, individually and collectively.

I will come back to these dynamics in greater detail when discussing the proposal of *subaltern cosmopolitanism* in the final section of this chapter.

In a timely critical analysis of liberal and what he calls 'poststructuralist' approaches to cosmopolitanism, Chandler (2009: 59) argues, 'For cosmopolitan human rights advocates there is no distinct difference between global, deterritorialized, human rights and territorial, sovereignty, bounded, democratic and civil rights. ... For critiques of cosmopolitan right regimes the extension of a discourse of rights and law merely enhances the power of liberal governance.' Though the critique of liberal cosmopolitanism certainly is inspired by a poststructuralist insight of cultural and social fragmentation (e.g. hybridity) and – in effect – the appearance of more complex notions of belonging beyond the national-territorial container, it is short sighted to understand this critique of liberal cosmopolitanism as an intellectual debate of Western post-modernity. Against the dominance of this Anglo-American or European perspective it is relevant to note that the Columbian philosopher Santiago Castro-Gómez, for example, calls the 'self-realization of modernity' (cited in Mendieta 2003[2]) the moment where 'the postmodern is really the re-discovery of history through the historization of

---

2   http://www.javeriana.edu.co/pensar/Rev27.html.

everyday experience' (ibid.). This kind of *cosmopolitan self-realisation* that is based on counter-historical knowledge and also refers to collective struggles against oppression and discrimination[3] can trigger utopian visions; it transcends local and concrete experiences and combines it with the struggle for the better in the sense of a cosmopolitan ambit. The particular Western perspective of post-structuralism as conveyed in Chandler's label of 'poststructuralist' cosmopolitanism tends to abandon the idea of a communitarian-collective perspective for global (human) social justice. However, the question Chandler rightly poses, and which is not vastly different to Mouffe's critique of (liberal) cosmopolitanism, is: Who should become the *democratically elected governmental agent* of our cosmopolitan global community if we do not foster local mediators as 'representative' or direct voices of cosmopolitan/global democracy? What kind of democratic procedures might be able to handle our utopian cosmopolitanism from the bottom up?[4] Or, alternatively phrased, is the *value laden* intent of cosmopolitanism counterproductive to more radical post-socialist and feminist inspired democratic movements? I will come back to this in a minute. For the moment it is important to acknowledge that human/women's rights debates predominantly tackle *violence* against women. The focus on violence engenders different levels of scandalising perpetrators: first, there is a certain warrior response undertaken as 'last' resort to systematic or endemic physical and *direct* violence that hurts people, particularly women and children; this is the context of war (civil and state enacted) abroad. Second, activists raise consciousness and also deliver acute help and practical relief for victims of predominantly male violence (intimate and public) and engage with themes such as trafficking, child prostitution or HIV (at home and abroad). Third, and more interesting to a proactive human rights' framework, is the question of 'structural violence' (Galtung 1969, 1996). In what ways can we call upon human rights if people are harmed by poverty, famine and the lack of 'goods' caused either systematically by capitalist exploitation or as its 'side-effect'?

In her detailed proposal of 'Cosmopolitan Feminism and Human Rights', Niamh Reilly (2007: 193) admits, 'Arguably, the struggle to achieve recognition of women's wider economic and social rights has lagged behind the feminist challenge to public-private divide – at least in relation to the issue of violence.' Though the five 'mutually constitutive moments' (Reilly 2007: 184) that characterise in her view 'cosmopolitan feminism as a transformative political framework'[5] (ibid.)

3	This is introduced above by the argument of Nwankwo (2005).

4	Critical to the possibility of democratic and participatory rule-making in the context of cosmopolitanism and democracy, Urbinati (2003); Gould (2004).

5	'1. A critical engagement with public international law. 2. A global feminist consciousness that challenges the systematic interplay of patriarchal, capitalist, and racist power relations. 3. Recognition of intersectionality and a commitment to cross-boundaries dialogue, networking, and social criticism. 4. The Development of collaborative advocacy strategies around concrete issues. 5. The utilization of global forums as sites of cosmopolitan solidarity and citizenship' (Reilly 2007: 184).

are relevant to an ethical-political understanding of feminist global action, these angles are not doing away with the dialectic positioning of *citizens of the world* and cosmopolitan outlaws. In particular, the second aspect of a 'global feminist consciousness' is most vulnerable to her argument as it attempts to harmonise rather opposite interests along the lines of class, race, ethnicity and faith creating antagonistic world views among feminists.

Nwanko's (2005: 13) reminds us of what cosmopolitanism entails, it is both 'hegemonic cosmopolitanism, exemplified by the material and psychological violence of imperialism and slavery (including dehumanisation) and a cosmopolitanism that is rooted in a common knowledge and memory of that violence.'

The scope of human rights in the context of global redistributive justice is discussed more directly by Onora O'Neill (1991; 2010). She focuses on the dialectics of 'obligation-rights' while bringing together debates on international distributive justice and the potential of human rights to support this claim. As she argues:

> Discussions of human rights often take no account of needs at all; and where they try to do so strains are placed in the basic structure of rights theory and the identification of needs is sketchy. A full account of international distributive justice would require a complete theory of human needs, which I shall not provide … It is not controversial that human beings need adequate food, shelter and clothing appropriate to their climate, clean water and sanitation, and some parental and health care. When these basic needs are not met they become ill and die prematurely. (2010: 62)

Given that these basic needs are *not met* in a global context, the controversial debates on the role and impact of new cosmopolitanism in Chapter 3 and 4 are confronted with the twin shadow of the 21st-century cosmopolitanism, cosmopolitans who could be alienated *Kosmopoliten*. When people are stuck in (refugee) camps or across deprived neighbourhoods, social anger can feed counter-cosmopolitan mobilisation: different expressions of counter-cosmopolitan mobilisation might imply nationalistic, racist or ethno-tribal rivalry depending on the social location and gendered state of its morally or physically humiliated actors. If 'the vocabulary of obligation looks at ethical relationships from the perspective of agency and the vocabulary of right looks at *them*[6] from the perspective of recipience' (O'Neill 2010: 66) it becomes clear that the 'right-ethical relationship' nexus, nevertheless, sustains an existing unjust *normative* framework. In the words of Christina Lafont (2008), who challenges the Kantian-Habermasian worldview as only protecting *limited* human rights, 'Now, if it is true that there is not hope for a global consensus on the need to prevent any massive human rights violations of economic origin, then there is not hope for a global domestic politics geared towards these goals' (2008: 52).

Despite obvious structural deficits in its regulatory power as argued here, most scholars remain optimistic of the lasting power of the Human Rights agenda. For

---

6   My emphasis.

example, in Sharon Anderson-Gold's (2001) view implementing global human rights could simultaneously help establish world peace and overcome racialised divisions between citizens and foreigners. According to Anderson-Gold, the European Union (EU) could be regarded as having an advanced form of regional integration while also promoting the 'internationalization of human rights' (2001; 129). Compared to the position of the hegemonic US she may be correct, but as made clear in Chapter 2 this tentatively optimistic view, written before 9/11, contrasts with the dichotomy of *normalising difference* and *outlawing otherness* in its aftermath. Coming back to the two EU countries, Britain and Germany, discussed more closely in the context of cosmopolitanism, the national mode of security-control runs smoothly in its non-contested domestic territory of 'law and order'.

Andrew Blick et al. (2006: 65) conclude in their report *The Rules of the Game – Terrorism, Community and Human Rights* that 'The European Convention, now largely incorporated into British Law, allows for a government to restrict some rights in a genuine national emergency.' The British Government responded to 9/11 and to the London 7/7 bombings of 2005, with tougher anti-terrorism legislation.[7] Furthermore, plans to issue biometric ID cards[8] and to digitalise surveillance technologies are said to be catching up with the implementation of an EU wide security order (Hayes 2006). The legal creation of a situation of 'genuine national emergency' complements these measures while taking the national security management beyond the British *Civil Contingencies Act 2004*, which specified as grounds for exemption 'a serious threat to human welfare, the environment or the case of war or terrorism'. According to Vertigans (2010: 31), 'Prevent, Pursue, Protect and Prepare (HM Government 2009)' has been implemented in Britain as a strategy of counter-terrorism. Though organisations such as the 'Equality and Human Rights Commission (EHRC 2008), Forum against Islamophobia and Racism (FAIR 2004a) and Human Rights Watch (HRW 2007) have uttered concerns about the ways Muslims are targeted and suspects are treated, there is 'little or no protest from the majority' (Vertigans 2010: 300).

In 2002 the German Government passed the '*Terrorismusgesetz*' (terrorism law) for a temporary period of five years. This law was formally passed into the legislature in 2007 and recently declared as permanent law. Further, the *ATDG*[9] (2006), (*Antiterrordateigesetz*: anti-terrorism data law) allows the gathering of personal information about terror suspects regarding their professions, education, the places where individuals stayed and lived, or even the *person's religion*. Above all, the data gathered is accessible to police, secret service and all national public authorities.

---

7   For details on various anti-terror legislation since 2000; i.e. the Terrorism Act, see http://tna.europarchive.org/20100419081706/http://security.homeoffice.gov.uk/ For a comparison of the experiences of Irish and Muslim communities with British anti-terrorism laws, see Birmingham Report 2006.

8   The costs are estimated at GBP 5.5 billion.

9   http://www.gesetze-im-internet.de/bundesrecht/atdg/gesamt.pdf.

These legislative developments bring to the fore the problematic bias of 'plurality'/'alterity' as argued in this book: these countries extended drastic surveillance and criminalising measures paradoxically along their anti-discrimination law following EU directives. They do so despite a 21st-century image of being cosmopolitan in outlook and open to difference.

In addition, the critique of human rights beyond Europe and the West looms around issues of particular 'cultural' units. Despite ambitious efforts to implement human rights all over the world, any idealistic vision concerning cosmopolitanism and universal human rights also is confronted with the criticism of Western primacy and its empirical record of failing inclusive goals of global justice. For instance, the 1990s controversy about specific (East) Asian values confronted the Western claim of impartial universality with reproaches condemning the economic and ideological purposes of its *individual* rights agenda. Political leaders (particularly in Malaysia, China and Indonesia) based their criticism of Western values on their different understanding of authority, community values and the importance of religious identity (Langlois 2001).[10] In a similar way, Brown (2009) refers to the politician Lee Kuan-Yew who underscores this ongoing controversy concerning human rights as individually based and contrasts it with communitarian interests such as 'communal obligations and cultural self-determination' (2009: 201). A political geo-cultural debate, however, sustains particular elite interests rather than tackling systems of discrimination within and across East Asian countries and elsewhere. Likewise, specific elite interests shape notions of liberalistic or communitarian ideals and practices inside single nation states, within Europe and across the West. We have to accept that there is a perplexity of views and agonistic interests that have to be taken seriously when discussing ideological controversies about the 'right' impact of human rights and global democracy (Vieten 2007, similarly Brown 2009). In contrast to political agendas attempting to define rights and cosmopolitan outlooks along a geographical plane I argue that contradictory cultural traditions reside in any part of the world as they do inside the West, above all in Europe.

As argued above, we should be sceptical of equating human rights rhetoric with cosmopolitan intent and leaving out the ambivalent role nationalism and nation state plays in these power and bonding games. As Calhoun (2007: 166) rightly critiques: 'Women and minority groups have been integrated into the political life of many modern states not simply despite nationalism (though certainly despite certain versions of nationalism), but through the transformation of nationalism. Nationalism then becomes in part the history of such struggles.' This ambivalence also means that neither feminists nor other politically 'progressive' identified

---

10   Firstly, the recognition of authority and order to which democracy must submit would be different in Asia. Secondly, and in keeping with this 'Confucian' argument, the community and universal principles to which individuals must commit themselves to submit to would be defined in more communitarian terms. Thirdly, the recognition of transcendence as re-emergence of a religious identity was stressed in contrast to a notion of secular society (Langlois 2001: 16).

subjects can unsubscribe to the *settled* formula of actually existing nation states; we are all part of the production of paradoxes.

Turning now again to the democratic uprisings in the Middle East in 2011: though the *national* liberation of civilians in Libya is welcomed, of course, it is the NATO's logistic and militaristic support of the counter-Gaddafi movement that helped to make this possible and further, one wonders why this sort of international intervention is not granted to the revolutionary movement in Syria or elsewhere. Apparently, *human rights* as rhetoric for cosmopolitan global law are encompassed by its endemic betrayal. These contradictions underscore that a *moral argument* for freedom and security (such as the absence of dictatorship and abusive law) intends to wash away its particular political-economic grounding. The 21st century is imprinted with another re-configuration of global political space that operates through different interwoven layers of national governments and local management strategies regarding populations (control of movement and settlement) and goods (porous economic frameworks and osmotic legal structures). As Fraser (2007b: 7) rightly emphasises, 'Legitimacy and Efficacy of Public Opinion' have to be scrutinised against another stage of transformed public sphere that is shaped and shaken by a post-Westphalian confusion of asymmetric global state power with transformed national territorial containers.

Given the link between global capitalism and commercial cosmopolitanism, in effect its interests work against global 'distributive justice' and therefore warrants the two dimensional cosmopolitan subjectivity of *culturalist* cosmopolitanism as explored in the previous chapters. In agreement with Boaventura de Sousa Santos[11] (2002), and argued elsewhere, 'increased alienation and deprivation enshrined in global capitalisms place us increasingly in direct confrontation with the broader phenomenon of *social fascism*' (Yuval-Davis et al. 2006: 7). This 'social fascism' is articulated locally in various forms of gendered and systemic violence. Thus, the critical analysis of two-fold dimensions of new cosmopolitanism and the problematisation of structural, individual and collective violence is an important element in understanding the tightening of community boundaries against the Other. As far as a shifting global political space is concerned, two functional dimensions have to be differentiated accordingly. Firstly, there is the institutional development of larger units of local governance (regionalism) and secondly, there is the timely construction of modified and extended, imagined political communities of *civic* bonding and belonging. The latter is corresponding to an increased process of transnational and institutionalised regional interests (i.e. Europeanism as advocated 'European cosmopolitanism').[12] Thinking about a global space of communication and accordingly, the meaning of cosmopolitan claims, Philip Schlesinger (2007: 416) argues, 'The EU is a conceptual anomaly. Less all-embracing than the globe,

---

11   De Sousa Santos (2001: 187) calls this form of socio-cultural deprivation 'societal fascism'; for detailed explanation see De Sousa Santos 2002.

12   I am referring here to a European discourse; in principal we could also think of African cosmopolitanism or Asian cosmopolitanism and so forth.

it is also much more territorially far-reaching than the state. And it is precisely this ambiguous figuration that makes it so open to a cosmopolitan temptation'. The 'cosmopolitan temptation' is referring to late modern and supra-national perceptions of being 'cosmopolitan'; however, this self-embracing image is more contradictory and jettisoned in terms of the overall presence of parochial, nationalistic and xenophobic attitudes of EU citizens (Pichler 2008).

I now turn to the assessment of some explicitly postcolonial/feminist interventions transgressing the new European regionalism debate.

Reading Postcolonial Feminism into Cosmopolitanism

When thinking about contemporary Europe, legacies of colonial racialisation come up that predate specific nationalisms and nation building processes as discussed above. It means we have to think about *racism* and *othering difference* in terms of a long lasting multi-layered history of administered violence as intrinsic element of state and cultural formations in Europe. A Eurocentric 'Civilisation' entangled with a mission of Christianity can be traced back to colonial roots of the 15th century. For example, both the Spanish conquest in South America, which initiated an era of European colonial discourse of the *Other outside Europe* and the re-conquest of Spain in 1492 by the Catholic Church, which initiated the murder and expulsion of Spanish Muslims and Jews against *the Other inside Europe*, can be regarded as contributing factors to the development of a modern racialising discourse towards otherness (Mignolo 2002).

As explained in this book, cosmopolitanism is gendered, as nationalism is; it is 'coloured' by national histories and has to be understood as a continuing human adventure leaving space for further speculations and collective actions towards a more equal and just world. As exposed in Chapters 3 and 4 the role of minority views (migrants; ethnic groups, sex/gender) challenging mainstream perspectives on cosmopolitanism emerged particularly in the disciplinary fields of *Culture and Postcolonial Studies* (Bhabha) in Britain and *Marxist Kulturwissenschaft* (Behrend) in East Germany. International Postcolonial Studies, therefore, open up an innovative discursive transnational field where marginalised and subaltern voices on new cosmopolitanism speak out. According to Hena Ahmad (2010: 5), 'The cosmopolitan attitudes that postcolonial women writers bring to their literary texts enable them to negotiate and construct new postcolonial identities for women in opposition to national and patriarchal ideologies, revealed in their antipatriarchal and antinational stances.'

The most promising anti-colonial and anti-capitalist concept of 'subaltern cosmopolitanism' was coined by Boaventura de Sousa Santos in the beginning of the 21st century[13] (2002, 2009). He started his intellectual project in Portugal

---

13　Glick-Schiller et al. (2011: 407) use the term 'subaltern cosmopolitanism' in reference to Lamont and Aksartova (2002).

(University of Coimbra), located in the South (West) of Europe, and also is academically affiliated with the US and Britain. What makes his work significant to a feminist alternative reading of cosmopolitanism is his consequent personal engagement with counter-hegemonic globalisation movements (Santos 2002: 459), e.g. with the *World Social Forum*, and further, his effort to retrieve forgotten and marginalised knowledge inside Europe (Santos 2009). Before discussing more in detail his proposal of a 'subaltern' cosmopolitanism and looking at the way this can contribute to a feminist reading of the postcolonial in response to Eurocentric imagination, I will briefly introduce his concept of the 'Diatopical hermeneutics' (Santos 2002: 273) as this precedes the idea of subaltern formulation. According to de Sousa Santos:

> Diatopical hermeneutics is based on the idea that the *topoi* of an individual culture, no matter how strong they may be, are as incomplete as the culture itself. Such incompleteness is not visible from the inside the culture itself, since aspiration to the universal induces taking a part as a whole. Incompleteness in a given culture must be assessed from another culture's *topoi*. More than as an inadequate answer to a given problem, cultural incompleteness manifests itself as an inadequate formulation of the problem itself. The objective of diatopical hermeneutics is, therefore, not to achieve completeness – which is admittedly an unachievable goal – but, on the contrary, to raise the consciousness of reciprocal incompleteness to its maximum possible by engaging in the dialogue, as it were, with one foot in one culture and the other in the other. (ibid.)

This version of *dialogue across different cultures* echoes some notions of Habermasian ideals of communicative dialogic spheres; however, as de Sousa Santos (2002: 274) explicitly emphasises, 'The recognition of reciprocal incompleteness and weakness is an essential condition of a cross-cultural dialogue'. From here, we can move to the content of a 'subaltern cosmopolitanism' which embraces the counter perspective of a cosmopolitanism that resist hegemonic and mainstream interests of elite cosmopolitanism. In de Sousa Santos's (2002: 460) wording:

> In sum, those socially excluded, victims of the hegemonic conception of cosmopolitanism, need a different type of cosmopolitanism. Subaltern cosmopolitanism is therefore an oppositional variety. Just as neo-liberal globalization does not recognize any alternative form of globalization, so also cosmopolitanism without adjectives denies its own particularity. Subaltern, oppositional cosmopolitanism is the cultural and political form of counter-hegemonic globalization. It is the name of the emancipatory projects whose claims and criteria of social inclusion reach beyond the horizon of global capitalism.

Under the umbrella of counter-hegemonic struggles feminist networks and different forms of political and cultural resistance can be shielded comfortably. In opposition to a moral-normative framework which is conveyed in mainstream cosmopolitanism a more revolutionary and affective cosmopolitan bonding is suggested in these lines. It is 'empathy' plus 'caring' plus 'critical political activism' that boost an alternative cosmopolitan engagement with the world towards global justice and fair redistribution to come. This alternative or counter-reading of cosmopolitan intent transgresses the global order of international politics, territorial solidarity and 'humanist interventionism'.

Taking this notion of 'subaltern cosmopolitanism' further, and equipping its critique with a postcolonial de-masking of Eurocentric sociological theory, Gurminder K. Bhambra (2010) proposes 'provincialised cosmopolitanism' (2010: 234), also echoing what Chakrabarty (2000) coined as a 'provincialisation of Europe'. Bhambra argues further, 'For postcolonial theorists, this ['the cultural homogeneity in to the sign of modernity', UMV] ultimately demonstrates the ethnocentric limitations of the concept; specifically the way in which a particularism becomes transformed into a universal' (ibid.).

It is worthwhile to note for the matter of following up *travelling* concepts and 'Traveling Theory' (Said 1983) that Hans Georg Gadamer (1965) had already described this process of Europe's loss of meaning in the period post-1914 (Santos 2010: 235). Unlike those postcolonial voices that are tempted to essentialise Europe as a homogeneous cosmos of Occidentalism, it is again de Sousa Santos who urges us to understand that 'dominant postcolonialism universalizes colonial experiences on the basis of British colonialism, and the emergent Latin-American postcolonialism somehow does the same, this time on the basis of Iberian colonialism' (ibid.). A similar argument is made by Suki Ali (2007) highlighting the lingual-cultural limits of these debates, that are largely not transferable to the Latin American, Chinese or situation of 'indigenous people' (2007: 197–198).

As argued elsewhere (Vieten 2009, Vieten 2011) it is too simplistic to equate the distinctive societies of more than 27 European countries to a single cultural signifier of a European Union identity-container as it is wrong to think of postcolonialism as a monolithic framework of a righteous anti-colonial critique. It remains to be discovered in what ways different European colonial regimes produced different postcolonial legacies, and to what degree post-communist states or differently framed Scandinavian historiographies, for example, produced their own 'subalternity'. These trajectories, however, are in need of an articulation of cosmopolitan consciousness that links the social locations we are born into with another broader imagination reaching out to a global scale. It is here where *listening* is necessary, but also learning different languages to foster translations and trying to outnumber those who marginalise or silence alternative voices.

Glick-Schiller's et al. (2011: 402) definition of 'cosmopolitan sociability as consisting of forms of competence and communication skills that are based on the human capacity to create social relations of inclusion and openness to the world' gives an idea of how this idea of subaltern complexity could be broken down to social practices where cosmopolitan engagement takes place. In addition, the spiritual (not only religious) motivation of individuals to socialise with Others is emphasised by these authors.

Agreeing with this line of argument 'cosmopolitan competence' should be regarded as futuristic critical thinking, sceptical of pre-defined group closure and characterised by curiosity towards the unknown. As a generic capacity it aims to open up social space for all-inclusive human bonds while situating roots and routes.

This attempt of grasping a more radical cosmopolitan attitude is inspired by the feminist idea of 'transversal politics' (Yuval-Davis 1997, 1999). 'Transversal politics' combines insights of feminist standpoint epistemology (Haraway 1988) with a critique of communitarian restricted multicultural policy or identity politics. According to Yuval-Davis (1999: 94–95), transversal politics 'recognizes that from each positioning the world is seen differently and thus that any knowledge based on just one positioning is unfinished.' Consequently, if we think of a dialogical and subaltern cosmopolitanism this engagement evolves by accepting differential positionings. Further, difference is encompassed by equality (ibid.). We are aware that this is an optimistic programme, but that is the idea of utopia.

While referring to Hollinger (2002) Nora Fisher Onar (2011: 13) rather sarcastically summarises:

> In recent years, a host of observers across the arts, humanities, and social and political scientists have endorsed the 'cosmopolitan outlook' as a promising formula how to live together despite our differences. We accordingly see a plethora of labels with which advocates of 'new' cosmopolitanism have sought to brand the frame. A far from exhaustive list includes: 'vernacular cosmopolitanism, rooted cosmopolitanism, critical cosmopolitanism, comparative cosmopolitanism, national cosmopolitanism, discrepant cosmopolitanism, situated cosmopolitanism, and actually existing cosmopolitanism' (Hollinger, 2002: 228).

Also, she adds her own label of 'cosmopolitan postmodernism' (ibid.)

Mendieta (2009) calls emanations of cosmopolitan labelling 'Babelian proliferation of modified, localized, and historicized forms of cosmopolitanism' (2009: 242), without hesitating to add another adjective in 'dialogical cosmopolitanism' (Mendieta 2009: 243). In a nutshell, this dialogical cosmopolitanism would be a synthesis of de Sousa Santos 'subaltern' and Mignolo's 'decolonial cosmopolitanism' (ibid.).

Concluding Remarks

As argued above a feminist reading of subaltern cosmopolitanism offers an alternative frame that combines postcolonial critique as perspectives from the South and critical knowledge in and across Europe with feminist transnational (transversal) inquiry. At the end of the day, all the labels for cosmopolitan activity or consciousness are less decisive as the message behind it. Some female gendered virtues of 'caring' for the Other lean to another site of boundary transitions; they imagine an even more inclusive view of a cosmopolitan bond that appreciates nature/ecology and children rights: according to Sanches-Flores (2010: 85),

> Nature and childhood are essential others to Western individuality and it is urgent that we decipher where this othering comes from. ... the world of individuals lies on one pole and that of nature (or those defined as close to nature) on the other. Women, children and 'barbarians' have been readily placed by the Western liberal tradition of thought in the proximity of nature, and thus have been seen as essentially underdeveloped, or worse, inferior.

While arguing that 'women and racialised others' have been 'set off' (ibid.) to (be) included, in her view it is nature and children that are most vulnerable. The project of 'setting off' to greater inclusion refers to some progress as far as EU anti-discrimination policy, equality legislation and measures such as 'positive action' are concerned. This is a beginning, and not the end to *her-story*. As long as we think of 'progress' as control towards a finite future we might miss the point of another infinite shared world. Coming back to Semetzky's (2010) feminist reading of the Tarot cards introduced in Chapter 1, it is *'The Star'* that follows *'The Tower'*. According to Semetzky (2010: 116) '"The Star" embodies the meaning of hope, healing, inspiration and the forthcoming of the Aquarian age; in fact, this card is often called "The Star of Hope": the hope for understanding!'

<h1 style="text-align:center">Bibliography</h1>

Acton, T. (1999) 'Globalization, the Pope and the Gypsies', in Avtar Brah, Mary Hickmann and Mairtin An McGhall (eds), *Global Futures*, London: Macmillan

Adam, B. and Van Loon, J. (2000) 'Introduction: Repositioning Risk: the Challenge for Social Theory', in Barbara Adam and Ulrich Beck and Joost van Loon (eds), *The Risk Society and Beyond – Critical Issues for Social Theory*, London: Sage, 1–31

Agamben, G. (1994) 'We Refugees' (www.egs.edu/faculty/agamben/agamben-we-refugees.html, p1.); accessed 1 Sept. 2011

Agamben, G (1998) *Homo Sacer: Sovereign Power and Bare Life*, Stanford, CA: Stanford University Press

Ahmad, H. (2010) *Postnational Feminisms – Postcolonial Identities and Cosmopolitanism in the Works of Kamala Markandaya, Tsitsi Dangarembga, Ama Ata Aidoo and Anita Desai*, New York, Washington – Bern – Frankfurt/ M/ Berlin – Brussels – Vienna – Oxford: Peter Lang

Ali, S. (2007) 'Introduction: Feminist and Postcolonial: Challenging Knowledge', *Ethnic and Racial Studies*, 30 (2), Special Issue Feminism and Postcolonialism: Knowledge/Politics: 191–212

Allen, S. and Macey, M. (1990) 'Race and Ethnicity in the European Context', in Crouch, Colin (ed.), *Britain as a European Society?*, special issue of *The British Journal of Sociology*, 41 (3): 375–393

Aly, G. (2005) *Hitlers Volksstaat – Raub, Rassenkrieg und nationaler Sozialismus*, Frankfurt am Main: S. Fischer

Aly, G. (2007) *Hitler's Beneficiaries –Plunder, Racal War and the Nazi Welfare State*, New York: Metropolitan Books

Amin, S. (1988) *Eurocentrism*, New York: Zed books

Anderson, A. (2001) *The Power of Distance – Cosmopolitanism and the Cultivation of Detachment*, New Jersey: Princeton University

Anderson-Gold, S. (2001) *Cosmopolitanism and Human Rights*, Cardiff: University of Wales Press

Anthias, F. (1990) 'Race and Class Revisited: Conceptualising Race and Racisms', *Sociological Review*, 38 (3): 19–42

Anthias, F (2001a) 'The Concept of 'Social Division' and Theorising Social Stratification: Looking at Ethnicity and Class', *Sociology*, 35 (4): 835–854

Anthias, F. (2001b) 'New Hybridities, Old Concepts: The Limits of "culture"', *Ethnic and Racial Studies*, 24, 4 July: 619–641

Anthias, F. and Yuval-Davis, N. in association with Harriet Cain (1992) *Racialized Boundaries: Race, Nation, Gender, Colour & Class and the Anti-Racist Struggle*, London, Routledge

Appiah, A. (1998) 'Cosmopolitanism, Universalism and the Divided Legacies of Modernity', in P. Cheah and B. Robbins (eds), *Cosmopolitics: Thinking and Feeling Beyond the Nation*, Minneapolis; London: University of Minnesota, 265–289

Archibugi, D. (1998) 'Principles of Cosmopolitan Democracy', in Daniel Archibugi, David Held and Michael Koehler (eds), *Re-imagining Political Community: Studies in Cosmopolitan Democracy*, Cambridge: Polity Press, 198–230

Archibugi, D. (2003) 'Principles of Cosmopolitan Democracy', in Archibugi, D; Held, D. and Köhler, M. (eds), *Re-imagining Political Community*, Cambridge: Polity Press, 198–228

Arenas, F. (2003) *Utopias of Otherness – Nationhood and Subjectivity in Portugal and Brazil*, London/Minneapolis: University of Minnesota Press

Arendt, H. (1951, 1986) *Elemente und Ursprünge totaler Herrschaft*, München: Beck Verlag

Asad, T. (2000) 'Muslims and European Identity: Can Europe Represent Islam?', in Elizabeth Hallam and Brian V. Street (eds), *Cultural Encounters – Representing 'Otherness'*, London: Routledge, 11–27

Balibar, È (2001) 'At the Borders of Europe', *Make World Festival 2001*, http://www.makeworlds.org/node/80 accessed 12 Sept. 2011

Balibar, È. (2003) 'Europe an "unimagined" Frontier of Democracy', Project Muse, *Diacritics*, 33 (3–4): 36–44

Balibar, È. (2006) 'Strangers as Enemies: Further Reflections on the Aprorias of Transnational Citizenship', Working Paper Series – Universitè de Paris and University of California, Irvine

Balibar, È. (2010) 'At the Borders of Citizenship: A Democracy in Translation?', *European Journal of Social Theory*, 13 (3): 315–322

Barth, F. (ed.) (1969) *Ethnic Groups and Boundaries: The Social Organization of Culture Difference*, Bergen, London: Allen & Unwin

Bauböck, R. and Rundall, J. (eds) (1998) *Blurred Boundaries: Migration, Ethnicity and Citizenship*, Aldershot: Ashgate

Bauman, Z. (1999) *In Search of Politics*, Oxford: Blackwell

Bauman, Z. (2000) *Liquid Modernity*, Cambridge: Polity Press

Bauman, Z. (2002) *Society under Siege*, Cambridge: Polity Press

Bauman, Z. (2004) *Wasted Lives. Modernity and its Outcasts*, Cambridge: Polity Press

Bauman, Z. (2005) 'Living in Utopia', *LSE Lecture* 27 October 2005 London

Bauman, Z. (2006) *Liquid Fear*, Cambridge: Polity Press

Baumann, G. (2004) 'Grammars of Identity/Alterity – A Structural Approach', in Gerd Baumann and Andre Gingrich (eds), *Grammars of Identity/Alterity – A Structural Approach*, New York/Oxford: Berghahn Books, 18–50

Beck, U. (1986) *Risikogesellschaft – Auf dem Weg in eine andere Moderne*, Frankfurt am Main: Suhrkamp

Beck, U. (1992) *Risk Society – Towards a New Modernity*, London: Sage

Beck, U. (1994) 'The Reinvention of Politics: Towards a Theory of Reflexive Modernization', in Ulrich Beck and Anthony Giddens and Scott Lash (eds), *Reflexive Modernization – Politics, Tradition and Aesthetics in the Modern Social Order*, Cambridge: Polity Press, 1–55

Beck, U. (1997) *The Reinvention of Politics – Rethinking Modernity in the Global Social Order*, Cambridge: Polity Press

Beck, U. (1998a) 'How Neighbours Become Jews: The Political Construction of the Stranger in the Age of Reflexive Modernity', in *Democracy without Enemies*, Cambridge: Polity Press, 122–140

Beck, U. (1998b) 'Nation-States without Enemies: The Military and Democracy after the End of the Cold War', in *Democracy without Enemies*, Cambridge: Polity Press, 141–153

Beck, U. (2000a) 'Risk Society Revisited: Theory, Politics and Research Programmes', in Barbara Adam, Ulrich Beck and Joost van Loon (eds), *The Risk Society and Beyond – Critical Issues for Social Theory*, London: Sage, 211–229

Beck, U. (2000b) 'Die Reflexivität der Zweiten Moderne', in Hans-Martin Schönherr-Mann (Hrsg) *Ethik des Denkens – Perspektiven von Ulrich Beck, Paul Ricoer, Manfred Riedel, Gianni Vattimo, Wolfgang Welsch*, München: Wilhelm Fink Verlag

Beck, U. (2000c) 'The Cosmopolitan Perspective: Sociology of the Second Age of Modernity', *British Journal of Sociology*, 51 (1): 79–106

Beck, U. (2002a) 'Kleine Grabrede an der Wiege des kosmopolitischen Zeitalters', in (2002b) *Macht und Gegenmacht im globalen Zeitalter – Neue weltpolitische Ökonomie*, Frankfurt am Main: Edition Zweite Moderne Suhrkamp, 407–448

Beck, U. (2002b) *Macht und Gegenmacht im globalen Zeitalter – Neue weltpolitische Ökonomie*, Frankfurt am Main: Edition Zweite Moderne Suhrkamp

Beck, U. (2002c) 'The Cosmopolitan Society and its Enemies', *Theory, Culture & Society* 19 (1–2): 17–44

Beck, U. (2002d) 'The Silence of Words and Political Dynamics in the World Risk Society', *Logos*, 1 (4): 1–18

Beck, U. (2002e) 'The Terrorist Threat. World Risk Society Revisited', *Theory, Culture & Society*, 19 (4): 39–55

Beck, U. (2003) 'Verwurzelter Kosmopolitanismus: Entwicklung eines Konzepts aus rivalisierenden Begriffspositionen', in Ulrich Beck, Natan Sznaider and Rainer Winter (Hg.), *Globales Amerika? Die kulturellen Folgen der Globalisierung*, Bielefeld: (transcript verlag) Cultural Studies

Beck, U. (2004a) 'Mobility and the Cosmopolitan Perspective', http://www.cosmobilities.net/Dokumente/download/Paper_Beck_Cosmopolitan Perspective_authorisiert_final.pdf: not accessible any longer

Beck, U. (2004b) 'Cosmopolitan Realism: On the Distinction between Cosmopolitanism in Philosophy and the Social Sciences', *Global Networks*, 4 (2): 131–156

Beck, U. (2004c) *Der kosmopolitische Blick: Krieg ist Frie*den, Frankfurt am Main: Suhrkamp

Beck, U. (2005) 'Das kosmopolitische Empire', *Internationale Politik* (IP) Nr. 7, 6–12

Beck, U. (2006a) 'Understanding the Real Europe: A Cosmopolitan Perspective', *Annual Neale Wheeler Lecture at the Nobel-Museum*, Stockholm, 1 June

Beck, U. (2006b) *The Cosmopolitan Vision*, Cambridge: Polity Press

Beck, U. (2009) 'Critical Theory of World Society: A Cosmopolitan Vision', Constellations, 16 (1): 4–22

Beck, U. (Hrsg.) (1977) *Die soziale Konstitution der Berufe*, Frankfurt am Main: Aspekte Verlag

Beck, U. and Brater, Michael (1978) *Berufliche Arbeitsteilung und soziale Ungleichheit: Eine historisch-gesellschaftskritische Theorie der Berufe*, Frankfurt am Main: Campus Verlag

Beck, U. and Brater, Michael/Daheim, Hansjürgen (1980) *Soziologie der Arbeit und der Berufe: Grundlagen, Problemfelder, Forschungsergebnisse*, Reinbek bei Hamburg: Rowohlt

Beck, U. and Grande, E. (2004) *Das kosmopolitische Europa*, Frankfurt am Main: Edition Zweite Moderne – Suhrkamp

Beck, U. and Grande, E. (2010) 'Varieties of Second Modernity: The Cosmopolitan Turn in Social and Political Theory and Research', *The British Journal of Sociology*, 61 (3): 409–443

Beck, U. and Sznaider, N. (2006) 'A Literature on Cosmopolitanism: An Overview', *The British Journal of Sociology*, 57 (1): 153–164

Becker, O.E.H. (1947) 'Weltbürgertum und Gegenwart', *Athena – Illustrierte Monatsschrift für Kunst und Literatur*, 2: 21–24

Behrend, H. (1992a) 'Women Catapulted into a Different Social Order: Women in East Germany', in *Women's History*, 1 (1): 141–153

Behrend, H. (1992b) 'East Germany under the Federal German Eagle', *New Politics*, Winter

Behrend, H. (1994a) 'Frauenemanzipation Made in GDR', in B. Butow and H. Stecker (Hg), *Eigenartige Ostfrauen: Frauenemanzipation in der DDR und den neuen Bundesländern*, Bielefeld

Behrend, H. (1994b) 'Keeping a Foot in the Door: East German Women's Academic, Political, Cultural and Social Projects', in Elizabeth Boa and Janet Wharton (eds), *Women and the 'Wende'. Social Effects and Cultural Reflections of the German Unification Process*, Amsterdam: Atlanta

Behrend, H. (1996a) 'Ruhmlose Deutsche Vereinigung', in Hanna Behrend (Hrsg.), *Die Abwicklung der DDR – Wende und deutsche Vereinigung von innen gesehen*, Köln: Neuer ISP Verlag, 11–54

Behrend, H. (1996b) 'East German Women Five Years after the Wende', in Mary Maynard and June Purvis (eds): *New Frontiers in Women's Studies: Knowledge, Identity and Nationalism*, London: Routledge

Behrend, H. (1997) 'The Rise and Fall of the East German Civil Rights Movement', *New Politics*, 6 (3): Summer

Behrend, H. (1999) 'Marxismus und Feminismus – inkompatibel oder verwandt?', in *UTOPIE kreativ*, H. 109/110, November/Dezember, 162–173

Behrend, H. (2000) 'Universalismus und Differenz', in *UTOPIE kreativ*, H. 121/122, November/Dezember, 1156–1161

Behrend, H. (2001a) 'Besprechung von Roger Bromley, Udo Göttlich, Carsten Winter (Hrsg.) (1999) Cultural Studies: Grundlagentexte zur Einführung', in *Hintergrund* II, 43–57

Behrend, H. (2001b) 'Die andere Tradition des Nationalen aus marxistisch-feministischer Sicht – Beitrag zur Internationalen Tagung *"Strategien neoliberaler Hegemonie – Kritische Erneuerung emanzipatorischer Standpunkte"'*, Hamburg HWP, 9.–11.02.2001, http://www.glasnost.de/autoren/habehrend/nenner.html checked 12 Sept. 2011

Behrend, H. (2001c) 'Die Tradition des Nationalen aus marxistisch-feministischer Sicht – Die nationale Frage: ein Kampffeld der Auseinandersetzung mit dem deutschen Nationalismus', http://www.glasnost.de/autoren/habehrend/nation.html checked 12 Sept. 2011

Behrend, H. (2001d) 'Die Linke und der neue Krieg der mächtigen weißen Männer', http://www.glasnost.de/autoren/habehrend/frauen.html checked 12 Sept. 2011

Behrend, H. (2002a) 'Der schriftstellernde Schildermaler, der sich Robert Tressell nannte und sein bemerkenswertes Buch "Die Menschenfreunde in zerlumpten Hosen" – Das kurze Leben des Robert Noonan', *Jahrbuch für Forschungen zur Geschichte der Arbeiterbewegung* III, 39–59

Behrend, H. (2002b) 'Arbeiterliteratur und "sozialistischer Realismus" – Eine alte Debatte von neuer Aktualität', in *Sozialistische Hefte* Nr. 2, 13–23

Behrend, H. (2002c) 'Kriegs- und Friedenskräfte in Deutschland in Zeiten der Globalisierung', http://www.glasnost.de/autoren/habehrend/thesenfrieden.html checked 12 Sept. 2011

Behrend, H. (2003) 'Rezension zu Andreas Hepp und Carsten Winter (Hg.): Die Cultural Studies Kontroverse, Lüneburg: Klampen Verlag', http://www.glasnost.de/autoren/habehrend/rezen-cskontroverse.html checked 12 Sept. 2011

Behrend, H. (ed.) (1995) *German Unification. The Destruction of an Economy?*, London: Pluto Press

Benhabib, S. (1986) *Critique, Norm and Utopia*, New York: Columbia University Press

Benhabib, S. (1992) *Situating the Self: Gender, Community and Postmodernism in Contemporary Ethics*, New York: Routledge

Benhabib, S. (2002) *The Claims of Culture – Equality and Diversity in the Global Era*, Princeton, NJ: Princeton University Press

Benhabib, S. (2004) *The Rights of Others – Aliens, Residents and Citizens*, Cambridge: Cambridge University Press

Benhabib, S. (2008) *Another Cosmopolitanism*, The Berkley Tanner Lectures, Oxford: Oxford University Press

Berl, H. (1947) 'Kosmopolitismus und Individualismus', *Neues Europa – Halbmonatsschrift für Völkerverständigung* 2 (10): 6

Berman, J. (2001) *Modernist Fiction, Cosmopolitanism, and the Politics of Community*, Cambridge: Cambridge University Press

Bhabha, H.K. (1994a) 'Articulating the archaic: Cultural difference and colonial nonsense', in *The Location of Culture*, London and New York: Routledge, 123–138

Bhabha, H.K. (1994b) 'DissemiNation: Time, Narrative and the Margins of the Modern Nation', in *The Location of Culture*, London and New York: Routledge, 139–170 also: Bhabha, Homi K. (1990) 'DissemiNation: Time, Narrative, and the Margins of the Modern Nation, in Homi K. Bhabha (ed.), *Nation and Narration*, London and New York: Routledge, 291–322

Bhabha, H.K. (1994c) 'Introduction: Locations of Culture', in *The Location of Culture*, London and New York: Routledge, 1–18

Bhabha, H.K. (1994d) 'The Other Question: Stereotype, Discrimination and the Discourse of Colonialism', in Homi K. Bhabha, *The Location of Culture*, London and New York: Routledge, 66–84

Bhabha, H.K. (1995) 'Translator Translated,' interview with W.J.T. Mitchell, *Artforum*, 33 (7), http://prelectur.stanford.edu/lecturers/bhabha/interview.html visited 9/12/2011

Bhabha, H.K. (1996) 'Unsatisfied: Notes on Vernacular Cosmopolitanism', in L. Garcia-Moreno and P.C. Pfeiffer (eds), *Text and Nation: Cross-disciplinary Essays on Cultural and National Identities*, Columbia: Camden House, 191–207

Bhabha, H.K. (1997a; 1999) Re-inventing Britain Manifesto – The Manifesto, *Wasafiri*, 14 (29): 38–39

Bhabha, H.K. (1997b) Minority Culture and Creative Anxiety (1–3), The British Council, http://www.counterpoint-online.org/themes/reinventing_britain/ minority1.html: not available any longer

Bhabha, J. and Shutter, S. (1994) *Women's Movement – Women Under Immigration, Nationality and Refugee Law*, London: Trentham Books Limited

Bhambra, G.K. (2010) 'Sociology after Postcolonialism: Provincialised Cosmopolitanisms and Connected Sociologies', in Encarnación Gutiérrez Rodríguez, Manuela Boatcă and Sérgio Costa (eds), *Decolonializing European Sociology – Transdisciplinary Approaches*, Farnham: Ashgate, 33–47

Bigo, D. (2002) 'Security and Immigration: Towards a Critique of the Governmentality of Unease' *Alternatives*, 21 (1): 63–92

Bigo, D. and Guild, E. (eds) (2005) *Controlling Frontiers: Free Movement Into and Within Europe*, Farnham: Ashgate

Bigo, D. et al. (2010) *Europe's 21st Century Challenge: Delivering Liberty*, Farnham: Ashgate

Blick, A., Choudhury, T. and Weir, St. (2006) *The Rules of the Game – Terrorism, Community and Human Rights*, a Report by Democratic Audit, Human Rights Centre University of Essex (For the Joseph Rowntree Reform Trust)

Bloch, A. (2002) *The Migration and Settlement of Refugees in Britain*, Basingstoke and New York: Palgrave

Borradori, G. (2003) *Philosophy in the Time of Terror: Dialogues with Jürgen Habermas and Jaques Derrida*, Chicago: University of Chicago Press

Bradiotti, R. (1994) *Nomadic Subjects*, New York: Columbia

Brah, A. and Phoenix, A. (2004) 'Ain't I am Woman? Revisiting Intersectionality', in *Journal of International Women's Studies*, 5 (3): 75–86

Brennan, T. (1997) *At Home in the World: Cosmopolitanism Now*, Cambridge, MA: Harvard University Press

Brennan, T. (2001) 'Cosmopolitanism and Internationalism', *New Left Review*, 2 (7): 75–84

Breuilly, J (2000) 'Nationalism and the History of Ideas', *Proceedings of the British Academy*, 105: 187–223

Breuilly, J. (2001) 'The State and Nationalism', in M. Gubernau and J. Hutchinson J. (eds), *Understanding Nationalism*, Cambridge: Polity Press, 32–52

Broeders, D. (2007) 'The New Digital Borders of Europe: EU Databases and the Surveillance of Irregular Migrants', *International Sociology*, 22 (1): 71–91

Brown G.W. and Held, D. (eds) (2010) *The Cosmopolitanism Reader*, Cambridge: Polity Press

Brown, G.W. and Kime, M. (2010) 'A Comprehensive Overview of Cosmopolitan Literature', in G.W. Brown and D. Held (eds), *The Cosmopolitanism Reader*, Cambridge: Polity Press, 444–464

Brown, W. (2006) 'Feminist Theory and the Frankfurt School', Introduction, *Differences: A Journal of Feminist Cultural Studies*, 17 (1): 1–5

Brubaker, R. (1992) *Citizenship and Nationhood in France and Germany*, Cambridge, London: Harvard University Press

Brubaker, R. (2004) 'Ethnicity Without Groups', in Stephen May, Tariq Madood and Judith Squires (eds), *Ethnicity, Nationality and Minority Rights*, Cambridge: Cambridge University Press, 50–77

Buck-Morss, S. (2003) *Thinking Past Terror – Islamism and Critical Theory on the Left*, London/New York: Verso

Buck-Morss, S. (2008) 'Sovereign Right and the Global Left', *Cultural Critique*, 69 (1): 145–171

Butler J. and Spivak, G.Ch. (2007, 2010) *Who Sings the Nation-State?* London/ NewYork/Calcutta: Seagull

Calhoun, C. (2002a) 'Imagining Solidarity: Cosmopolitanism, Constitutional Patriotism and the Public Sphere', *Public Culture*, 14 (1): 147–171

Calhoun, C. (2002b) 'Constitutional Patriotism and the Public Sphere: Interests, Identity, and Solidarity in the Integration of Europe' in Pablo De Greiff (ed.), *Social Solidarity and Transnational Politics*, Cambridge MA: MIT Press

Calhoun, C. (2007) *Nations Matter: Culture, History and the Cosmopolitan Dream*, New York: Routledge

Canfora, L. (2006) *Democracy in Europe – A History of an Ideology*, Oxford: Blackwell Publisher

Cavallar, G. (2005) 'Cosmopolis – Supranationales und kosmopolitisches Denken von Vitoria bis Smith', in *Deutsche Zeitschrift für Philosophie* 1, Berlin: Akademie Verlag, 49–67

Cesarini, D. (1997) 'The Changing character of Citizenship And Nationality in Britain', in David Cesarini, and Mary Fulbrook (eds), *Citizenship, Nationality and Migration in Europe*, London: Routledge, 17–29

Chakrabaty, D. (2000, 2007) *Provincializing Europe: Postcolonial Thought and Historical Difference*, 2nd edn, Princeton, NJ: Princeton University Press

Chandler, D. (2002) *From Kosovo to Kabul – Human Rights and International Intervention*, London: Pluto Press

Chandler, D. (2006) 'National Interests, National Identity and 'Ethical Foreign Policy', in Nira Yuval-Davis, Kalpana Kannabiran and Ulrike M. Vieten (eds), *The Situated Politics of Belonging*, London: Sage, 161–175

Chandler, D. (2009) 'Critiquing Liberal Cosmopolitanism? The Limits of the Biopolitical Approach', *International Political Sociology*, 3 (1): 53–70

Cheneval, F. (2002) *Philosophie in weltbürgerlicher Bedeutung – Über die Entstehung und die philosophischen Grundlagen des supranationalen und kosmopolitischen Denkens der Moderne*, Basel: Schwete & Co AG Verlag

Chernilo, D. (2006) 'Social Theory's Methodological Nationalism', *European Journal of Social Theory*, 9 (1): 5–22

Cohen, R. (1994) *Frontiers of Identity – The British and the Others*, London and New York: Longman

Colley, L. (1994) *Britons – Forging the Nation 1707–1837*, London: Vintage

Crenshaw, K. (1989) *Demarginalizing the Intersection of Race and Sex: A Black Feminist Critique of Antidiscrimination Doctrine, Feminist Theory and Antiracist Policies*, Chicago, IL: University of Chicago Legal Forum, 139–167

Crossley, N. (2004) 'On Systematically Distorted Communication: Bourdieu and the Socio-Analysis of Publics', in Nick Crossley and John Michael Roberts (eds), *After Habermas – New Perspectives On The Public Sphere*, Oxford: Blackwell Publishing, 88–112

Cunningham, H. (2004) 'Nations Rebound? Crossing Borders in a Gated Globe', *Identities: Global Studies in Culture and Power*, 11 (3): 329–350

Cusack, A. (2010) 'The Wanderer as *Weltbürger*: *Die Harzreise* and the Genesis of Heine's Cosmopolitanism', in Patrick O'Donovan and Laura Rascaroli (eds), *The Cause of Cosmopolitanism – Dispositions, Models, Transformations*, Oxford, Bern, Berlin, Brussels, Frankfurt am Main, New York and Vienna: Peter Lang, 153–171

Dabag, M. (2000) 'Genozid und weltbürgerliche Absicht. Perspektiven', in Norbert Bolz, Friedrich Kittler und Reimar Zons (Hrsg.), *Weltbürgertum und Globalisierung*, München: Wilhelm Fink Verlag, 43–70

Davis, G. (1991) *The Irish in Britain – 1815–1914*, Dublin: Gill and Macmillan

Davis, M. and Moctezuma, A. (1999) 'Policing the Third Border', *Colorlines – the national newsmagazine on race and politics* Fall 1999, http://www.colorlines.com/article.php?ID=98&limit=750&limit2=15002page=2

De Greiff, P. (2002) 'Habermas on Nationalism and Cosmopolitanism', *Ratio Juris*, 15 (4): 418–438

Dean, J. (ed.) (2000) *Cultural Studies & Political Theory*, Ithaca/London: Cornell University Press

Dean, M. (2006) 'A Political Mythology of World Order: Carl Schmitt's *Nomos*', *Theory, Culture & Society*, 23 (5): 1–22

Delanty, G. (1996) 'The Frontier and Identities of Exclusion in European History', *History of European Ideas*, 22 (2): 93–103

Delanty, G. (2006) 'The Cosmopolitan Imagination: Critical Cosmopolitanism and Social Theory', *British Journal of Sociology*, 57 (1): 25–46

Delanty, G. (2009) *The Cosmopolitan Imagination – The Renewal of Critical Social Theory*, Cambridge: Cambridge University Press

Deleuze, G and Guattari, F. (1987) *A Thousand Plateaus: Capitalism and Schizophrenia*, trans. B. Massoli, Minneaopolis: University of Minnesota Press

Derrida J. (2001) *On Cosmopolitanism and Forgiveness*, London: Routledge

Dirlik, A. (1994) 'The Postcolonial Aura: Third World Criticism in the Age of Global Capitalism', *Critical Inquiry*, 20 (2): 328–356

Dorfman, B. (2008) 'Writing History, Writing Resistance. History, Narrative and the Political', in Wojciech H. Kalaga and Marzena Kubisc (eds), *Multicultural Dilemmas – Identity, Difference, Otherness*, Frankfurt am Main: Peter Lang GmbH, 13–22

Douglas, M. and Wildavsky, A. (1983) *Risk and Culture*, Berkeley: University of California University

Douzinas, C. (2002) 'Identity, Recognition, Rights: What can Hegel Teach us about Human Rights, *Journal of Law and Society*, 29 (3): 379–405

Douzinas, C. (2007) *Human Rights and Empire – The Political Philosophy of Cosmopolitanism*, Abingdon: Routledge Cavendish

Dunraven, Earl of, K.P., C.M.G. (1920) *The Crisis in Ireland –Federal Union, through Devolution*, London: Hodder and Stoughton

Dussel, E. (1995) *The Invention of the Americas: Eclipse of "the Other" and the Myth of Modernity*, New York: Continuum

Dussel, E. (2000) 'Europe, Modernity and Eurocentrism', *Nepantla: Views from the South*, 1 (3): 465–478

Edmunds, J. (2011) 'The Limits of Post-National Citizenship: European Muslims, Human Rights and the *Hijab*', *Ethnic and Racial Studies*, 1: 1–19

Eisenberg, A. (2006) 'Education and the Politics of Difference: Iris Young and the Politics of Education', *Educational Philosophy and Theory*, special issue

'Citizenship, Inclusion and Democracy: A Symposium on Iris Marion Young', guest Editor Mitja Sardoc, 38 (1): 7–23

Eisenstein, Z. (2004) *Against Empire*, London: Zed Press

Elliott, A. (2003) *Critical Visions – New Directions in Social Theory*, Oxford: Rowman & Littlefield Publishers, inc.

Erel, U. (2003) 'Gendered and Racialized Experiences of Citizenship in the Life Stories of Women of Turkish Background in Germany', in Jacqueline Andall (ed.), *Gender and Ethnicity in Contemporary Europe*, Oxford/New York: Berg Publishers, 155–176

Etzioni, A. (2007) 'The Community Deficit', *Journal of Common Market Studies*, 45 (1): 23–42

Falk, R (1995) *On Human Governance: Towards a New Global Politics*, University Park: Pennsylvania State University Press

Fehr, S. (2011) 'Intersectional Discrimination and the Underlying Assumptions in the French and German Headscarf Debates: An Adequate Legal Response?', in Dagmar Schiek and Anna Lawson (eds), *European Union Non-Discrimination Law and Intersectionality – Investigating the Triangle of Racial, Gender and Disability Discrimination*, Farnham: Ashgate, 111–124

Fine, R. (2007) *Cosmopolitanism*, New York/London: Routledge

Fine, R. and Chernilo, D. (2004) 'Between Past and Future: The Equivocations of the New Cosmopolitanism', *Studies in Law, Politics, and Society*, 31: 25–44

Fine, R. and Cohen, R. (2002) 'Four Cosmopolitanisms Moments', in Steven Vertovec and Robin Cohen (eds), *Conceiving Cosmopolitanism – Theory, Context, and Practice*, Oxford: Oxford University Press, 137–162

Fine, R. and Smith, W. (2003) 'Jürgen Habermas's Theory of Cosmopolitanism', *Constellations*, 10 (4): 469–487

Fisher Onar, N. (2011) '"Europe", "Womanhood" and "Islam" – Re-aligning Contested Concepts via the Headscarf Debate', *RECON online working paper* 2011. 12, 1–22

Fleming, M. (1995) 'Women and the "Public Use of Reason"', in Johanna Meehan (ed.), *Feminists Read Habermas – Gendering the Subject of Discourse*, New York/London: Routledge, 117–138

Forman-Barzilai, F. (2002) 'Adam Smith as Globalization Theorists', *Critical Review*, 14 (4): 391–419

Forman-Barzilai, F. (2005) 'Sympathy in Space(s)', *Political Theory*, 33 (2): 189–217

Forman-Barzilai, F. (2010) *Adam Smith and the Circles of Sympathy: Cosmopolitanism and Moral Theory*, Cambridge: Cambridge University Press

Francke, K. (1928) *Weltbürgertum in der deutschen Literatur von Herder bis Nietzsche*, Berlin: Weidmannsche Buchhandlung

Fraser, N. (1992) 'Rethinking the Public Sphere: A Contribution to the Critic of Actually Existing Democracy', in Craig Calhoun (ed.), *Habermas and the Public Sphere*, Cambridge, MA: MIT Press

Fraser, N. (1995) 'What's Critical about Critical Theory?', in Johanna Meehan (ed.), *Feminist Read Habermas – Gendering the Subject of Discourse*, New York; London: Routledge, 21–56

Fraser, N. (1997) *Justice Interruptus – Critical Reflections on the "Postsocialist" Condition*, London: Routledge

Fraser, N. (2005) 'Reforming Justice in a Globalising World', 36 *New Left Review*, 69

Fraser, N. (2007a) 'Reframing Justice in a Globalizing World', in David Held and Ayse Kaya (eds), *Global Inequality – Patterns and Explanations*, Cambridge: Polity Press, 252–272

Fraser, N. (2007b) 'Transnationalizing the Public Sphere – On the Legitimacy and Efficacy of Public Opinion in a Post-Westphalian World', *Theory, Culture & Society* 24 (4): 7–30

Friedman, J. (1999) 'The Hybridization of Roots and the Abhorrence of the Bush', in Mike Featherstone and Scott Lash (eds), *Spaces of Culture: City – Nation – World*, London: Sage, 230–256

Frisby, D. and Featherstone, M. (eds) (1979) *Georg Simmel 1958–1918. Simmel on Culture. Selected Writings.* London: Sage

Fulbrook, M. (1999) *German National Identity after the Holocaust*, Cambridge: Polity

Galtung, J. (1969,1996) *Peace by Peaceful Means: Peace and Conflict Development and Civilisation.* London: Sage

Gavinson; R. (1992) 'Feminism and the Public/Private Distinction', *Stanford Law Review*, 45 (1): 1–45

Geras, N. (1998) *The contract of Mutual Indifference – Political Philosophy after the Holocaust*, London/New York: Verso

Ghorashi, Halleh (2010) 'From absolute invisibility to extreme visibility: Emancipation trajectory of migrant women in the Netherlands', *Feminist Review* 94: 75–92

Gibney, M.J. (2004) *The Ethics and Politics of Asylum – Liberal Democracy and the Response to Refugees*, Cambridge: University Press

Giddens, A. (1990) *The Consequences of Modernity*, Stanford, California: Stanford University Press

Giddens, A. (1998) *The Third Way. The Renewal of Social Democracy.* Cambridge. Cambridge University Press

Gilroy, P. (1987) *There Ain' t no Black in the Union Jack*, London: Century Hutchinson

Gilroy, P. (1993) *The Black Atlantic: Modernity and Double Consciousness*, Cambridge: Harvard University Press

Gilroy, P. (2004) *After Empire: Melancholia or Convivial Culture?*, London: Routledge

Glick-Schiller, N., Darieva, T. and Gruner-Domic, S. (2011) 'Defining Cosmopolitan Sociability in a Transnational Age. An introduction, *Ethnic and Racial Studies* 34 (4): 399–418

Goldberg, D.T. (2002) *The Racial State*, Malden, MA/Oxford: Blackwell

Goldberg, D.T. (2006) 'Racial Europeanization', in *Ethnic and Racial Studies*, 29 (2): 331–364

Goodwin, M. (2009) 'Multidimensional Exclusion: Viewing Romani Marginalisation through the Nexus of Race and Poverty', in D. Schiek and V. Chege (eds), *European Union Anti-Discrimination Law: Comparative Perspectives on Multidimensional Equality Law*, London: Routledge-Cavendish, 137–161

Grabham, E., Cooper, D., Krishnadas, J. and Herman, D. (eds) (2009) *Intersectionality and Beyond – Law, Power and the Politics of Location*, New York/Abingdon: Routledge-Cavendish

Green, B. (2003) 'The New Woman's Appetite for "Riotous Living": Rebecca West, Modernist Feminism, and the Everyday', in Ann L. Ardis and Leslie W. Lewis (eds), *Women's Experience of Modernity, 1875–1945*, Baltimore and London: The Johns Hopkins University Press, 221–236

Green, S. (2001) 'Citizenship Policy in Germany: The Case of Ethnicity over Residence', in Randall Hansen and Patrick Weill (eds), *Towards a European Nationality – Citizenship, Immigration and Nationality Law in the EU*, Basingstoke: Palgrave, 24–51

Green, S. (2004) *The Politics of Exclusion: Institutions and Immigration Policy in Contemporary Germany*, Manchester: Manchester University Press

Habermas, J. (1962, 1985) *Theorie des kommunikativen Handelns, Band 2 – Zur Kritik der funktionalistischen Vernunft*, 3. durchgesehene Auflage, Frankfurt am Main: Suhrkamp

Habermas, J. (1970) *Towards a Rational Society: Student Protest, Science, and Politics*, Boston: Beacon Press

Habermas, J. (1981, 1987) *Theory of Communicative Action*, Cambridge: Polity Press

Habermas, J. (1988) 'Concerning the Public Use of History', *New German Critique*, 44: 40–50

Habermas, J. (1989, 1992) *The Structural Transformation of the Public Sphere – An Inquiry into a Category of Bourgeois Society*, Cambridge: Polity Press

Habermas, J. (1991) 'Yet Again: German Identity – A Unified Nation of Angry DM-Burghers?', *New German Critique*, 52: 84–101

Habermas, J. (1992) *Between Facts and Norms*, Cambridge: Polity Press

Habermas, J. (1994) 'The Asylum Debate (Paris Lecture, 14 January 1993)', in Max Pensky (ed.), *Jürgen Habermas Interviewed by Michael Haller*, Lincoln, London: University of Nebraska Press

Habermas, J. (1996, 2000) 'The European Nation-state – Its Achievements and Its Limits. On the Past and Future of Sovereignty and Citizenship', in Gopal Balakrishnan (ed.), *Mapping the Nation*, London and New York: Verso, 281–294

Habermas, J. (1997) *Die Einbeziehung des Anderen – Studien zur politischen Theorie*, Frankfurt am Main: Suhrkamp

Habermas, J. (1998a) *The Inclusion of the Other – Studies in Political Theory*, Cambridge, MA: The MIT Press

Habermas, J. (1998b) *Die postnationale Konstellation – Politische Essays*, Frankfurt am Main: Suhrkamp

Habermas, J. (1999) 'Der europäische Nationalstaat unter dem Druck der Globalisierung', *Blätter für deutsche und internationale Politik*, 4: 425–436

Habermas, J. (2001a) *The Postnational Constellation – Political Essays*, Cambridge: Blackwell Publishers Ltd.

Habermas, J. (2001b) 'Von der Machtpolitik zur Weltbürgergesellschaft', in *idem. Zeit der Übergänge*, Frankfurt am Main: Suhrkamp, 27–39

Habermas, J. (2003) 'What does the Felling of the Monument Mean?', Habermas, (translation of 'Was bedeutet der Denkmalsturz?', *Frankfurter Allgemeine Zeitung*, 17. April)

Habermas, J. (2004) 'Solidarität jenseits des Nationalstaats. Notizen zu einer Diskussion', in Jens Beckert, Julia Eckert, Martin Kohle and Wolfgang Streeck (Hrsg.), *Transnationale Solidarität – Chancen und Grenzen*, Frankfurt am Main: Campus Verlag, 225–235

Habermas, J. (2005) 'Eine politische Verfassung für die pluralistische Weltgesellschaft', *Kritische Justiz*, 3: 222–247

Habermas, J. (2008) What is Meant by a Post-Secular Society? A Discussion on Islam in Europe', in *Europe – The Faltering Project*, Cambridge: Polity Press, 59–77

Habermas, J. and Derrida, J. (2004) *Philosophie in Zeiten des Terrors*, Berlin/ Wien: Philo Verlag

Halas, Elzbieta (2008) 'Issues of Social Memory and their Challenges in the Global Age, *Time & Society*, 17 (1): 103–118

Halbwachs, M. (1950, 1992) *The Collective Memory*, Chicago: The University of Chicago Press

Hall, Kim (1997) 'Sensus Communis and Violence: A Feminist Reading of Kant's Critique of Judgement', in Robin Schott (ed.), *Feminist Interpretations of Kant*, University Park: Pennsylvania State University Press

Hall, St. (1984) 'The Rise of The Representative/Interventionist State', in Gregor McLennan, David Held and Stuart Hall (eds), *State and Society in Contemporary Britain – A Critical Introduction*, Oxford: Polity Press, 7–49

Hall, St. (2004) 'Divided City: The Crisis of London', *Open Democracy – free thinking for the world* (website)

Hannerz, U. (1990) 'Cosmopolitans and Locals in World Culture', in Mike Featherstone (ed.), *Global Culture: Nationalism, Globalisation and Modernity*, London: Sage, 237–252

Hannerz, U. (1996) *Transnational Connections*, London: Routledge

Hansen, R (2000) *Citizen and Immigration in Postwar Britain. Institutional Origins of a Multicultural Nation*, Oxford: Oxford University Press

Hansen, R. (2001) 'From Subjects to Citizens: Immigration and Nationality Law in the United Kingdom', in Randall Hansen and Patrick Weill (eds), *Towards a European Nationality – Citizenship, Immigration and Nationality Law in the EU*, Basingstoke: Palgrave, 69–94

Haraway, D. (1988) 'Situated Knowledge: The Science Question in Feminism and the Privilege of Partial Perspective', *Feminist Studies*, 14 (3): 575–599; https:// faculty.washington.edu/pembina/all_articles/Haraway1988.pdf accessed 13 Sept. 2011

Hardt, M. and Negri, A. (2000) *Empire*, Harvard: Harvard University Press

Haritaworn, J. (2008) 'Loyal Repetitions of the Nation: Gay Assimilation and the War on Terror', *DarkMatter* (web journal), issue 3, May. Accessed on 13 Sept. 2011

Harris, L. (1984) 'State and Economy in the Second World War', in Gregor McLennan, David Held and Stuart Hall (eds), *State and Society in Contemporary Britain – A Critical Introduction*, Oxford: Polity Press, 50–76

Hayes, B. (2006) *Arming Big Brother – The EU's Security Research Programme*, Amsterdam: TNI/Statewatch.

Haymann, F. (1924) *Weltbürgertum und Vaterlandsliebe in der Staatslehre Rousseaus und Fichtes*, Berlin: Pan Verlag Rolf Heise

Heater, D. (2000) 'Does Cosmopolitan Thinking have a Future?' *Review of International Studies*, 26 (5): 179–197

Held, D (2004a) *Global Covenant – The Social Democratic Alternative to the Washington Consensus*, Cambridge: Polity Press

Held, D. (1982) 'Crisis Tendencies, Legitimation and the State', in John B. Thompson and David Held (eds), *Habermas – Critical Debates*, London: Macmillan Press Ltd, 181–195

Held, D. (1984) 'Power and Legitimacy in Contemporary Britain', in Gregor McLennan and David Held and Stuart Hall (eds), *State and Society in Contemporary Britain – A Critical Introduction*, Cambridge: Polity Press, 299–369

Held, D. (1995) 'Democracy and the New International Order', in Daniele Archibugi and David Held (eds), *Cosmopolitan Democracy – An Agenda for a New World Order*, Cambridge: Polity Press, 96–120

Held, D. (1996) 'Political Community and the Cosmopolitan Order', in *Democracy and the Global Order*, Cambridge: Polity Press, 221–238

Held, D. (2002a) 'Cosmopolitanism: Ideas, Realities and Deficits', in David Held and Anthony McGrew (eds), *Governing Globalization – Power, Authority and Global Governance*, Cambridge: Polity Press, 305–324

Held, D. (2002b) 'Violence, Law and Justice in a Global Age', *Constellations*, 9 (1); also published in 2003, in Daniele Archibugi (ed.), *Debating Cosmopolitics*, London: Verso, 184–202

Held, D. (2004) 'Towards a Global Covenant: Global Social Democracy', in *Global Covenant – The Social Democratic Alternative to the Washington Consensus*, Cambridge: Polity Press

Held, D. (2010a) *Cosmopolitanism – Ideals and Realities*, Cambridge: Polity Press

Held, D. (2010b) 'Cosmopolitanism after 9/11', *International Politics*, 47 (1): 52–61

Held, D. and Kaya, A. (2007) 'Introduction', in David Held and Ayse Kaya (eds), *Global Inequality – Patterns and Explanations*, Cambridge: Polity Press, 1–25

Held, D. and Koenig-Archibugi, M. (2004) 'Introduction: Whither American Power?', in David Held and Mathias Koenig-Archibugi (eds), *American Power in the 21st Century*, Cambridge: Polity Press, 1–20

Heller, A. (1998) 'Self-Representation and the Representation of the Other', in Rainer Bauböck and John Rundell (eds), *Blurred Boundaries: Migration, Ethnicity, Citizenship*, European Centre Vienna, Aldershot: Ashgate, 341–354

Hickman, M.J. (1998) 'Reconstructing Deconstructing 'Race': British Political Discourses about the Irish in Britain', *Ethnic and Racial Studies*, 21 (2): 288–307

Hofmann, H. (2003) '"Die Welt ist keine politische Einheit sondern ein politisches Pluriversum" (54–58) Menschenrecht im Pluriversum?', in Manemann, Jürgen (2002), *Carl Schmitt und die Politische Theologie – Politischer Anti-Monotheismus*, Münster: Aschendorff Verlag, 111–123

Hollinger, D. (2002) 'Not Universalists, Not Pluralists: The New Cosmopolitans Find their own Way', in Stephen Vertovec and Robin Cohen (eds), *Conceiving Cosmopolitanism. Theory, Context, and Practice*, Oxford: Oxford University Press, 227–239

Holub, R.C. (1991) *Jürgen Habermas – Critic in the Public Sphere*, New York/London: Routledge

Honig, B. (2001) *Democracy and the Foreigner*, Princeton, NJ: Princeton University Press

Horkheimer, M. and Adorno Th. W. (1947, 1979) *Dialektik der Aufklärung*, London: Verso

Horneffer, R. (1926) *Die Lehre von der Demokratie bei Hans Kelsen, Ein Beitrag zur Kritik der Demokratie*, Erfurt: Stenger

How, A. (1995) *The Habermas–Gadamer Debate and the Nature of the Social*, Aldershot: Ashgate

Huddart, D. (2006) *Homi K. Bhabha*, London/New York: Routledge

Humpel-Ulrich, A. (2000) *Der unabhängige Frauenverband, ein frauenpolitisches Experiment im deutschen Vereinigungsprozeß*, Berlin: Berliner Debatte Wissenschaftsverlag

Ifekwunigwe, J.O. (2006) 'An Inhospitable Port in the Storm: Recent Clandestine West African Migrants and the Quest for Diasporic Recognition', in Nira Yuval-Davis, Kalpana Kannabiran and Ulrike M. Vieten (eds), *The Situated Politics of Belonging*, London: Sage, 84–99

Jacob, M.C. (2006) *Strangers Nowhere in the World – The Rise of Cosmopolitanism in Early Modern Europe*, Philadelphia, PA: University of Philadelphia Press

James, W. (1909) *A Pluralistic Universe – Hibbert Lectures at Manchester College on the Present Situation in Philosophy*, London: Longmans, Green and Co.

Jervis, J. (1999) *Transgressing the Modern – Explorations in the Western Experiences of Otherness*, Oxford: Blackwell

Johnson, R. (2003) *British Imperialism*, London: Palgrave Macmillan

Joseph, M. (1999) *Nomadic Identities – the Performance of Citizenship*, Minneapolis: University of Minnesota Press

Kaldor, M. (2010) 'Humanitarian Intervention: Towards a Cosmopolitan Approach', in G.W. Brown and D. Held (eds), *The Cosmopolitanism Reader*, Cambridge: Polity Press, 334–350

Kannabiran, K. (2006) 'A Cartography of Resistance: The National Federation of Dalit Women', in Nira Yuval-Davis, Kalpana Kannabiran and Ulrike M. Vieten (eds), *The Situated Politics of Belonging*, London: Sage, 54–71

Kannabiran, K., Vieten, U.M. and Yuval-Davis, N. (2006) 'Introduction to the special issue 'Boundaries, Identities and Borders: Exploring the Cultural Production of Belonging', *Patterns of Prejudice*, 40, (3): 189–195

Kant, I. (1795) 'Perpetual Peace: a Philosophical Sketch', http://www.mtholyoke.edu/acad/intel/kant/kant1.htm

Kant, I. (1797; 1970) *Metaphysische Anfangsgründe der Rechtslehre*, Königsberg: Friedrich Nicolonius; Nachdruck des Verlages Ferdinand Keip

Kant, I (1884) *A Philosophical Treaty on Perpetual Peace*, trans. J.D. Morell, London: Hodder & Stoughton

Kaufmann, E. (2003) 'The Rise of Cosmopolitanism in the Twentieth Century West. A Comparative and Historical Perspective on the United States and the European Union', *Global Society*, 17 (4): 359–383; http://eprints.bbk.ac.uk/449/1/Binder1.pdf checked 13 Sept. 2011

Kearns, G. (2003) 'Nation, Empire and Cosmopolis: Ireland and the Break with Britain', in David Gilbert, David Matless and Brian Short (eds), *Geographies of British Modernity*, Oxford: Blackwell Publishing Ltd, 204–228

Kiernan, V.K. (1995) *The Lords of Human Kind – European Attitudes to Other Cultures in the Imperial Age*, London: Serif

Kleingeld, P. (1998) 'Kant's Cosmopolitan Law: World Citizenship for a Global Order', *Kantian Review*, 2: 72–90

Kleingeld, P. (1999) 'Six Varieties of Cosmopolitanism in Late Eighteenth-Century Germany', *Journal of the History of Ideas*, 60 (3): 505–524

Kleingeld, P. (2005) *Wereldburger in eigen Land: Over Kosmopolitisme en patriottisme, Inaugural Lecture*, 30 September 2005, Universiteit Leiden – Faculteit der Wijsbegeerte

Kleingeld, P. and Brown, E. (2006) 'Cosmopolitanism', in *Stanford Encyclopedia of Philosophy*, Zalta, E.N. (ed.), http://www.seop.leeds.ac.uk/entries/cosmopolitanism/ visited 9/13/2011

Kleinwellfonder, B. (1996) *Der Risikodiskurs – Zur gesellschaftlichen Inszenierung von Risiko*, Opladen: Westdeutscher Verlag

Klinger, Cornelia (1995) 'The Concepts of the Sublime and the Beautiful in Kant and Lyotard', *Constellations*, 2 (2): 207–224

Kofman, E., Phizacklea, A, Raghuram, P. and Sales, R. (2000) *Gender and International Migration in Europe, – Employment, Welfare and Politics*, London and New York: Routledge

Kofman, Eleonore (2005) 'Figures of the Cosmopolitan – Privileged Nationals and National Outsiders', *Innovation*, 18 (1): 83–97

Köhler, B. (2006) *Soziologie des Neuen Kosmopolitanismus*, Wiesbaden: Verlag für Sozialwissenschaften

Koldinská, K. (2011) 'EU Non-Discrimination Law and Politics in Reaction to Intersectional Discrimination against Roma Women in Central and Eastern Europe', in D. Schiek and A. Lawson (eds), *European Union Non-Discrimination Law and Intersectionality – Investigating the Triangle of Racial, Gender and Disability Discrimination*, Farnham: Ashgate, 241–258

Kress, G. and van Leeuwen, T. (1996) *Reading Images: The Grammar of Visual Design*, London: Routledge

Kristeva, J. (1993) *Nations without Nationalism*, New York: Columbia Press

Kymlicka, W. and Straehle, Ch. (1999) 'Cosmopolitanism, Nation-States, and Minority Nationalism: A Critical Review of Recent Literature', *European Journal of Philosophy*, 7 (1): 65–88

Laclau, E. and Mouffe, Ch. (1985) *Hegemony & Socialist Strategy – Towards a Radical Democratic Politics*, 1st edn, London and New York: Verso

Laclau, E. and Mouffe, Ch. (2001) 'Preface to the Second Edition', in *Hegemony & Socialist Strategy – Towards a Radical Democratic Politics*, 2nd edn, London and New York: Verso, vii–xix

Ladwig, B. (2003) 'Die Unterscheidung von Freund und Feind als Kriterium des Politischen' (26–28), in Reinhard Mehring (Hrsg.), *Carl Schmitt – Der Begriff des Politischen – Ein kooperativer Kommentar*, Berlin: Akademie Verlag, 45–60

Lafont, C. (2005) 'Religion in the Public Sphere. Remarks on Habermas's Conception of Post-secular Societies.' *A reply to Habermas's speech at the Holberg Prize*. 28. November

Lafont, C. (2008) Alternative Visions of a New Global Order: What Should Cosmopolitan Hope For?' *Ethics & Global Politics*, 1 (1–2): 41–60

Lamont, M. and Aksartova, S. (2002) 'Ordinary Cosmopolitanisms: Strategies for Bridging Racial Boundaries among Working-Class Men', *Theory, Culture & Society*, 19 (4): 1–25

Landes, J.B. (1995) 'The Public and the Private Sphere: A Feminist Reconsideration', in Johanna Meehan (ed.), *Feminist Read Habermas – Gendering the Subject of Dicourse*, New York; London: Routledge, 91–116

Langlois, A. (2001) *The Politics of Justice and Human Rights: South-East Asia and Universalist Theory*, Cambridge and New York: Cambridge University Press

Lara, M.P. (2007) 'The Vertigo of Secularization: Narratives of Evil', in Robin May Schott (ed.), *Feminist Philosophy and the Problem of Evil*, Bloomington: Indiana University Press, 228–244

Lash, S. (2000) 'Risk Culture', in Barbara Adam, Ulrich Beck and Joost van Loon (eds), *The Risk Society and Beyond – Critical Issues for Social Theory*, London: Sage, 47–61

Lash, S. (2002) 'Foreword: Individualization in a non-linear mode', in Ulrich Beck and Elisabeth Beck-Gernsheim (eds), *Individualization*, London: Sage

Latour, B. (2004) 'Whose Cosmos, Which Cosmopolitics? Comments on the Peace Terms of Ulrich Beck', http://www.ensmp.fr/~latour/articles/article/92-BECK-CK.html

Lehmann-Rossbueldt, O. (1950) 'Neue Weltbürger', *Geist und Tat – Monatsschrift für Recht, Freiheit und Kultur*, 5: 201

Lenz, G.H. and Dallmann, A. (2007) 'Justice, Governance, Cosmopolitanism, and the Politics of Difference – Reconfigurations in a Transnational World', *Distinguished W.E.B. DU Bois Lectures 2004/2005 by Kwame Anthony Appiah, Seyla Benhabib, Iris Marion Young and Nancy Fraser*, Berlin-HU Heft 152, 5–15

Leonard, M. (1997) *Britain™ – Renewing our Identity*, London: DEMOS

Lettinga, D. (2011) 'Framing the *Hijab*: The Governance of Intersecting Religious, Ethnic and Gender Differences in France, the Netherlands and Germany', PhD Thesis VU Amsterdam

Levinas, E (1974; 1991) *Otherwise than Being or Beyond Essence*, Dordrecht and Boston: Kluwer Academic Publisher

Levitt, P. and Glick-Schiller, N. (2004) 'Conceptualising Simultaneity: A Transnational Social Field Perspective on Society', *International Migration Review*, 38: 595–629

Levy, D. and Sznaider, N. (2002) 'Memory Unbound – The Holocaust and the Formation of Cosmopolitan Memory', *European Journal of Social Theory*, 5 (1): 87–106

Levy, J.T. (2010) 'Multicultural Manners', Michel Seymour (ed.), *The Plural States of Recognition*, Basingstoke: Palgrave Macmillan, 61–77

Lewis, P. (1997) 'Arenas of Ethnic Negotiation: Cooperation and Conflict in Bradford', in Tariq Modood and Pnina Werber (eds), *The Politics of Multiculturalism in the New Europe – Racism, Identity and Community*, London and New York: Zed Books, 126–146

Liebert, U. with Stephanie Sifft et al., (eds) (2003) *Gendering Europeanization?*, Series Multiple Europes, No. 19, Brussels: Peter Lang

Link, J. and Hall, M.M. (2004) 'From the Power of the Norm to "Flexible Normalism": Considerations after Foucault', *Cultural Critique*, 57: 14–32

Linklater, A. (1998) *The Transformation of Political Community: Ethical Foundations for a Post-Westphalian Era*, Cambridge: Polity Press

Lister, R. (1997a*); Citizenship – Feminist Perspectives*, London: Macmillan Press Ltd

Lister, R. (1997b) 'Dialectics of Citizenship', *Hypathia*, 12 (4): 6–26

Lollini, M. (2002) 'Postscript', in Steven Shankman and Massimo Lollini (eds), *Who, Exactly, Is The Other? Western and Transcultural Perspectives*, Oregon: University of Oregon Press, 65–70

Lutz, H., Herrera Vivar, M.T. and Supik, L. (eds) (2011) *Framing Intersectionality – Debates on a Multi-Faceted Concepts of Gender Studies*, Farnham: Ashgate

Lysaker, J.T. (2002) 'A Liberal Sense of Alterity', in Steven Shankman and Massimo Lollini (eds), *Who, Exactly, Is the Other? Western and Transcultural Philosophical Perspectives*, Oregon: University of Oregon, Part I, 5–14

McGhee, D. (2005) *Intolerant Britain? Hate, Citizenship and Difference*, Berkshire: Open University Press

McGoldrick, Dominic (2006) *Human Rights and Religion: The Islamic Headscarf Debate in Europe*, Portland: Hart Publishing

McLaughlin, L. (2004) 'Feminism and the Political Economy of Transnational Public Space', in Nick Crossley and John Michael Roberts (eds), *After Habermas: New Perspectives on the Public Sphere*, Oxford: Blackwell Publishing, 156–175

Maharajin, S. (2001) 'Perfidious Fidelity – The Untranslatability of the Other', in Stuart Hall and Sarat Maharajin (eds), *Annotations – Modernity and Difference*, London: Institute of International Visual Arts, 26–35

Mahler, S.J. and Pessar, P.R. (2010) 'Gendered Geographies of Power: Analyzing Gender across Transnational Spaces', *Identities*, 7 (4): 441–459

Mandel, R.E. (2008) *Cosmopolitan Anxieties*, Duke University Press

Mann, M (2005) *The Darkside of Democracy: Explaining Ethnic Cleansing*, Cambridge: Cambridge University Press

Marshall, T.H. (1950) *Citizenship and Social Class*, Cambridge: Cambridge University Press

Marshall, T.H. (1981) *The Right to Welfare and other Essays*, London: Heinemann Educational Books

Martinez, M. (2009) 'On Immigration Politics in the Context of European Societies and the Structural Inequality Mode', in Ann Ferguson and Mechthild Nagel (eds), *Dancing with Iris – The Philosophy of Iris Marion Young*, Oxford: Oxford University Press, 213–227

Marwick, A. (1977) *Women at War – 1914–1918*, Glasgow: Collins Sons & Co. Ltd.

Mason, D. (1995, 1st edn; 2000, 2nd edn), *Race & Ethnicity in Modern Britain*, Oxford: University Press

Meinecke, F. (1906, 1928) *Weltbürgertum und Nationalstaat*, München: Oldenbourg

Mendieta, E. (1997) 'The Othering of the Other – Santiago Castro-Gómez's Critique of Latin American Reason', in *Dissens, Revista International de Pensamiento Latinoamericano No.3*, 117–123

Mendieta, E. (2009) 'From Imperial to Dialogical Cosmopolitanism', *Ethics & Global Politics*, 2 (3): 241–258

Meskimmon, M. (2011) *Contemporary Art and the Cosmopolitan Imagination*, London: Routledge

Metzger, W. (1912) *Untersuchungen zur Sitten- und Rechtslehre Kants und Fichtes*, Habilitationsschrift; Heidelberg: Carl Winter's Universitätsbuchhandlung

Migdal, J.S. (2004) *Boundaries and Belonging*, Cambridge: Cambridge University Press

Mignolo, W.D. (2000) *The Many Faces of Cosmo-polis: Border Thinking and Critical* Cosmopolitanism, http://www.duke.edu/~wmignolo/InteractiveCV/Publications/ManyFacesCosmopolis

Mignolo, W.D. (2002) 'The Many Faces of Cosmo-polis: Border Thinking and Critical Cosmopolitanism', in Carol A. Breckenbridge and Sheldon Pollock, Homi K. Bhabha and Dipesh Chakrabarty (eds), *Cosmopolitanism*, Durham and London: Duke University Press, 157–187

Mignolo, W.D. and Tlostanova, M.V. (2006) 'Theorizing from the Borders: Shifting to Geo-and Body-Politics of Knowledge', *European Journal of Social Theory*, 9 (2): 205–221

Mitrovic, L. (1999) 'New Social Paradigm: Habermas's Theory of Communicative Action, *Philosophy and Sociology*, 2 (6/2): 217–223

Modood, T. and Werbner, P. (1997) (eds), *The Politics of Multiculturalism in the New Europe: Community, Identity, Racism*, London: Zed Books

Moller-Okin, S. (1999) 'Is Multiculturalism Bad for Women?', http://bostonreview.net/BR22.5/okin.html accessed on 13 Sept. 2011

Monnet, J. (2005) 'Modernism, Cosmopolitanism and Catastrophism in Los Angeles and Mexico City', Article 136 *Cybergeo* (WebSite)

Mouffe, Ch. (1990a) 'Radical democracy or liberal democracy?' *Socialist Review*, May, 57–66

Mouffe, Ch. (1990b) 'Rawls: Political philosophy without politics', in David Rasmussen (ed.), *Universalism vs. Communitarianism – Contemporary Debates in Ethics*, Cambridge, MA: The MIT Press, 217–236

Mouffe, Ch. (1992a) 'Preface – Democratic Politics Today', in Chantal Mouffe (ed.), *Dimensions of Radical Democracy – Pluralism, Citizenship, Community*, London and New York: Verso, 1–16

Mouffe, Ch. (1992b) 'Democratic Citizenship and the Political Community, in Chantal Mouffe' (ed.), *Dimensions of Radical Democracy – Pluralism, Citizenship, Community*, London and New York: Verso, 225 – 239; reprinted in Chantal Mouffe (1993), *The Return of the Political*, London and New York: Verso, 60–73

Mouffe, Ch. (1993a) 'Introduction: For an Agonistic Pluralism', in Chantal Mouffe (1993), *The Return of the Political*, London and New York: Verso, 1–8

Mouffe, Ch. (1993b) 'Pluralism and Modern Democracy: Around Carl Schmitt', in Chantal Mouffe (1993) *The Return of the Political*, London and New York: Verso, 117–134

Mouffe, Ch. (1996) 'Deconstruction, Pragmatism and the Politics of Democracy', in Chantal Mouffe (ed.), *Deconstruction and Pragmatism – Simon Critchley,*

Jaques Derrida, Ernesto Laclau & Richard Rorty, London and New York: Routledge, 1–12

Mouffe, Ch. (1999a) 'Carl Schmitt and the Paradox of Liberal Democracy', in Chantal Mouffe (ed.), *The Challenge of Carl Schmitt*, London and New York: Verso, 38–53

Mouffe, Ch. (1999b) 'Introduction: Schmitt's Challenge', in Chantal Mouffe (ed.), *The Challenge of Carl Schmitt*, London and New York: Verso, 1–6

Mouffe, Ch. (2000) *The Democratic Paradox*, London: Verso

Mouffe, Ch. (2003) *Politics and Passions: The Stakes of Democracy*, paper given on the 7.3.2003 at the Zentrum für Medientechnologie (ZKM), Karlsruhe, Germany

Mouffe, Ch. (2004) 'Cosmopolitan Democracy or Multipolar World Order?', *Soundings*, 28 (Winter): 62–74

Mouffe, Ch. (2005) Eine kosmopolitische oder eine multipolare Weltordnung?, *Deutsche Zeitschrift für Philosophie, Berlin*, 53, I, 69–81

Mouffe, Ch. (2006) 'Cosmopolitanism and its Problems', in Stephen F. Schneck (ed.), *Letting Be – Fred Dallmayr's Cosmopolitical Vision*, Notre Dame, IN: University of Notre Dame Press, 272–285

Mouffe, Ch (2007) 'Democracy as Agonistic Pluralism', in Elizabeth Deeds Ermarth (ed.), *Rewriting Democracy – Cultural Politics in Postmodernity*, Aldershot: Ashgate, 36–45

Müller, J.W. (2005) 'A "Thick" Constitutional Patriotism for the EU? On Morality, Memory and Militancy', http://www.iue.it/LAW/ResearchTeaching/Cidel/pdf/Muller.pdf

Munro, D. (1997) *Mediating Difference: The Politcal Theories of Jürgen Habermas and Charles Taylor*, MA Dissertation, The University of Western Ontario

Nagle, J. (2009) *Multiculturalism's Double Bind – Creating Inclusivity, Cosmopolitanism and Difference*, Farnham: Ashgate

Nava, M. (2002) 'Cosmopolitan Modernity – Everyday Imaginaries and the Register of Difference', *Theory, Culture & Society*, 19 (1–2): 81–99

Nava, M. (2006) 'Domestic Cosmopolitanism and Structures of Feeling: the Specificity of London', in Nira Yuval-Davis and Kalpana Kannabiran and Ulrike M. Vieten (eds), *Situated Politics of Belonging*, London: Sage, 42–53

Nava, M. (2007) *Visceral Cosmopolitanism – Gender, Culture and the Normalisation of Difference*, London: Berg Publishers

Nederveen Pieterse, J. (1985) *Empire & Emancipation – Power and Liberation on a World Scale*, London: Pluto Press

Nederveen Pieterse, J. (2007) *Ethnicities and Global Multiculture – Pants for an Octopus*, Plymouth: Rowman & Littlefield Publishers, inc.

Nowicka, M. and Rovisco, M. (eds) (2009) *Cosmopolitanism in Practice*, Farnham: Ashgate

Nussbaum, M.C. (1996) 'Patriotism and Cosmopolitanism', in J. Cohen (ed.), *For Love of Country: Debating the Limits of Patriotism*, Boston: Beacon Press, 2–17

Nussbaum, M.C. (1997) 'Kant and Cosmopolitanism' in James Bohman and Mathias Lutz-Bachmann (eds), *Perpetual Peace: Essays on Kant's Cosmopolitan Ideal*, Massachusetts Institute of Technology, 25–51; reprinted in Garrett Wallace Brown and David Held (eds), *The Cosmopolitanism Reader*, 2010, Cambridge: Polity Press, 27–44

Nwanko, I.K. (2005) *Black Cosmopolitanism – Racial Consciousness and Transnational Identity in the Nineteenth-Century Americas*, Philadelphia: University of Pennsylvania Press

O'Neill, O. (1991; 2010) 'A Kantian Approach to Transnational Justice', in Garrett Wallace Brown and David Held (eds), *The Cosmopolitan Reader*, Cambridge: Polity Press, 61–80; reprint from David Held (1991) *Political Theory Today*, Stanford University

O'Reilly, M. (2006) 'Die Berlinerin and the Politics of Metaphor', paper given at the second conference on '*Rethinking German Modernities*', USA (website)

Pateman, C. (1986) *Feminist Challenge: Social and Political Theory*, Sydney and London: Allen and Unwin

Pateman, C. (1989) *The Disorder of Women: Democracy, Feminism and Political Theory*, Cambridge: Polity Press

Penny, H.G. (2003) 'Wissenschaft in einer polyzentrischen Nation – Der Fall der deutschen Ethnologie', in Ralph Jessen und Jakob Vogel (Hg.), *Wissenschaft und Nation in der Europäischen Geschichte*, Frankfurt am, Main and New York: Campus Verlag, 80–94

Pichler, F. (2008) 'How Real is Cosmopolitanism in Europe? *Sociology*, 42 (6): 1107–1126

Pincus, F.L. (2006) *Understanding Diversity – an Introduction to Class, Race, Gender & Sexual Orientation*, Colorado and London: Lynne Rienner Publishers

Pitcher, Ben (2009) *The Politics of Multiculturalism – Race and Racism in Contemporary Britain*, Basingstoke: Palgrave Macmillan

Pollock, Sh. and Bhabha, H.K. and Breckenbridge, C. and Chakrabarty, D. (2002) 'Cosmopolitanisms', in Carol A. Breckenbridge and Sheldon Pollock and Homi K. Bhabha and Dipesh Chakrabarty (eds), *Cosmopolitanism*, Durham, NC and London: Duke University Press, 1–14

Porter, B. (1968) *Critics of Empire – British Radical Attitudes to Colonialism in Africa 1895–1914*, London: Macmillan

Postone, M. (1992) 'Political Theory and Historical Analysis', in Craig Calhoun (ed.), *Habermas and the Public Sphere*, Cambridge, MA and London: The MIT Press, 164–177

Poupeau, F. (2005) 'Reasons for Domination, Bourdieu versus Habermas', in Derek Robbins (ed.), *Pierre Bourdieu vol. II*, London: Sage, 91–113, previously in B. Fowler (ed.) (2000) *Reading Bourdieu on Society and Culture*, Oxford: Blackwell, 69–87

Prins, B. (2006) 'Narrative Accounts of Origins: A Blind Spot in the Intersectional Approach?', *European Journal of Women's Studies*, 13: 277–290

Puar, Jasbir K. (2007) *Terrorist Assemblages – Homonationalism in Queer Times*, Durham, NC and London: Duke University Press

Puwar, N. (2006) 'Im/possible Inhabitants', in Nira Yuval-Davis and Kalpana Kannabiran and Ulrike M. Vieten (eds), *The Situated Politics of Belonging*, London: Sage, 75–83

Puxon, G. (2000) 'The Romani Movement' Rebirth and the First World Romani Congress in Retrospect', in Thomas Action (ed.), *Scholarship and the Gypsies Struggle – Commitment in Romani Studies*, Hatfield: University of Hertfordshire Press, 94–112

Radstone, S. (2002) 'The War of the Fathers: Trauma, Fantasy, and September 11', *Signs*, 28 (1), special issue *Gender and September 11: A Roundtable: Cultural Amnesia: Memory, Trauma and War*: 467–469

Randeria, S., Fuchs, M. and Linkenbach, A. (Hrg.) (2004) *Konfigurationen der Moderne: Diskurse zu Indien*, Soziale Welt Sonderband, 15, Baden-Baden: Nomos Verlag.

Ray, L. (2002) 'Crossing Borders? Sociology, Globalization and Immobility', *Sociological Research Online*, 7 (3), http://www.socresonline.org.uk/7/3/ray.html

Reilly, N. (2007) 'Cosmopolitan Feminism and Human Rights', *Hypatia*, 22 (4): 180–198

Reiss, H.S. (ed.) (1970) *Kant: Political Writings, Cambridge Texts in the History of Political Thought*, Cambridge: Cambridge University Press

Rile Hayward, C. (2004) 'Constitutional Patriotism and Its Others', paper (draft) prepared for the 2004 Annual Meeting of the American Political Science Association, Chicago II, 2–5 September, http://psweb.sbs.ohio-state.edu/intranet/poltheory/Constitutional_Patriotism.pdf accessed 11 Sept. 2011

Roberts, J.M. and Crossley, N. (2004) 'Introduction', in Nick Crossley and John Michael Roberts (eds), *After Habermas – New Perspectives on the Public Sphere*, Oxford: Blackwell

Robins, K. (2006) *The Challenge of Transcultural Diversities: Transversal Study on the Theme of Cultural Policy and Cultural Diversity*, Council of Europe

Robinson, W.I. (2002; 2006) 'Capitalist Globalization and the Transnationalization of the State', in Richard Little and Michael Smith (eds), *Perspectives on World Politics*, 3rd edn, London and New York: Routledge, 260–269; originally published in Rupert, M and Smith H. (eds), *Historical Materialism and Globalization*, London: Routledge, 211–221

Rumford, Ch. (2000) *European Cohesion? Contradictions in EU Integration*, Palgrave Macmillan

Rumford, Ch. (2002) *The European Union: A Political Sociology*, Oxford: Blackwell

Rumford, Ch. (2006) 'Introduction: Theorizing Borders', *European Journal of Social Theory*, 9 (2): 155–169

Rumford, Ch. (2009) *Citizens and Borderwork in Contemporary Europe*, London: Routledge

Rundell, J. (2004) 'Strangers, Citizens and Outsiders: Otherness, Multiculturalism and the Cosmopolitan Imaginary in Mobile Societies', *Thesis Eleven*, 78 (1): 85–101

Ryan, Ch. (2002) 'The Difference between Difference and Otherness', in Shenkman, St. and Lollini, M. (eds), *Who Exactly the Other? Western and Transcultural Perspectives*, Oregon: University of Oregon Press

Sahgal, G. and Yuval-Davis, N. (1992, 2000) *Refusing Holy Orders – Women and Fundamentalism in Britain*, London: WLUML

Said, E.W. (1978) *Orientalism: Western Conceptions of the Orient.* London: Routledge

Said, E.W. (1983) 'Traveling Theory', in Edward W. Said, *The World, the Text and the Critic*, Cambridge: Cambridge University Press, 226–247

Samuel, R. (1989) 'Introduction – Exciting to be English', in Raphael Samuel (ed.), *Patriotism – The Making and Unmaking of British National Identity*, Vol. I History and Politics, London and New York: Routledge

Santos, B.S. (2002) *Toward a New Legal Common Sense*, 2nd edn, London: Butterworths

Santos, B.S. (2009) 'A Non-Occidentalist West: Learned Ignorance and Ecology of Knowledge', *Theory, Culture and Society*, 26: 103–126

Santos, B.S. (2010) 'From the Postmodern to the Postcolonial – And Beyond Both', in Encarnación Gutiérrez Rodríguez, Manuela Boatcă and Sérgio Costa (eds), *Decolonializing European Sociology – Transdisciplinary Approaches*, Farnham: Ashgate, 225–242

Saunders, R. (2001) 'Uncanny Presence: The Foreigner at the Gate of Globalization', *Comparative Studies of South Asia, Africa and the Middle East*, vol. XXI, no. 1–2, 88–98

Scheler, M. (1915) *Der Genius des Krieges und der Deutsche Krieg*, Leipzig

Schiek, D. (2002) 'Torn between Arithmetic and Substantive Equality? Perspectives on Equality in German Labour Law', *International Journal of Comparative Labour Law and Industrial Relations*, 18 (2): 149–167

Schiek, D. (2005) 'Broadening the Scope and the Norms of EU Gender Equality Law: Towards a Multidimensional Conception of Equality Law', *Maastricht Journal of European and Comparative Law*, 12 (4): 427–466

Schiek, D. (2011) 'Organising EU Equality Law around the Nodes of 'Race', Gender and Disability', in Schiek, D. and Lawson, A. (eds), *European Union Non-Discrimination Law and Intersectionality – Investigating the Triangle of Racial, Gender and Disability Discrimination*, Farnham: Ashgate, 11–27

Schiek, D. and Chege, V. (eds) (2009) *European Union Anti-Discrimination Law: Comparative Perspectives on Multidimensional Equality Law*, London: Routledge-Cavendish

Schiek, D. and Lawson, A. (eds) (2011) *European Union Non-Discrimination Law and Intersectionality – Investigating the Triangle of Racial, Gender and Disability Discrimination*, Farnham: Ashgate

Schlesinger, P. (2007) 'A Cosmopolitan Temptation', *European Journal of Communication*, 22: 413–426

Schmitt, C. (1938) *Der Leviathan in der Staatslehre des Thomas Hobbes – Sinn und Fehlschlag eines politischen Symbols*, Hamburg: Hanseatische Verlagsanstalt

Schmitt, C. (1950) *Der Nomos der Erde im Völkerrecht des Jus Publicum Europaeum*, Köln: Greven Verlag

Schott, R.M. (2000) 'Kant', in Alison M. Jaggar and Iris Marion Young (eds), *A Companion to Feminist Philosophy*, Oxford: Blackwell Publishing, 39–48

Schütz, A. (1967) *The Phenomenology of the Social World*, Chicago: Northwestern University Press

Schütz, A. (1971) *Collected Papers vol.1: The Problem of Social Reality*, The Hague: Martinus Nijhoff

Schwarz, B. (1996) *West Indian Intellectuals in Britain*, Manchester: Manchester University Press

Scott, A. (1999) 'War and the Public Intellectual: Cosmopolitanism and Anti-Cosmopolitanism in the Kosovo Debate in Germany', *Sociological Research Online*, 4, no.2 (website)

Scott, A. (2000) 'Risk Society or *Angst* Society? Two Views of Risk, Consciousness and Community', in Barbara Adam, Ulrich Beck and Joost van Loon (eds), *The Risk Society and Beyond – Critical Issues for Social Theory*, London: Sage, 33–46

Seidel-Pielen, E. (1995) *Unsere Türken. Annäherung an ein gespaltenes Verhältnis*, Berlin: Elefanten Press

Semetsky, I. (2010) 'Interpreting the Signs of the Times: Beyond Jung', *Social Semiotics*, 20 (2): 103–120

Senders, S. (1996) 'Laws of Belonging: Legal Dimensions of National Inclusion in Germany', *New German Critique*, 67: 147–176

Simmel, G. (1890) *Über soziale Differenzierung – soziologische und psychologische Untersuchungen*, Leipzig: Duncker & Humblott

Sinfield, A. (ed.) (1983) *The Context of English Literature – Society and Literature 1945–1970*, London: Methuen & Co

Slezkine, Y. (2004) *The Jewish Century*, Princeton: Princeton University Press

Smith, A. (1759) The *Theory of Moral Sentiments*, London: printed for A. Millar; and A. Kincaid and J. Bell, in Edinburgh; http://www.adamsmith.org/smith/tms/tms-index.htm

Smith, A. (1776) *An Inquiry into the Nature and Causes of the Wealth of Nations*, London: Printed for A. Strahan and T. Cadell jun. and W. Davies (successors to Mr. Cadell)

Smith, A.M. (2001) *Nationalism – Theory, Ideology, History*, Cambridge: Polity Press

Solomos, J. and Back, L. (1998); *Race, Politics and Social Change*, London: Routledge

Sondhi, R. (1987) *Divided Families – British Immigration Control in the Indian Subcontinent*, London: Runnymede Trust

Sontag, S. (2009, 1961) 'The Imagination of Disaster', in *idem, Against Interpretation and other Essays*, Penguin Modern Classics, 209–225

Spinner-Halev, J. (1994) *The Boundaries of Citizenship: Race, Ethnicity and Nationality in the Liberal State*, Baltimore: Johns Hopkins University Press

Spivak, G. (1988) 'Can the Subaltern Speak?', in Nelson, C. and Rossberg, L. (eds), *Marxism and the Interpretation of Culture*, Chicago: University of Illinois Press, 271, 313

Squires, J. (2005) 'Is Mainstreaming Transformative? Theorizing Mainstreaming in the Context of Diversity and Deliberation', *Social Politics*, 12(3): 366–388.

Steinbeck, W. (1941) *Johann Gottlieb Fichte – Politik und Weltanschauung – Sein Kampf um die Freiheit in einer Auswahl seiner Schriften*, Stuttgart: Alfred Körner Verlag

Stenglin, M. (2008) 'Binding: a Resource for Exploring Interpersonal Meaning in Three-Dimensional Space', *Social Semiotics*, 18 (4): 425–447

Stevenson, N. (2003) *Cultural Citizenship: Cosmopolitan Questions*, Maidenhead: Open University Press

Sturgis, J. (1984, *Britain and the New Imperialism*, in Eldridge, C.C. (ed.) (1984), British Imperialism in the Nineteenth Century, London: Macmillan Education Ltd, 85–105

Sznaider, N. (2008) *Gedächtnisraum Europa – die Visionen des europäischen Kosmopolitanismus – eine jüdische Perspective*, Bielefeld: transkript – Verlag für Kommunikation, Kultur und soziale Praxis

Taylor, Ch, Walker, M., Habermas, J. and Rockefeller, St. C. (eds) (1994) *Multiculturalism – Examining the Politics of Recognition*, Princeton: Princeton University Press

Thaler, M. (2010) 'The Illusion of Purity: Chantal Mouffe's Realist Critique of Cosmopolitanism', *Philosophy and Social Criticism*, 36 (7): 785–800

Thielking, S. (2000) *Weltbürgertum*, Habilitation 1999, Universität Essen, München: Fink Verlag

Torfing, J. (1999) *New Theories of Discourse – Laclau, Mouffe and Zizek*, Oxford: Blackwell

Touraine, A. (1997) *What is Democracy?* Colorado: Westview Press

Triandafyllidou, A. (2002) *National Identity Reconsidered. Images of Self and Other in a 'United' Europe*, Lampeter: Edwin Mellen Press

Ugarteche, O. (2007) 'Transnationalizing the Public Sphere – A Critique of Fraser', *Theory, Culture & Society*, 24 (4): 65–9

Urbinati, N. (2003) 'Can Cosmopolitical Democracy Be Democratic? In Daniel Archibugi (ed.) (2003) *Debating Cosmopolitics*, London: Verso; http://www.politicaltheory.info/essays/urbinati.htm accessed 11 Sept. 2011

Urry, J. (2000) *Sociology beyond Societies*, London: Routledge

Van der Veer, P. (2002) 'Colonial Cosmopolitanism', in Cohen, R and Vertovec, St. (eds), *Conceiving Cosmopolitanism*, Oxford: Oxford University Press, 165–179

Varsamopoulou, E. (2009) 'The Idea of Europe and the Ideal of Cosmopolitanism in the Work of Julia Kristeva', *Theory, Culture & Society*, 26 (1): 24–44

Verloo, M. (2006) 'Multiple Inequalities, Intersectionality and the European Union', *European Journal of Women's Studies*, 3: 211–229

Vertigans, S. (2010) 'British Muslims and the UK Government's "war on terror" within: Evidence of a clash of civilizations or emergent de-civilizing processes', *The British Journal of Sociology*, 61 (1): 24–44

Vertovec, S. (2007) 'Super-diversity and its Implications', *Ethnic and Racial Studies*, 30 (6): 1024–1055

Vieten, U.M. (2006) '"Out in the Blue of Europe": Modernist Cosmopolitan Identity and the Deterritorialization of Belonging', in Kalpana Kannabiran, Ulrike M. Vieten and Nira Yuval-Davis (eds), *Boundaries, Identities and Borders: Exploring the Cultural Production of Belonging*, special issue of Patterns of Prejudice vol. 40, number 3, July, 259–279

Vieten, U.M. (2007) *Situated Cosmopolitanisms: Notions of the Other in Contemporary Discourses on Cosmopolitanism in Britain and Germany*, University of East London: PhD Thesis

Vieten, U.M. (2009) 'Intersectionality Scope and Multidimensional Equality within the European Union: Traversing National Boundaries of Inequality?', in Dagmar Schiek and Victoria Chege (eds), *European Union Non-discrimination Law: Comparative Perspectives On Multidimensional Equality Law*, London: Routledge-Cavendish, 93–113

Vieten, U.M. (2010) 'Situating Contemporary Discourses on Cosmopolitanism in Britain and Germany: Who is the Other, Anyway?', in Patrick O'Donovan and Laura Rascaroli (eds), *The Cause of Cosmopolitanism – Dispositions, Models, Transformations*, Bern: Peter Lang Publishers, 89–114

Vieten, U.M. (2011) 'Tackling the Conceptual Order of Multiple Discrimination: Situating Different and Difficult Genealogies of Race and Ethnicity', in; Dagmar Schiek and Anna Lawson (eds), *European Union Non-Discrimination Law and Intersectionality – Investigating the Triangle of Racial, Gender and Disability Discrimination*, Farnham: Ashgate, 63–76

Vieten, U.M. (2012 forthcoming) '"When I land in Islamabad I feel home and when I land in Heathrow I feel home" – Gendered belonging and diasporic identities of South Asian British citizens in London and North England', in Georgina Tsolidis (ed.), *Living Diaspora – Family, Education and Identity*, Netherlands: Springer

Viscount Hythe, D.C.L. (1913) (ed.) *The Case For Devolution and A Settlement of the Home Rule Question by Consent – Extracts from Speeches*, London: P.S. King & Son, Orchard House, Westminster

Walby, S. (2004) 'The European Union and Gender Equality: Emergent Varieties of Gender Regimes', *Social Politics*, 11 (1): 4–29

Walby, S. (2007) 'Complexity Theory, System Theory and Multiple Intersecting Social Inequalities', *Philosophy of the Social Science*, 37: 449–470

Waldron, J. (1995) 'Minority Cultures and the Cosmopolitan Alternatives' in W. Kymlicka (ed.), *The Rights of Minority Cultures*, Oxford: Oxford University Press, 93–119

Walker, J. (2006) 'The Critical Image: Heinrich Heine and a Liberal German Identity', in Mary Anne Perkins and Martin Liebscher (eds), *Nationalism versus Cosmopolitanism in German Thought and Culture, 1789–1914*, Lewinston, Queenston, Lampeter: The Edwin Mellen Press, 131–157

Walker, N. (2005) 'Making a World of Difference? Habermas, Cosmopolitanism and the Constitutionalization of International Law, *European University Institute (EUI) Working Paper LAW No. 2005/17*, San Domenico di Fiesole, http://cadmus.iue.it/dspace/index.jsp

Walkowitz, R.L. (2006a) 'Virginia Woolf's Evasion', in Douglas Mao and Rebecca L. Walkowitz (eds), *Bad Modernisms?*, Durham, NC: Duke University Press, 119–144

Walkowitz, R.L. (2006b) 'Rushdie's Mix-Up', in Rebecca L. Walkowitz (2006) *Cosmopolitan Style – Modernism Beyond the Nation*, New York: Columbia University Press, 131–152

Walzer, M. (1980) *Radical Principles – Reflections of an Unreconstructed Democrat*, New York: Basic Books, Inc.

Weindling, P. (1993) *Health, Race and German Politics between National Unification and Nazism 1870 – 1945*, New York: Cambridge University Press

Wemyss, G. (2006) 'The Power to Tolerate: Contests over Britishness and Belonging', in Kalpana Kannabiran and Ulrike M. Vieten and Nira Yuval-Davis (eds), *Boundaries, Identities and Borders: Exploring the Cultural Production of Belonging*, Patterns of Prejudice 40, no.3, July, 215–236

Wemyss, G. (2009) *The Invisible Empire – White Discourse, Tolerance and Belonging*, Farnham: Ashgate

Werbner, P. (1999) 'Global Pathways, Working Class Cosmopolitans and the Creation of Transnational Ethnic Worlds', in *Social Anthropology*, 7 (1): 17–35

Werbner, P. (2006) 'Vernacular Cosmopolitanism', in Mike Featherstone (ed.), *Problematizing Global Knowledge*, special issue of *Theory, Culture & Society*, 23 (2–3): 496–498

Werbner, P. (2011) 'Paradoxes of Postcolonial Vernacular Cosmopolitanism in South Asia and the Diaspora', in Maria Rovisco and Magdalena Nowicka (eds), *The Ashgate Research Companion to Cosmopolitanism*, Farnham: Ashgate, 107–123

Werbner, P. (ed.) (2008) *Anthropology and the New Cosmopolitanism: Rooted, Feminist and Vernacular Perspective*. ASA Monograph No. 45. Oxford: Berg Publishers.

Westwood, S. (2001) 'Complex Choreography – Politics and Regimes of Recognition', *Theory, Culture & Society*, 18 (2–3): 247–264

Westwood, S. (2001) Complex Choreography: Politics and Regimes of Recognition, *Theory, Culture & Society*, 18 (2–3): 247–264

Williams, H. (2003) *Kant's Critique of Hobbes*, Cardiff: University of Wales Press

Wimmer, A. and Glick-Schiller, N. (2002) 'Methodological Nationalism and Beyond: Nation-state Building, Migration and the Social Science', *Global Networks*, 2 (4): 301–334

Winkler, H.-A- (1993) *Weimar 1918 bis 1933: Die Geschichte der ersten deutschen Demokratie*, München: Beck

Wirtz, Michaela (2006) *Patriotismus und Weltbürgertum – Eine begriffsgeschichtliche Studie zur deutsch-jüdischen Literatur 1750–1850*, Tübingen: Max Niemeyer Verlag

Wong, E. (2010) 'Anti-Slavery Cosmopolitanism in the Black Atlantic', *Victorian Literature and Culture*, 38: 451–466

Wyschogrod, E. (2003) 'Autochthony and Welcome: Discourses on Exile in Levinas and Derrida', *Philosophy and Scripture*, 1 (1): 1–9

Young, I.M. (1987) 'Impartiality and the Civic Public: Some Implications of Feminist Critiques of Moral and Political Theory', in Seyla Benhabib and D. Cornell (eds), *Feminism as Critique*, Oxford: Polity Press, 56–76

Young, I.M. (1990) *Justice and the Politics of Difference*, Princeton: Princeton University Press

Young, I.M. (1995) 'Polity and Group Difference: A Critique of the Ideal of Universal Citizenship', in R. Beiner (ed.), *Theorizing Citizenship*, Albany; State of New York

Young, I.M. (2000) *Inclusion and Democracy*, Oxford: University Press

Young, I.M. (2003) 'Polity and Group Difference: A Critique of the Ideal of Universal Citizenship', in Derek Matravers and Jon Pike (eds), *Debates in Contemporary Political Philosophy – An Anthology*, London: Routlege in association with Open University, 219–239

Young, I.M. (2006) 'Education in the Context of Structural Injustice: A Symposium Response', in Mitja Sardoc (ed.), *Citizenship, Inclusion and Democracy: A Symposium on Iris Marion Young /Educational Philosophy and Theory 2006*, vol. 38, no.1, 93–103

Young, I.M. (2009) 'Structural Injustice and the Politics of Difference', in Emily Grabham, Davina Cooper, Jane Krishnadas and Didi Herman (eds), *Intersectionality and Beyond – Law, Power and the Politics of Location*, Abingdon: Routledge-Cavendish, 273–298 (post-mortem published)

Young, R.J.C. (1995) *Colonial Desire – Hybridity in Theory, Culture and Race*, London and New York: Routledge

Yuval-Davis, N (1997a) *Gender & Nation*, London: Sage

Yuval-Davis, N (1997b) 'Women, Citizenship and Difference', *Feminist Review*, 57: 4–27

Yuval-Davis, N. (1999a) 'Institutional Racism, Cultural Diversity and Citizenship: Some Reflections on Reading the Stephen Lawrence Inquiry Report', *Sociological Research Online*, http://www.socresonline.org.uk/socresonline/4/Lawrence/Yuval-Davis.html

Yuval-Davis, N (1999b) 'The Multi-layered Citizen – Citizenship in the Age of Globalization', *International Feminist Journal of Politics*, 1: 119–136

Yuval-Davis, N. (1999c) 'What is "Transversal Politics"?' *Soundings*, 12, summer: 94–98

Yuval-Davis, N. (2000) 'Multi-layered Citizenship and the Boundaries of the 'Nation-State', in *HAGAR International Social Science Review*, 1 (1): 112–127

Yuval-Davis, N. (2002); 'Borders, Boundaries And The Politics Of Belonging', in S. May, T. Modood and J. Squires (eds), *Nationalism, Ethnicity and Minority Rights*, Cambridge: Cambridge University Press

Yuval-Davis (2004) 'Jewish Fundamentalisms and Women', in Ayesha Imam, Jenny Morgan and Nira Yuval-Davis (eds), *Warning Signs of Fundamentalism*, London: WLUM, 27–32

Yuval-Davis, N. (2005) 'Racism, Cosmopolitanism and Contemporary Politics of Belonging', *Soundings*, 30, Summer: 166–178

Yuval-Davis, N. (2006) 'Intersectionality and Feminist Politics', *European Journal of Women's Studies*, 13 (3): 193–209

Yuval-Davis, N. and Stoetzler, M. (2002) 'Imagined Boundaries and Borders – A Gendered Gaze', *The European Journal of Women's Studies*, 9 (3): 329–344

Yuval-Davis, N. and Werbner; P. (eds) (1999) *Women, Citizenship and Difference*, London, Zed Books

Yuval-Davis, N., Anthias, R. and Kofman, E. (2005) 'Secure Borders and Safe Haven and the Gendered Politics of Belonging: Beyond Social Cohesion' *Ethnic and Racial Studies*, 28 (3): 513–535

Yuval-Davis, N., Kannabiran, K. and Vieten, U.M. (2006) 'Introduction – Situating Contemporary Politics of Belonging', in Nira Yuval-Davis, Kalpana Kannabiran and Ulrike M. Vieten (eds), *The Situated Politics of Belonging*, London: Sage, 1–14

Zimmerer, J. (2004) *Deutsche Herrschaft über Afrikaner – Staatlicher Machtanspruch und Wirklichkeit im kolonialen Namibia*, Münster. LIT-Verlag

Zons, R. (2000) ‚Weltbürgertum als Kampfbegriff', in Norbert Bolz, Friedrich Kittler und Rainmar Zons (Hg.), *Weltbürgertum und Globalisierung*, München: Fink, 9–28

Zweig. St. (1990) *Gesammelte Werke in Einzelbänden* (Hrsg: Beck, K.), Frankfurt am Main: Fischer

Index

Individualism 19, 36, 42, 83–84, 96,
    111–112, 121, 125, 127–130
Integration 24, 55, 58, 72, 131–132, 146
  Cultural 51, 130
  Market 138
  Social 5, 54, 59, 70, 90
  State 44, 49, 52, 114
    Federal 51, 78, 126–128
Internationalism 24, 46–47, 58–59, 87, 92
Intertextuality 72, 125

James, William 47, 114
Jews 3, 23, 26, 45, 48, 51, 55, 60, 67,
    87–88, 126, 137, 149
Justice 1, 11, 30, 38, 40, 94, 115, 117, 120,
    130
  Court of Justice (international) 70
  Distributive 4, 36, 102, 142, 145, 148
    Redistribution 1, 142, 145
  Global 24, 147, 151
  Injustice 30, 35, 58, 135, 138
  Post-Westphalian democratic 112
  Social 18, 35, 41–42, 63, 80, 83–84,
    101, 118, 122, 144

Kant, Immanuel 1, 28–31, 36, 41–43, 47,
    56, 80, 85, 96, 111–114, 116–117,
    130, 142
  Habermasian 110, 145
Kaufman, Eric 92, 133
Kleingeld, Pauline 29–30, 85
Kofman, Eleonore 77, 90, 115, 125, 134
Koldinska, Kristina 39–40

Levinas, Emmanuel 7, 17–18, 104, 141
London 9, 33, 84–86, 90–91, 93, 105–106,
    108, 110, 116, 121, 127, 129, 131,
    135
  Post-2005 16, 135, 146
  Visceral cosmopolitan 4, 87

Mann, Thomas 48, 61
Meinecke, Friedrich 45
Memory 5, 11–12, 62, 69–70, 76, 98, 145
Migration 5, 7, 31, 78, 93, 122, 132,
    133–134
  Alterity 132
  Immigration 7, 35, 50–51, 88–91

  Anti- 50
  Security- 94
Mobility 5, 26, 51, 67, 78, 119, 133–134, 136
  Cosmopolitanism 106
  /plurality 132
  Social 122
Mouffe, Chantal 7, 9–10, 29, 46–47, 83,
    93–94, 100–102, 109–110, 112–
    115, 120, 122–123, 132, 136–137,
    142, 144
Multiculturalism 9, 32–33, 36, 41, 51,
    54–55, 76–77, 83, 92–93, 106,
    118–119, 121, 126–127, 129, 135
Multiversum 47, 101, 113–114, 122

Nationalism 3, 7–10, 44, 46–47, 51–52, 58,
    75, 78, 85, 88, 92, 118, 126, 142,
    147, 149
  Anti- 58–59
  Homo- 38
  Methodological 5
Nava, Mica 1, 4, 84, 86–87, 110, 119, 134
Nijab 8, 27, 41
Nwanko, Ifeoma Kiddoe 142, 145

Paradox 3, 28, 32–33, 49, 51, 105, 109,
    136, 138, 147–148
Plurality 8–9, 18, 22–23, 25, 41–42, 76, 78,
    80, 83, 110, 114, 121, 146–147
  Difference/ 12
  /Mobility 132
Post-Westphalian 112, 148

Redistribution/Recognition 36, 41
Representation 5, 14, 16–17, 21, 25–26,
    96, 119, 135
Roma 8, 19, 36, 39–42, 48–49, 51, 55, 87,
    126
Risk Society 7, 64–66, 69
Rushdie, Salman 91, 98, 105, 121–122,
    129
Ryan, Cheny 17, 22–23

Schmitt, Carl 29, 46, 101–102, 114–115,
    122
Secularism 3, 28, 31, 91, 105, 122
  Post- 31, 109